the SECRET
to Finishing *Well*

QUEST FOR AUTHENTIC LEADERSHIP

Anna,
May God continue to bless you
as you are a blessing to others

AGITU WODAJO

PRESS

Table of Contents

Acknowledgements

First, I am extremely grateful to God for the opportunity to serve Him and for His greatest investment in me to present this book the way it appears. I have countless reasons to thank Him.

I thank God for the wonderful children He blessed me with. Beyond the support they provided me with, their achievements and personal quality make me boast in the Lord, from whom all good things come.

I thank Professor Tomas O' Connell for giving me the holistic image of leadership and opening my eyes to see the details with which this book is framed. In his teachings, he introduced me to Gary Will's sixteen types of leadership examples including: Electoral, Radical, Reform, Diplomatic, Military, Charismatic, Business, Traditional, Constitutional, Intellectual, Church, Sports, Artistic, Rhetorical, Opportunistic and Saintly leaders.

I am very grateful to my long time friend Ertra Namarra for her meticulous job in reviewing my manuscript and giving me useful critics. Indeed, I benefitted from her wisdom in shaping the content of this book. Xulon Press's editor provided a tremendous support in editing my manuscript.

I am very thankful and appreciative of Professor Thomas O' Connell and Professor Tesfaye Biftu who carefully read my manuscript and gave me very encouraging feedback that boosted my confidence. I am grateful to Yoseph Petros who translated some of the appendixes and also gave me useful comments on my manuscript.

All Scripture quotations in this book are from the *New King James Version* translation. My Ethiopian history references in this book are mostly from Harold G. Markus's book titled, *A History of Ethiopia* 2002 edition.

List of Pictures

1. House of Slaves on Gore Island
2. Crown Prince, Regent Ras Tafari Makonnen (later Emperor Haile Sellassie I), Ethiopian Princes and nobility he took with him on their first trip to Europe, and the Vatican secretary of State who accompanied him, waiting to meet Pope Pius XI and clergy and nobility of the Vatican state in Italy in 1923.
3. Baoshan Iron and Steel Corporation near the port of Shanghai, China
4. Kum Lung Textile Holding/Company Ltd.(Hong Kong owned) in Shantou, China
   4 Garment workshops holding 1,500 machines in Shantou, China
5. Terracotta warriors in battle formation
   Terracotta worriers' archer kneeling for shooting
   Terracotta worriers' chariot
   Terracotta worriers' chariot driver
6. Dr. Nkrumah's Statue at the African Union (AU) Headquarters in Addis Ababa
7. Temporary shelters in Bole, Addis Ababa, Ethiopia
8. Women's Self-Reliance Association WSRA)'s leather crafts training in the Kebele's conference hall, Bole, Addis Ababa

9. WSRA's milling and food processing workshop
   WSRA's Pattern Construction and Sewing workshop
10. WSRA's leather workshop
    WSRA's leather products sample
11. Picture in front of Moody Bible institute, Chicago
12. International Self-reliance Agency for Women, Inc. (ISAW) computer training, ISAW Resource Bank, Minneapolis, USA

Introduction

A call to write books came to me twenty-four years ago in the 1980s through two ministers who closely watched my life as a Christian woman going through difficulty in my marriage, career, and religious life in Ethiopia. They encouraged me to write a book, telling me that my life example could touch many lives and make a huge difference. However, for quite a long time, I was blinded and unable to respond to the challenge until I experienced a very painful and humiliating wake-up call. The trauma I faced in my last job, which was with an adoption agency, finally opened my eyes to respond to the call. Although I paid a price for not paying attention to this call sooner, the delay offered me the opportunity to gain broader experience and learn more. The process enabled me to produce a better book that speaks to all kinds of audiences, alerting them to global problems and to our shared responsibility in addressing those needs.

What we see and hear from around the world today reveals that the world is not a good place and is not getting any better. All media sources bring us everyday news of evil doings, corruption, violence, and more. The Bible tells us that the end times will be exactly like that:

> But know this, that in the last days perilous times will come: For men will be lovers of themselves, lovers of money, boasters, proud, blasphemers, disobedient to

parents, unthankful, unholy, unloving, unforgiving, slanderers, without self-control, brutal, despisers of good, traitors, headstrong, haughty, lovers of pleasure rather than lovers of God.

—2 Timothy 3:1–4

People all over the world are victims of such a time as Timothy described and are crying out for solutions to our global problems. As a result of the interconnectedness of the world's population, what happens in one part of the world affects the rest. There is a need for strong leadership that will bring the changes necessary to restore the liberty and rights that human beings were granted by their creator and thereby make the world a better place. In this book, we will examine leadership examples in both the developing world and the Western world to aid in our selection of such leadership.

God granted me His grace to lead a life full of testimonies, and He blessed me with the opportunity for global exposure to learn from and serve people of diverse backgrounds. This book is a result of those two things, and I believe that it will help you discover the realities of life in most developing countries and thereby inspire you to do your part towards making the world a better place.

I was introduced to Western culture early in life, and as I grew up, life took me on a global journey. I was born in Wollega, an area in western Ethiopia, in a small town called Nedjo. Soon after I was born, my father accepted the Protestant Christian faith and purchased property adjacent to a Swedish mission school and church. He did so with a determination that his children would be educated and grow up in the faith he had accepted.

Because of the proximity of the school to my parents' house (about four hundred meters away), I was admitted to the first grade just before I turned six, although it was against the school's policy to accept students under age seven. After completing eighth grade at the age of thirteen, I had to leave my parents' home and travel to a different town in order to attend high school. This school was located eighty-five kilometers from my hometown of Nedjo. While attending high school, I lived with families that I was not acquainted with. This experience was very difficult for me, as it was for all the girls in the same situation. I ended up in that situation, however, because a corrupt director of the Swedish mission school I had attended in my earlier years gave his brother's girlfriend a scholarship intended for me, a scholarship that would have allowed me to attend a private Christian high school. Sad but true, that young woman did not benefit from the fraudulent opportunity. She failed in the ninth grade and was dismissed.

Since my childhood, spirituality has always shaped my life. The desire to do the most good for the most people was instilled in me when I was quite young. As the firstborn child among five siblings, I grew up with a keen sense of responsibility. After obtaining an associate degree in community nursing from a public health college in northern Ethiopia, I joined Western missionaries and served as a nurse, where I further discovered my passion. My career journey took me through diverse routes, including working for Western missionaries, the government of Ethiopia, and international Non-Governmental Organizations (NGOs. In these organizations, I served in various capacities as a nurse practitioner and as a social worker prior to moving to the United States. These extensive experiences exposed me to social, political, and economic life in many diverse societies on an international level.

I received a call to serve God in the early eighties while I was yet suffering from a very abusive marriage to an ungodly man who immersed himself in outrageous immorality. I had to keep my struggle secret from my children and endure it until I eventually left Ethiopia for good. In response to my call, I joined a choir, because that was the ministry I had participated in since a young age. Although messages for me to move one step forward kept coming, the call to serve God was confusing to me, as I thought it was only spiritual—working in Christian settings, preaching the gospel, singing, etc. To that end, I applied for enrollment at Moody Bible Institute in Chicago.

For the next three years, I struggled to discern God's will for me. Then the Lord gave me a clear vision to serve displaced women and their families in Addis Ababa, the capital city of Ethiopia, through a holistic approach addressing both their spiritual and physical needs. These women had been displaced during the great famine of 1973 and had no livelihood. God gave me the guidance and resources to establish the first-of-its-kind women's nongovernmental organization (NGO), which I named Women's Self-Reliance Association (WSRA). WSRA provided training in marketable skills, including leatherwork/crafts, sewing and food processing, as well as management and marketing. The organization soon became a best-practice model and eventually opened the doors for me for international involvements.

I came to Minnesota in August 1994, along with my five children. My sister Tsehai Wodajo was a great encouragement in helping me make a decision on that move. While resettling in Minneapolis, I found myself in a new social class, moving from a wealthy neighborhood in Addis Ababa to an unfavorable neighborhood in south Minneapolis. Ms. Kathleen Moore, an American woman from Minneapolis, was a tremendous support in my family's resettlement effort in Minnesota. We had hosted Kathleen in Addis Ababa in 1993, and she paid it back tenfold, although she doesn't see it that way. When I hosted her, I had no previous acquaintance with her or even knew that I would one day be moving to Minnesota. But as Hebrews 13:2 says, "Do not forget to entertain strangers, for by so doing some have unwittingly entertained angels."

My second divine connection from south Minneapolis was a Straitgate Church member, Mr. Jerry Khan, who took me to that church. He and his family were a great help towards my adjusting to my new life in Minneapolis. Their pastor, Dr. Roger Magnuson, was also a great encouragement towards my heeding my call. He is so unique in that he wears so many hats. He is a highly regarded copartner and attorney of Dorsey & Whitney LLP and has been recognized as one of the top trial lawyers in the United States. He is also a prolific author, the dean of Oak Brook College of Law and Government Policy, and a well-revered pastor who knows very well the law of the land and the Scriptures. Although I don't understand how he affords the time, he works diligently in reaching the unreached neighborhoods of southern and northern Minneapolis through his church. His church even provided me with office space in 1995 for starting a nonprofit organization to help immigrant women from around the world and their families.

Soon after moving to Minnesota, I enrolled at Metropolitan State University (MSU) on an F-1 student visa and obtained a BA degree in human services. MSU was indeed a new beginning towards my future. As a community-centered educational institution, MSU equipped me with necessary skills and empowered me to make a difference. The leadership course that was offered by Professor Thomas O'Conner gave me the broad knowledge of leadership with which this book is framed. As part of my internship work at Metro State University, I founded a nonprofit organization that helped immigrant women help themselves, similar to the NGO that I had founded in Ethiopia. My tour of China in early 1997, through a course of study at MSU titled "Case Studies in International Business, Asia I," was an additional opportunity to explore the world from a different angle. Just one year after obtaining my BA, I was blessed with another opportunity, the Bush Leadership Fellowship grant, with which I obtained a master's degree from the Humphrey Institute (presently School) of Public Affairs of the University of Minnesota.

My children have been my greatest encouragement in my journey in life. I have been blessed with five well-accomplished children who have obtained undergraduate and advanced degrees in engineering (computer, software), architecture, and business. The fact that my children and I have succeeded proves that anybody can achieve whatever he or she desires in this land of opportunity. When I say "this land of opportunity," I want to make clear that the opportunity is not a handout that teaches dependency. Rather, it is a "use it or lose it" hands-up venture that is made possible because Americans are willing to teach and encourage others who are where they started and help them achieve what they have achieved or go even farther. They do so by helping others activate and develop whatever they bring to the table and thus facilitate their success. This is what makes America different. This is why it is a country of innovation.

During my early years in Minnesota, an American immigration attorney asked me, "Do you know why our country is great?" and then gave the answer herself, saying, "It is because countries like yours lose their great people and we welcome them." In my native country, I was taken advantage of and mistreated for my contributions towards bringing a positive change. I found the United States so different in that this country provided me with approval and encouragement for my commitment to serving others. Furthermore, I was motivated and empowered through numerous awards and recognitions that I received from the governor of Minnesota, Metropolitan State University, the Department of Homeland Security, KARE 11 TV, the City of Minneapolis, and the Bush Foundation's generous grant towards my graduate degree.

"For everyone to whom much is given, from him much will be required; and to whom much has been committed, of him they will ask the more," says Luke 12:48. As I mentioned above, God has granted me the opportunity to experience all areas of life: religious, social, political, and even gender inequality—all with a purpose. I have explored and seen enough to witness the differences that exist between the developing countries of the world and the nations of the developed world. While living in Ethiopia, I experienced three different forms of governments: (1) the emperor Haile Selassie I's aristocratic reign of the monarchy (1930–1974), (2) the Communist rule of the People's Democratic Republic of Ethiopia under President Mengistu Haile Mariam (1974–1991), and (3) the Federal Democratic Republic of Ethiopia (1991–present). I have also experienced the democratic government of the United States. By the way, the name *United States* does not reveal that it is a democratic country, but its actions do; and actions speak louder than words.

As can be seen from the lives of leaders in the Bible and leaders in many countries of the world, starting well does not guarantee finishing well. In this book, we will explore different forms and effects of government leadership, ranging from God's original system of government to the different government leadership styles of Ethiopia, a three-thousand-year-old east African country, to how the Constitution of the United States of America relates to God's system of government in our quest for authentic leadership and finishing well. To do that, I will rely on evidence from the Bible (all quotations are from the New King James Version), my extensive experience studying, working, and living in Ethiopia and the United States of America; and my global exposure and reading of literature and resources related to the topics addressed in this book.

My aim is as follows:

- To enlighten readers to the details of the facts so together we can do our share towards making the world a better place as God intended it to be
- To revisit the ideologies underlying the principles upon which the Founding Fathers established the New World after liberation from British rule
- To examine America's alliance with foreign nations in our examination of what works best towards faring well and finishing well

The Constitution of the United States and the Declaration of Independence can be related to the biblical leadership model that I will briefly discuss in the pages to follow. These two documents were crafted by men who were refined by British tyranny and who gained extensive knowledge, wisdom, and deep conviction to set the stage for democracy and liberty for all. The United States Declaration of Independence, with which America declared freedom from tyranny and became a refuge for those who flee the same, is based upon the ideas of natural rights and individual liberty. The beginning of the document states:

All men are created equal, that they are endowed by their Creator with certain unalienable Rights, that among these are Life, Liberty, and the pursuit of Happiness.

The preamble to the Constitution of the United States reads:

We the People of the United States, in Order to form a more perfect Union, establish Justice, insure domestic Tranquility, provide for the common defence, promote the general Welfare, and secure the Blessings of Liberty to ourselves and our Posterity, do ordain and establish this Constitution for the United States of America.

Based on these facts, I can say that the foundation on which America was built instilled in its citizens dedication to focusing on the good of the country. For example, before he was hung as a spy by the British, Nathan Hale, who worked for the Patriots during the American Revolution, said, "I regret that I have but one life to give for my country." In a similar vein, President Kennedy said, "Ask not what your country can do for you—ask what you can do for your country."

As part of my introduction, I would also like to mention that this book is just an introductory one and will be further enriched through my future writings. I am not a historian, and the stories included in this book are merely a reflection of my personal experiences and insights that I believe serve as case studies for the topics addressed in this book. I would also like to point out that my life experience is too long to be covered in this one book. It requires a separate writing, which will follow this one.

1

The Origin of Leadership

If we go back to the beginning of human creation, we find that upon creating the living creatures after their kinds, God saw that it was all good. Then He created Adam and Eve, the first human beings, in His own image and placed them in the Garden of Eden, or Paradise. It was a perfect place where there was no problem or want. Then He granted them full freedom and dominion over everything that He had created for them to enjoy (Genesis 1:27–28). After creating Adam and Eve, God saw that everything was very good indeed: "Then God saw everything that He had made, and indeed it was very good" (Genesis 1:30). As a just leader, He gave the couple instructions by which they could avoid evil and death.

After the fall of Adam and Eve, however, the story changed. Things had not gone the way God intended. Adam and Eve misused their God-given freedom and displeased God by making wrong choices. In their disobedience, they ate the forbidden fruit, and God had to remove them from the Garden of Eden.

Adam and Eve brought to the world the fruit of their rebellion, making it a difficult place to live. Their firstborn son, Cain, murdered his younger brother out of jealousy. I believe that this jealousy was the fruit of his parents' discontent, which led them to eat the forbidden fruit. Although they lacked nothing, they desired to become like God and thus disobeyed Him.

Humankind continued to be rebellious, to the extent that God regretted that He had created man:

> Then the LORD saw that the wickedness of man was great in the earth, and that every intent of the thoughts of his heart was only evil continually. And the LORD was sorry that He had made man on the earth, and He was grieved in His heart.
> —Genesis 6:5–6

But their disobedience did not cause God to reverse His eternal plan for human beings. He has always guided them in the right direction by giving them leaders like Moses, who listened to God and led His people according to His directions. In the Bible, the story of the Israelites displays God's system of government. The first written laws and instructions from God's system of government came into existence when He gave the Israelites the Ten Commandments and the instructions called the Torah, also known as the Book of Moses (Exodus 20–23). Through the wise counsel of his father-in-law, Moses developed a democratic type of leadership with which he led the Israelites in the wilderness to the Promised Land:

> And Moses chose able men out of all Israel, and made them heads over the people: rulers of thousands, rulers of hundreds, rulers of fifties, and rulers of tens. So they judged the people at all times; the hard cases they brought to Moses, but they judged every small case themselves.
> —Exodus 18:25–26

Moses made a big mistake at the last minute when he was just a few miles away from finishing his long leadership journey (Deuteronomy 34: 1-4). Ultimately, he did not cross over and take the assembly of Israel into the Promised Land (Numbers 20:12, (Deuteronomy 34: 1 – 4). After the death of Moses, Joshua led the children of Israel with wisdom and finished the journey well because he learned from the past and followed God's instruction. He also followed the leadership style of Moses in the decision-making process:

> This Book of the Law shall not depart from your mouth, but you shall meditate in it day and night, that you may observe to do according to all that is written in it. For then you will make your way prosperous, and then you will have good success.
>
> —Joshua 1:8

> Then Joshua gathered all the tribes of Israel to Shechem and called for the elders of Israel, for their heads, for their judges, and for their officers; and they presented themselves before God.
>
> —Joshua 24:1

Eventually the Israelites asked Samuel to give them a king like all the other nations had, a king to reign over them and protect them from their enemies. They made this request, they said, because Samuel's sons were corrupt and did not follow in the ways of their father: "But his sons did not walk in his ways; they turned aside after dishonest gain, took bribes, and perverted justice" (1 Samuel 8:3). Though his sons did not walk in God's ways, Samuel himself had led the Israelites in a godly fashion. However, his leadership style was very different from that of a king, like the Israelites wanted. He thus had Israel evaluate him and proved himself blameless in their eyes:

"Here I am. Witness against me before the LORD and before His anointed: Whose ox have I taken, or whose donkey have I taken, or whom have I cheated? Whom have I oppressed, or from whose hand have I received any bribe with which to blind my eyes? I will restore it to you."

And they said, "You have not cheated us or oppressed us, nor have you taken anything from any man's hand."

— 1 Samuel 12:3–4

Samuel was not pleased by Israel's request for a king because a king's rule was not the best option for them. Yet they insisted on a king, though they should have used their right to bring their case first to their leaders and then to Samuel. God, however, respected their freedom and told Samuel to fulfill their request, even though He knew they had made a wrong choice. He instructed Samuel to educate the Israelites about the way a king rules his nation:

"Now therefore, heed their voice. However, you shall solemnly forewarn them, and show them the behavior of the king who will reign over them."

So, Samuel told all the words of the LORD to the people who asked him for a king. And he said, "This will be the behavior of the king who will reign over you: He will take your sons and appoint them for his own chariots and to be his horsemen, and some will run before his chariots. He will appoint captains over his thousands and captains over his fifties, will set some to plow his ground and reap his harvest, and some to make his weapons of war and equipment for his chariots. He will take your daughters to be perfumers, cooks, and bakers. And he will take the best of your fields, your vineyards, and your olive groves, and give them to his servants. He will take a tenth of your grain and your vintage, and give it to his officers and servants. And he will take your male servants, your female servants, your finest young men and your donkeys, and put them to his work. He will take a tenth of your sheep. And you will be his servants. And you will cry out in that day because of your king whom you have chosen for yourselves, and the LORD will not hear you in that day."

—1 Samuel 8:9–18

The Israelites chose to subject themselves to exploitation and oppression by asking for a king against the will of God. They did not listen to God's warning, and consequently, Saul was appointed as their first king, outside their sacred tradition. The king of their choice soon disobeyed God, however, and did not finish well. God, who knew in advance that their choice would not work, had in store a godly man, David, whom He was coaching until the death of their first king, Saul. But Saul was so obsessed with power that his heart was filled with jealousy against David immediately after David killed Goliath, Israel's greatest threat, and won victory for them. From that time on, Saul worked hard to find a way to kill David, although David was only a shepherd boy at the time. Here we can see that God's leadership style grants full freedom; in which case He is always in control, His followers reap the consequences of the decisions they make.

Chosen by God, David became the king of Israel after the death of King Saul. Because of David's obedient and law-abiding heart, God called him a man after His own heart. David followed God's ways in his leadership and thereby gained God's favor. "Your word is a lamp to my feet and a light to my path," he declared in Psalm 119:105. "I delight to do Your will, O my God, and Your law is within my heart," he stated in Psalm 40:8.

The eternal king, Jesus Christ, who descended from the line of King David, came to earth and modeled the desired leadership style to the generations of the New Testament. This leadership style perfectly displayed God's initial leadership design in His system of government:

> But Jesus called them to Himself and said, "You know that the rulers of the Gentiles lord it over them, and those who are great exercise authority over them. Yet it shall not be so among you; but whoever desires to become great among you, let him be your servant."
> —Matthew 20:25–26

This is the leadership style that the United States has developed as a nation. As a person who has experienced autocratic leadership, I am moved when American leaders running for office say, "I will serve you," indicating that they are in the hands of those they serve. As I pointed out earlier in this chapter, God instructed Samuel to heed the voice of those he led, and that is how democracy works in the United States:

> In a democracy, supposedly, the leader does not pronounce God's will to the people but carries out what is decided by the people. Some might object that the leader is, in that case, mainly a follower—he or she does what the community says when it "speaks" through elections, through polls, through constituent pressure. Such leaders are not like the Pericles of Thucydides, able to displease their followers. They compromise their principles. They are bribed, if not with money, then with acceptance, or office, or ego satisfaction. [1]

God uses various methods to turn human beings from their wrong ways. Foremost among these, He puts His law into their hearts. If they follow it, they make their way prosperous (Joshua 1: 8) and protect themselves from evil:

> For when Gentiles, who do not have the law, by nature do the things in the law, these, although not having the law, are a law to themselves, who show the work of the law written in their hearts, their conscience also bearing witness, and between themselves their thoughts accusing or else excusing them.
>
> —Romans 2:14–15

All human beings have natural law in their hearts, and it whispers warnings to their ears before they act. *Collins English Dictionary* defines natural law as follows:

1. A law or body of laws that derives from nature and is believed to be binding upon human actions apart from or in conjunction with laws established by human authority.
2. (Philosophy) an ethical belief or system of beliefs supposed to be inherent in human nature and discoverable by reason rather than revelation.
3. (Philosophy) the philosophical doctrine that the authority of the legal system or of certain laws derives from their justifiability by reason, and indeed that a legal system which cannot be so justified has no authority.

Several Oromo proverbs from my culture provide examples as well:

- You can't climb two trees at the same time just because you have two legs.
- One shouldn't sleep on the road and pray to God for protection.

- One who has never experienced "burn" runs towards fire.

The government leadership styles that will be discussed in the following pages have their roots in the above-mentioned biblical leadership style. In fact, most of the laws of Western countries revolve around the Ten Commandments and the instructions in the books of Moses, the Torah (the first five books in the Bible). It has been said that "David's court historian has a good claim to be the founding father of western history" [2]

The laws of Europe were codified around the concept of the divine right of kings, which asserted that a king of a given country was placed there by God's will and thus received direct guidance from God. With this mind-set, kings used religion to retain full power; this in turn gave way to the rule of tyranny, from which the Founding Fathers of the United States of America fled. In its place, they established a new world free from such rule.

As you can see from the lessons Samuel taught the Israelites on a king's rules and regulations, the Communists got the idea of "stateless government" from the Bible, although they did not acknowledge it.

2

The Culture of Government Leadership in Ethiopia

Located in the tropical zone of east Africa, between the equator and the Tropic of Cancer, Ethiopia is one of the oldest countries in the world—over three thousand years old. It is the only African nation that has never been colonized by foreign forces, with the exception of the five-year invasion by Italy from 1935 to 1941. Known as the Horn of Africa, Ethiopia has a total area of 1,127,127 square kilometers (935,183 square miles). The country became landlocked after Eritrea gained its independence from Ethiopia in 1991. According to the 2007 Census from the Ethiopian Central Statistical Agency (CSA), the population of Ethiopia was 73,750,932. The 2012 estimate suggests that the population has reached 84,320,987, making it thwe second-most populous nation in Africa.

Archaeological findings confirm that Ethiopia is the origin of humankind [3] A 3.5-million-year-old complete human skeleton, Lucy, was discovered in 1974 in the Awash region of Ethiopia, 224 kilometers from Addis Ababa, the capital city, by an American paleoanthropologist, Dr. Donald

C. Johnson. Lucy is her American name, while her Ethiopian name is *Dinknesh* (Amharic word for "you are wonderful"). Lucy's skeleton toured museums in the United States for five years, then returned to Ethiopia on May 1, 2013.

Following the unearthing of Lucy, archaeologists also discovered a human skeleton that the scientists named *Idaltu*, meaning "elder," dating back 5.8 million years. Whether Lucy is Eve or Idaltu is Adam, I suppose that the Garden of Eden was not far from Ethiopia, although I don't know, of course, how far God moved Adam and Eve when He banished them from the garden. Perhaps that is why the Nile River was named after the biblical Gihon (Nile): "The name of the second river is Gihon; it is the one which goes around the whole land of Cush" (Gencis.2:3).

Ethiopia is also the place where coffee originated. Furthermore, according to legend, Ethiopia is the resting place of the ark of the covenant that lies in St. Mary of Zion's church in Axum.

Ethiopia has three different climate zones that vary depending on the elevation. They are as follows: (1) The *kolla* (tropical zone) lies below 1,830 meters and has an average annual temperature of 27 degrees Celsius. It is the hottest region in Ethiopia, with temperatures up to 50 degrees Celsius. The Danakil Depression (Danakil Desert) is located here and lies about 125 meters below sea level. The region also includes the Eritrean lowlands, the eastern Ogaden, the deep tropical valleys of the Tekezé and Blue Nile Rivers, as well as the peripheral areas along the Sudanese and Kenyan borders. (2) The *woina dega* (subtropical zone) covers the highland areas, with an elevation of 1,830–2,440 meters and an average annual temperature of about 22 degrees Celsius. (3) The *dega* is the cool zone, with an elevation above 2,440 meters and an average annual temperature of about 16 degrees Celsius. The cool zone consists of the central parts of the western and eastern sections of the northwestern plateau and a small area around Harer. The elevation of Addis Ababa, the capital city, ranges from 2,200 to 2,600 meters, and the maximum temperature is 26 degrees Celsius, while the minimum is 4 degrees Celsius.

Ethiopian seasons are as follows: (1) *Kiremt* or *meher* (the summer season) covers the months of June, July, and August. The country receives heavy rainfalls in these three months. (2) *Tseday* (spring) is also called the "harvest season" and includes the months of September, October, and November. (3) *Bega* (winter) is known as the dry season and covers the months of December, January, and February. (4) *Belg* (autumn) covers the months of March, April, and May. There is occasional rain in this season, and May is the hottest month in Ethiopia.

Thousands of books have been written on leadership, and people define leadership in different ways. Leadership differs greatly from country to country and from situation to situation. The leadership style of a particular country is a result of that country's background, the principles by which it was established, and the way it adheres to those principles. From my observation, the way a given leader comes to power, as well as the motives of the leader and those he leads, determines the definition and the outcome of his leadership. Only those who come to leadership, not by might, nor by power, but humbled by the spirit of serving others, meet the original goal of leadership—the type of leadership that I highlighted in chapter 1. I think Nelson Mandela described it well: "Lead from the back—and let others believe they are in front."

A common definition of leadership in the United States is mobilizing others towards a shared goal. This definition is clearly seen in how the president of the United States gains his presidency. The president's party does not decide his presidency, but rather, endorses him for the election campaign. After assuming office in the government of the people, by the people, and for the people, he is governed by the Constitution

31

of the United States and controlled by the general public that made his leadership possible and with whom he shares the goals for which he was elected.

In Ethiopia, however, the situation is different. Emperor Haile Sellassie I had a modern constitution adopted for the first time in the nation's history. His successors formulated their own constitutions after coming to power. With the current government of Ethiopia (FDRE[1]), the general public votes for the ruling party, and the party decides the leader (head of state). In 2005, the Ethiopian people participated in democratic voting for the first time in their history.

According to Article 69 of the FDRE constitution, the President is the head of state, but his role is mostly ceremonial. Article 74 gives the Prime Minister all executive power. Article 74 Sub-Article 1 states, "The Prime Minister is the Chief Executive, the Chairman of the Council of Ministers, and the Commander-in-Chief of the national armed forces." Article 72 sub-Article 3 states that the term of office of the Prime Minister is for the duration of the mandate of the House of Peoples' Representatives. Article 74, Sub-Article 4 specifies the term of office of the President to be six years and no person shall be elected President for more than two terms.

The Prime Minster presents high-level leaders (ministers, deputy ministers, and the like) to the parliament for their approval while the President shall, upon recommendation by the Prime Minister, appoint ambassadors and other envoys to represent the country abroad (Article 71 sub-Article 3). Sub-Article 6 states, "The president, upon recommendation by the Prime Minister and in accordance with law, shall grant high military titles.

In the pages that follow, I will walk you through the different government leaderships that Ethiopia has experienced. In so doing, I will share briefly my personal experiences with

---

[1] FDRE: Federal Democratic Republic of Ethiopia

three regimes in Ethiopia: (1) Emperor Haile Selassie I of the monarchy, (2) the Derg's (Peoples Democratic Republic of Ethiopia) Communist junta, and (3) the current Federal Democratic Republic of Ethiopia. In discussing the reign of Emperor Haile Selassie I, I will use references from my readings as well. My discussion of the latter two governments will concentrate on my broad-ranged personal experiences.

The ancient monarchy's ruling line that governed Ethiopia until Emperor Haile Selassie I was deposed in 1974 claimed direct descent from King Menilek I, the son of the biblical King Solomon of Israel and the queen of Sheba of Ethiopia. According to legend, his mother, Queen Makeda (the queen of Sheba), traveled to Jerusalem in the tenth century BC to learn of King Solomon's wisdom. There she conceived Menilek I, the first emperor of Ethiopia. The legendary story of his birth is found in *Fetha Nagast*[2] (*The Law of the Kings*). Article 2 of the Ethiopian constitution that was revised in 1955 states that the ruling line descended from Emperor Menelik I, the son of Makeda, queen of Ethiopia, and Solomon, king of Israel[4] Here is Article 2 of the Ethiopian constitution:

> The Imperial dignity shall remain perpetually attached to the line of Haile Selassie I, descendant of King Sahle Selassie, whose line descends without interruption from the dynasty of Menelek I, son of the Queen of Ethiopia, the Queen of Sheba, and King Solomon of Jerusalem.

---

[2] "*Fetha Nagast*" is 4th-century's accounts written in Ge'ez on how Queen Makeda/the Queen of Sheba of Ethiopia met King Solomon of Israel and the birth of their son Menelek I, how the Ark of the Covenant came to Ethiopia, the Solomonic line of the Ethiopian Emperors' and Ethiopians' conversion to the Israelites faith.

Ethiopia is a nation that has exercised a variety of leadership styles, including aristocratic, autocratic, and federalist democratic. I have witnessed these myself and feel that Ethiopia serves as a good case study for the topic of this book. In my discussion, I have divided Ethiopian leaders into three groups: (1) heads of state, (2) executive leaders, and (3) subordinate leaders who report to their given leaders, depending on the hierarchy. Those whom I classify as executive leaders include ministers, vice ministers, the current government's federal president, and presidents of regional-national states. Those whom I classify as subordinate leaders consist of department heads; heads of various positions; *kebele* (district), city, and regional administrators; and other such leaders. Under Emperor Haile Selassie I's feudal system, the leaders included feudal lords (*balabat* in Amharic), nobles, the clergy, and government officials.

The three heads of state of Ethiopia in whose regimes I was a subject displayed unique differences. President Mengistu Haile Mariam differed from the two wise intellectual leaders, Emperor Haile Selassie I and Prime Minister Meles Zenawi, in that his actions were based on his feelings rather than on thinking and reasoning. The leadership style of all three varied, depending on the nature of the leadership that gave a tendency to hold on to power "until death do us part." For Emperor Haile Selassie I, the leadership position was a birthright passed to him by the tradition of the monarchy, which was further confirmed by Article 4 of the 1955 revised constitution. It reads as follows:

By virtue of His Imperial Blood, as well as by the anointing which He has received, the person of the Emperor is sacred, His dignity is inviolable and His Powers indisputable. He is consequently entitled to all the honors due to Him in accordance with tradition and the present Constitution. Any one so bold as to seek to injure the Emperor will be punished.

For the emperor's successors, leadership was earned with military power, making it hard to easily transfer power to a party that had not labored for it. The late Prime Minister of Ethiopia, Meles Zenawi, fought a guerilla war against the brutal Marxist junta led by President Mengistu Haile Mariam for seventeen years and gained victory through military might and sacrifice. In a speech he delivered at a UN-sponsored referendum held at the UN/ECA in Addis Ababa in April 1993, he referred to this effort when he said, "Thanks to our greater and mighty struggle" ("Letalakuna ena lehayalu tiglachin misgana yigbawuna " in Amharic) For that matter, we could say that Emperor Haile Selassie I also had to earn his leadership, because he fought a bloody war against a well-prepared and well-armed modern foreign invader, Italy, by which he regained and restored the monarchy.

In reality, no head of state in any country has obtained that high post without a struggle. Even in the United States, the battles that candidates fight in running for office have never been easy, although no one pulls a trigger for it. To even dare to run for office, candidates must first be confident that their personal lives are clean enough to pass the public's test. Second, they must meet the criteria set by the Constitution in order to gain the endorsement of their parties (Republican and Democrat) for their campaigns. After being endorsed, they are seriously scrutinized and grilled on the campaign trail (I call it "grill trail") for many months.

In most cases, the mentality of the leaders in Ethiopia has been shaped by the aristocratic tradition of the monarchy that ruled the country for centuries. The Amhara was the ruling class of the aristocracy then, and they had a saying that gave way to much corruption: "*Sishom yalbelabet sishar yikochewal*" in Amharic, meaning "one who doesn't eat when appointed will regret it when deposed." In far too many cases, soon after Ethiopian leaders assume power, they begin strategizing how to manipulate and use the law to suit their needs, using their leadership power to "eat." Consequently, corruption and poverty have become part of the culture in Ethiopia, although there is no law that endorses corruption. The historian and moralist Lord Acton, in an opinion in a letter to Bishop Mandell Creighton in 1887, put it this way:

> Power tends to corrupt, and absolute power corrupts absolutely. Great men are almost always bad men.

Instead of implementing with honesty the government policies they are entrusted with, power-hungry individuals strategize on how to take advantage of the very policies that govern their country. To cover up their illegal deeds, such leaders apply premeditated tactics, including false evidence that is masqueraded by legal provisions. This practice bears negative effects that undermine the efforts of others in leadership to bring positive change. The situation is worsened when the top leaders are reluctant or unwilling to control the subordinate leaders or are themselves beneficiaries of the corruption. Since subordinate leaders exercise dual power as government appointees and as members of the ruling political party, in most cases they have the power to take advantage of their direct access on the grassroots level and corruptly exploit available resources. In such instances, the top leaders are used as a shield for their corruption. This type of leadership renders a negative image of the governance of the country and affects the outcome of its leadership. As Mr. Jeremy Pope, head of anticorruption watchdog group, Transparency International, has stated:

What has been revealed is a hopelessly corrupt political elite—a political class across the spectrum that simply sees politics as a way of becoming wealthy. . . . As long as politics is seen as the path to wealth, then Africa is on a downward path. [5]

3

Emperor Haile Selassie I
of the Monarchy
(Regent/Prince, 1917–1930; Emperor, 1930–1974)

The ancient Ethiopian monarchy did not have a formal constitution with religious and traditional laws as its basis until Emperor Haile Selassie introduced one. During those earlier periods, the *Feetha Negest*[3] meaning "The Law of the Kings"), a written document that was the law of the land, was used as a source for the traditions and rules followed in the imperial court as well as in legal, ceremonial, religious, and routine matters.

I will begin my discussion of Emperor Haile Selassie I's reign with Emperor Menilek II, the grandson of King Sahle Selassie, whose reign extended from 1795 to 1847.

---

[3] Compiled by an Egyptian Coptic Christian, Abdul Fada'il Ibn al-'Asad around 1240, "*Fətha Nägäśt*" (in <u>Ge'ez</u>), was translated into <u>Ge'ez</u> and adopted to the Ethiopia 's national context during the reign of emperor Zar'a Ya'kob. 'Ibn al-Assal took the laws partly from apostolic writings and the codes of law of the Byzantine rulers. "Fətha Nägäśt combines spiritual and secular matters and was used by Coptic Orthodox Church and the state.

In order to expand and centralize his government, Emperor Menilek II established his headquarters in Addis Ababa. His expansion motive and strategy had its root in that of Emperor Amde Tsion, who ruled Ethiopia from 1314 to 1344, after the Solomonic dynasty was restored. In consolidating that new dynasty's power, Emperor Amde Tsion made the Amharic language and Christianity integral parts of the imperial government, establishing an unbreakable relationship between the church and the crown. Under his rule, Ethiopia expanded to the south through military might. Military power and evangelism were both used to control the newly conquered southern lands and for exploitation of the same:

> As imperial control grew, so did the economy, which delivered gold, ivory and slaves from the south and central Ethiopia to the cost for export to the Middle East. . . . Amda Syion shrewdly invited the Muslim communities that dominated commerce and the trade routes into a symbiotic relationship. To continue their activities, they had to recognize his suzerainty, pay him taxes on trade, and otherwise conform to his administration. [6]

Under feudal autonomy, Emperor Amde Tsion gained ownership of all land and thereby allocated *gult*[4] to his followers or servicemen as a reward for their service. In turn, they became gult lords. The gult lords administered their localities, supplied soldiers and animals during wartime, demanded service from their subjects, and collected taxes and tributes.[6] The gult was transferred from father to son and became a hereditary right (p. 20). Amde Tsion's administrative system was further modified by his successors and was sustained until the monarchy was totally abolished in 1975.

---

[4] "Gult"is "land tenure," or "fiefs" that was introduced by emperor Amdetsion

Emperor Menilek II used that same system in his territorial expansion and administration. Under him, land tenure took the form of *rist*[5] and *"gult"*. *Rist"* is a communal type of land tenure that could be transferred to family members. *Gult* rights were granted by the emperor or his designated representative to loyalists and service men as a reward for service and to Ethiopian Orthodox churches as endowments.

The rights of *rist* lords were maintained for the emperor's designees and the nobility, while loyalists and servicemen received *gult*[6]. "Gult" holders were entitled to collect tribute and demand labor from the use of the land they held. Emperor Menelik II extended gult rights and allocated substantial gult to local chiefs and other non-Amharas who were assigned low-level administrative positions among their own people. These were classified as *balabat*[7], while the peasants became *gebari*.[8] The Amhara service men from the north who were granted land rights among indigenous people of the south were called *"neftegna"*[9] The Ethiopian Orthodox Church and its monasteries were also granted rist as endowments, thus enabling Orthodox clergy to receive and enjoy gult rights from the church.

Emperor Menilek II started his territorial expansion to the south while he was the king of Showa and Emperor Yohannes II in Tigray was in control of Ethiopia. The aim of his expansion was to Christianize the heathen as well gain the abundant wealth of the south and use it to acquire the imperial throne. Of course, Emperor Yohannes II was unaware of this:

---

[5] "Rist" is a communal land tenure that was practiced in Northern Ethiopia (Among the Amharas and Tigres)

[6] *"Gult"* was not transferable under Emperor Menelik II's rule

[7] *"Balabat"* is an Amharic term for "Lords"

[8] *"Gebari"* is an Amharic word in relation to "serfs."

[9] *"Neftegna"* is an Amharic word for "a person who owns a gun" referring to those settlers who were granted right over land and the people in southern Ethiopia.

Not so obvious to the emperor was Menelik's realization that he needed new sources of wealth to purchase weapons that one day he might use to acquire the Solomonic throne. [7]

Emperor Menilek II's ambition of expansion to the south was fulfilled through his most faithful and diligent fighter, Dejazmach[10] (later elevated to *ras*[11]) Gobena Danchi, an Oromo who conquered his fellow Oromos for Menelik II and forced the entire south to submit. The tributes that the then-king Menelik II paid to Emperor Yohannes II came from the wealth that he exploited from the south through his other Oromo agent, Abba Jifar of Jimma. Abba Jifar of Jimma paid him large tributes in return for autonomy. The wealth came through slave trade from the southwest and the exploitation of gold and ivory, as noted below:

Abba Jifar II's (r.1878 – 19320) wealth and the well-being of his state were intimately tied up with the slave trade from the southwest and slavery as a mode of production. He facilitated the trade through Jima as a source of transit revenues and as a way to obtain ivory from the south; and he and other officials used salves on the large farms they had formed from land appropriated from the traditional users. Abba Jifar's exploitation of slaves supported his court and government and paid Menelik his tribute. Similar situation in Leka, Guma and Gera benefitted Menelik who also taxed sales of slaves in Showa or their transit through the province or both. Meanwhile, Yohannes was busy safeguarding Ethiopia's independence. [8]

[10] *"Dejazmach"* is and Amharic term for "commander of the gate" and was a title given to a distinguished nobility

[11] *"Ras"* is an Amharic term meaning head. It is a title equivalent to duke and was given to nobility

Categorically, those with very dark skin, thick lips, and kinky hair were classified as slaves (Negros) at the time, but Abba Jifar indiscriminately targeted the Oromos, his own tribe, for the slave trade. My paternal grandmother told me what she personally witnessed about the slave trade. Her brother-in-law, who was involved in that business, would bring young men to her house, one at a time, and tell them to wait for him, while unknown to them, he was arranging their sale to his customers. Once my grandmother realized the secret, she informed the young men who were brought to her house and helped them escape. She packed them food for their journey home and escorted them to ensure their safe exit. Her brother-in-law was never successful in any of his attempts, but he kept trying.

Since I personally never saw slavery in Ethiopia and didn't even know much about it, I never imagined how bad the slave trade really was until I learned its horrifying story during my visit to the House of Slaves in Senegal, Dakar, in 1993 and 1994. My visit to the House of Slaves left me with a lifetime memory of the crime against humanity that took place there. Built in 1776, the House of Slaves is located on Goree Island, a forty-five-acre island off the coast of Senegal, just four miles from the city of Dakar. The House of Slaves displays two completely different features. Upstairs is a luxurious residence that housed the slave traders, while downstairs is a warehouse with very narrow rooms where men, women, and children slaves were held separately. Through an exit door at the back, the slaves boarded the ships that took them to their final destinations. West African men, women, and children were forcibly taken from their homes, brought to Goree Island, sold into slavery, held practically naked in the warehouse (with only a small piece of cloth covering their genitals), and then shackled and chained neck to neck.

The male slaves were shackled, chained neck to neck, and placed in two separate rooms. These eight-square-feet rooms each held thirty to fifty men. Women, girls, and children were held in separate cells. These narrow cells had a very tiny window to let light in and held from 150 to 200 slaves total. The slaves lived in these conditions for about three months until they were shipped off.

The slaves had to sit naked, chained neck to neck and shackled, with their backs against the walls. There was not enough space for them to lie down to sleep. Their living conditions were so unhygienic that many died in their cells. If a male slave rebelled, he was shackled chin to ankle and shoved into a very small room under the stairs as punishment. Sick slaves were thrown into the ocean and eaten by sharks. I saw the unimaginably terrible condition these slaves faced in their temporary stay at the House of Slaves. They could only imagine how much worse the permanent house of slavery would be under masters who purchased them as commodities to make profits. After all, if their own brothers sold them into such astounding dehumanization, what could they expect from their foreign owners?

House of Slaves on Gore Island

"Door of no return" rear side

Goree Island

After Emperor Menilek II's death, his daughter, Empress Zewditu, was crowned and proclaimed Elect of God, Conquering Lion of the Tribe of Judah, and Queen of Kings, on September 27, 1916. Upon her coronation, Ras Tafari Makonnen (later Emperor Haile Selassie I), was proclaimed heir to the throne and crown prince. Soon after he gained his regency, Ras Tafari Makonnen introduced widespread ambitious reforms to modernize the country, although Empress Zewditu had the final say and the Ras's power was limited.

As a strategy to get direct knowledge from the West as well as convince the nobility of the empire that modernization and progress would lead Ethiopia to prosperity and guarantee the empire's continued independence, Prince Regent Ras Tafari took the leading nobles and aristocrats to Europe. [9]

Crown Prince, Regent Ras Tafari Makonnen, preparing to meet Pope Pius XI in audience, accompanied by the Vatican secretary of State, Ethiopian Princes and nobility, and with clergy and nobility of the Vatican state, 1923.

Since Ethiopia had been so isolated, it was the first experience for many of them to travel to Western countries.

However, in the beginning, Europeans didn't trust Prince Regent Ras Tafari:

> Europeans thought Tafari corrupt and venal, though his behavior was completely understandable in traditional terms, since he redistributed the proceeds of his venture to Addis Ababa's poor, including the soldiery. [10]

Prince Regent Ras Tafari Makonnen placed major importance on education as a building block to modernize his country. Eventually he opened Ethiopia's doors to Western countries to utilize their expertise towards achieving his goals. Placing his trust in the younger generation, he staffed his modern administration with educated leaders to transform the nation. Eventually, while he was still a regent, he began building new schools in Addis Ababa. On April 25, 1925, he opened a boarding school in Addis Ababa named Tafari Makonnen School, with a plan to have young boys from all over the country receive a high-quality modern education. According to Mr. Emmanuel Abraham, one of the first students of the school, the prince regent and his wife, Princess Menen (later empress), looked after the students at Tafari Makonnen School like a mother and a father:

> The Prince then arrived surrounded by a group of retainers...... His Highness made the following remarks: "Do not fear because you left your home district or because you are separated from your relatives. We shall make every effort to look after you like a father and a mother."

> At first all the meals were prepared and sent to us at the Heir Apparent's palace. Sweets which we called "sugar" and cakes used to be sent regularly to "the

Wollega boys" by the order of His Highness. As the numbers of boarders grew.....our meals were cooked in the school compound. Even then, on Thursday of every week our Lady Woizero Menen (Later Her Majesty the Empress) used to bring us specially cooked food and honey water. She would sit at the head of one of the tables and watch us while we ate. The Prince would drop in and move from table to table, talking to some of the boys and encouraging us. In this way, both the Prince and the Princess took care of us like father and mother, and we pursued our studies in comfort with a sense of well-being.[11]

Having Ethiopia obtain membership with the League of Nations (presently the United Nations) was at the top of his priority list because he strongly believed this would enable Ethiopia to sustain its sovereignty under international law. In order for Ethiopia to qualify for membership in the League of Nations, he eventually proclaimed the end of slavery in 1923. He had yet to face strong hostility to his modernizing zeal from the conservative nobility. When the opposition did come, it was quite vocal:

They rigorously opposed his every move towards modernizing the administration of the Empire, raising objections, saying that the things the Prince wanted to do were "un-Ethiopian." Particularly, when told that slaves were to be freed, Fitawrari Hapte Giorgis is said to have sputtered with outrage, "So is my wife to carry water on her back from the springs herself?" [9]

Empress Zewditu elevated Ras Tafari to kingship on September 22, 1928, granting him full power. Upon the death of Empress Zewditu, the crown council proclaimed Tafari emperor. [12] Ras Tafari was crowned emperor of Ethiopia on November 2, 1930, and took his baptismal name Haile Selassie, meaning "the might of Trinity," and assumed the title of King of Kings, Elect of God, Conquering Lion of the Tribe of Judah, from the monarchical tradition.

While still a regent, Haile Selassie had greatly desired for Empress Zewditu to proclaim a constitution. However, not everyone shared his wish:

> Some of the great nobles, to whose advantage it was to rule the country without a constitution, had pretended that it would diminish the dignity and authority of Queen Zewditu if a constitution were set up.[13]

Just one year after his coronation, in 1931, Emperor Haile Selassie spearheaded the adoption of the first modern constitution of Ethiopia, thereby establishing the rule of law. That constitution was promulgated from the Meiji Constitution of Japan and contained fifty-five articles arranged in seven chapters [14] Not only did the constitution affirm the emperor's power and reserve succession to his line, but it also gave certain power to the two-house parliament in that they had to approve finances and taxes and were allowed to question ministers as well as disapprove imperial decrees. [15] In the preface to his translation of this constitution into English, William Stern stated, "It is worthy of note that this was the first instance in history where an absolute ruler had sought voluntarily to share sovereign power with the subjects of his realm [16] Harold G. Marcus also states, "Never before had a monarch achieved such a broad national consensus" (p. 134). The constitution was revised in 1955 and contained 131 articles.

Immediately after his coronation, the emperor began implementing his modernization plan. He hired seven Western advisers from six Western countries in Europe and one from the United States Rome. [17] Many schools were built, most of them in Addis Ababa.

The monarchy's deep-rooted aristocratic tradition left a legacy of persistent leadership problems. What Emperor Haile Selassie I inherited from his predecessors was a society characterized by gross inequality between the aristocratic elite ruling class consisting of land lords, royal family, clergy fundamentalists, and government officials, and the larger majority of illiterate, impoverished peasants. After Emperor Menilek II's Christianization efforts, the Coptic Orthodox church was given a great deal of power in the governmental system, thus establishing an unbreakable marriage between church and state. For example, the Crown Council, which Emperor Menilek II instituted as an executive body of the aristocracy, was composed of leading noblemen, ranking church officials, and government ministers [18]

The Orthodox Church and the state worked hand in hand in the centralization and building of the Ethiopian Empire, and they remained bonded until the disgraceful fall of Emperor Haile Selassie I in 1974, which brought monarchy rule to an end. As mentioned above, the Orthodox Church was given land that was appropriated from the local peasantry inhabitants, who became serfs, or *gebari*. The gebari were obliged to give the clergy and the gult holders fiefs or tribute from their agricultural products, which were generated through old-style arduous farming techniques. Concerning the church's role in the empire, Gebru Tareke, states:

> Central to the Church's code of morality was the belief in divine omnipotence, the sanctity of the royal authority, and the justness over lordship. Supported by the tradition of awesome antiquity, enjoying direct access to land and to the products of the peasants, and exercising the virtual monopoly in education, the Church affected nearly every facet of rural life. . . .

By providing a code of ethics that stressed habits of conformity, deference to authority, and reverence for tradition, there can be little doubt that it helped in maintenance of tranquility in a world otherwise filled with misery and tension.[19]

Funded by the state, Orthodox churches that displayed a deep Amharic culture were planted all over the newly occupied territories of the south and southwest. Consequently, the word *Amhara* came to be oftentimes used interchangeably with the word *Christian*. The Orthodox churches also established schools, named "Priest-schools" (Yekes timhirt in Amharic), all over the country. These schools were run by Orthodox priests who were assigned from Gojam (Amhara region) and who taught the Ge'ez language as well as literacy skills. Students learned to recite the book of Psalms in Ge'ez without any knowledge of the meaning in their own language and were trained to become deacons. The main focus of the Orthodox Church was Christianizing the heathens and teaching the people to be law-abiding and loyal to the king because of his mandate from heaven. Christianization was imposed, and Christianized individuals were expected to carry the Christian names given to them, such as *Gebre Mariam*, meaning "slave of Mary" (*Walate Mariam* for a female). Un-Christianized Oromos were called *Galla* and ostracized.

Let me share with you the story my parents told me about their experience in that regard. My mother was not Christianized until the age of twelve. One day before she was a Christian, she went to the river to fetch water, and on her way home, the water jar that she was carrying broke. She was scared of being punished by her mother and said she wanted to die rather than face the punishment. She then remembered that she had been told not to mention the name of the Trinity before she was Christianized, lest she die. Nonetheless, she started saying repeatedly, *"Bassumaa waalde"* (in the name of the Father, the Son), and she didn't die. The words were in Amharic, a language she had never learned, and she didn't even say the words correctly when she related her story to me; she said *bassumaa waalde* instead of *besimeAb beWold*. When my parents accepted Protestant Christianity, they were labeled "unholy" and "thread breakers," a reference to the thread that the Orthodox priest tied on the neck of a Christianized individual during the Christianization ritual, and other derogatory names.

Coptic Orthodox Christianity remained the state religion, and the bishop and clergy retained a great deal of power in the government until the end of Emperor Haile Selassie I's regime. As a result, the Amhara tribe, which was the ruling class then, and the Orthodox Christianity of the Amhara culture maintained supremacy that still has not totally disappeared. Evangelical Christians often face persecution from Orthodox churches.

Let me make clear, however, that the problem is not Orthodox Christianity, but rather, the role it was given in the government since the reign of Emperor Amde Tsion in the fourteenth century. In fact, some Orthodox monks, who were greatly concerned about the integrity of Christianity and wanted to uphold the ethical values and dogma of the church in the mid fourteenth century, were the first to face persecution from their own church, which was the state's top ally. Let me give you a few examples.

First, Abba Ewostatewos (ca. 1273–1352) and his followers were severely persecuted for their stand against secular clergy and the monarchy. Abba Ewostatewos stressed spiritual independence in order to be isolated from corrupting state influence:

> He accused the secular clergy of their loose morality
> and the aristocracy of their venality by participating
> in the lucrative slave trade to Arabia, Sudan, and
> Egypt. . . . Abba Ewostatewos and his followers were

actively persecuted, and the unyielding leader was forced into exile, first in the Holy Land and later in Armenia, where he died in 1352.[20]

Second is the example of Rev. Gebre Ewostatewos, an evangelical priest from Eritrea, who converted to Protestant Christianity, and his friend, Daniel, a former Oromo slave who was freed in Masawa (Eritrea). They were the first indigenous missionaries to bring evangelical Christianity to the Oromo people at Bodji in Wollega, which is in western Ethiopia, in 1898. These two heroes of faith were persecuted by Orthodox clergy and priests. They were accused of rejecting Virgin Mary's intercessory role and the feast of *Taskar*[12]. After Daniel's death in 1905, his house was set on fire. Rev. Gebre Ewostatewos and two of his assistants died in the burning house while trying to rescue the mules of Daniel's family.[21]

The third example is Onesimos Nesib, a former slave who faced great suffering and persecution in bringing the Protestant Christian faith and educational opportunities to Wollega in southwestern Ethiopia around the end of the 1800s and the beginning of the 1900s. The Swedish missionaries first came to Nedjo, Wollega, in the early 1890s through Onesimos Nesib (previously named Hika), a former Oromo slave whom they evangelized and educated in his early life.

Hika was born at Hurumu, a small village in Illubabor in western Oromia, Ethiopia. Hika was kidnapped from his mother when he was around four years of age and was sold into slavery. He was given a new name, Nesib, and taken to Imkulu, a village near Port Masaw in Eritrea, which was then the northern part of Ethiopia. A French consulate official bought Hika from the slave traders, freed him from slavery, and gave him to the head of the Swedish Evangelical Mission

---

[12] *"Tascar"* is feast offered by a deceased person's family and relatives for the salvation of that person's soul, according to Orthodox Christianity.

(SEM) boys' school at Imkulu. In 1870, Hika was admitted to the SEM boys' school as one of six new students.

Hika was a brilliant student, and upon his request at age sixteen, he was baptized at the Swedish mission and took the Christian name Onesimos. Since he expressed a desire to evangelize the Oromo people someday in the future, the Swedish Evangelical Mission sent him to the seminary training institute of Johanneunld in Sweden, where he studied for five years. The above mentioned Reverend Gebre Ewostatewos, an Eritrean convert, and Daniel, the former slave who like Onesimos, had been freed by a French consulate official in Masawa, were his classmates at the Imkulu Swedish Evangelical Mission School.

In the fall of 1881, as soon as he completed his education in Sweden, Onesimos returned with a volunteer Swedish classmate to reach the Oromo people with the gospel of Jesus Christ. Onesimos's wife, her father, and three others joined him for his journey to Wollega. Because of travel restrictions imposed on Western missionaries, they had to take the longest and most difficult route. As they traveled south and west, their journey to Wollega was hindered by the raiding armies of Emperor Menilek II that were led by Degazmatch (later promoted to *ras*) Gobena Danchi in the campaign to expand the Ethiopian empire. [22]

In 1882, a second expedition also failed to reach Wollega. This journey went by way of the Sudan, traveling through the Nubian Desert to Egypt and then on to Khartoum. They faced unbelievable hardship. As there was no road, they used mules and camels and also sailed. They suffered illness in the desert to the point of death, and one of the group members, the Swedish doctor, died on their way back from the second unsuccessful expedition. Egyptian authorities who enjoyed slave trade with Abba Jifar, Emperor Menilek II's agent, as well as dishonest advisers, misled them so that they did not find their way.

In 1885, Onesimos received a green light to make a third attempt. Emperor Menilek II sent Onesimos, his wife, and three others to Aliu Amba in Showa to provide medical treatment for over two thousand people. They used that opportunity to proclaim the gospel in that town while waiting for permission to travel to Wollega. However, when they were asked to convert to Orthodox belief or leave, they returned to Imkulu, Eritrea.

After returning to Imkulu and while waiting for another possibility to travel to Wollega, Onesimos continued to preach the gospel to Oromos in Eritrea and translated the Bible into Afaan Oromo, an Oromo language. An Oromo young woman named Aster Ganno, who had been liberated from slavery and knew the Oromo language better than he did, helped him with the translation. Among those touched by Onesimos's burning desire to reach the Oromo people were Rev. Gebre Ewostatewos and Daniel. At Boji, Rev. Ewostateus evangelized in Afaan Oromo, the language he had learned from Onesimos. Onesimos also wrote a collection of a hundred hymns in Afaan Oromo, titled *Galata Waqayo Gofta Macha* (*Glory to God, the Lord of Hosts*), which was published in 1887. Needless to say, I grew up singing these hymns and still know most of them by heart.

Finally Onesimos was allowed by the government to carry out his mission in Wollega and received the blessing of the Asmara congregation to take with him five people, including Aster Ganno, his assistant translator, as missionaries. Onesimos left for Wollega on December 6, 1903, together with his family of four and the five missionaries from the Asmara congregation. They arrived at Nekemte on April 15, 1904. The journey took so long because there were no roads. After obtaining the approval of the archbishop of Ethiopia and Emperor Menilek II, Onesimos and his group launched their mission work of literacy education and evangelism at Nedjo and Bodji in western Wollega.

It was not with full freedom that Onesimos and his group started their work at Nedjo, however. He soon faced persecution from the Orthodox clergy, who opposed the spread of evangelical Protestant Christianity and preaching in the Oromo language rather than in Amharic. As mentioned earlier, Orthodox Christianity was the state religion, and its priests and clergy wielded much influence. Soon after Onesimos's work began to grow and two more missionary families from the Asmara church joined him, Onesimos was accused by the Orthodox priests at Nedjo of evangelizing and teaching in Afaan Oromo. He was taken to Addis Ababa, where he was tried on several false charges. Fortunately, the brutal charges were lifted through a decision of Emperor Menilek II, but only on the condition that Onesimos be banned from teaching and preaching and live only in Nekemte, capital city of Wollega. However, Onesimos continued his evangelism work in Nekemete, underground. The work that he had started in Nedjo was closed until a Swedish missionary obtained permission from Lij Iyasu in 1916 and renewed the good work.

The situation changed for Onesimos after the death of Emperor Menilek II. In 1916, Onesimos received permission from Lij Iyasu to preach and teach with full freedom, but he could preach only in Amharic with an interpreter into the Oromo language. Soon Lij Iyasu was succeeded by Ras Prince Tafari Makonnen, later known as Emperor Haile Selassie I, whose modernization program and reforms favored Onesimos and Western missionaries. Following his coronation, Emperor Haile Selassie I continued with his modernization plan, but he needed the help of foreign experts, especially in the areas of education and health care.

The situation was now greatly conducive for Onesimos and his team to carry out their mission the way Onesimos had initially intended, but he still had to speak in Amharic with an interpreter. Emperor Haile Selassie I's proclamation that "religion is private; country is shared" (Haymanot yegil

55

newu, hager yegara newu in Amharic) also made the situation better. The hostility of the Orthodox Church leaders towards the missionaries gradually faded after the death of the archbishop, and Onesimos and his team continued their work peacefully. However, persecution against evangelical believers was not totally eliminated, and like Onesimos, they too had to teach and preach in Amharic with an Oromo interpreter [23]

Eventually the missionaries established Evangelical Mekane Yesus churches in Nekemte, Nedjo, and Bodji, and they achieved great success in expanding their work to many parts of the country beyond Wollega. Their ministry incorporated a holistic approach committed to reaching the unreachable with evangelism, education, health care, and rural development. Presently the number of believers exceeds five million, and there are many renowned scholars all over the world who are the fruit of that Nedjo Swedish mission school. Here are two examples: (1) Professor Ephraim Isaac, the first professor to be hired at Harvard in Afro-American studies (1969–1977), was voted best teacher each year, and the Ephraim Isaac Prize for Excellence in African Studies was named in his honor. (2) Dr. Bekele Geleta was the first black secretary general of the International Federation of Red Cross and Red Crescent Societies (IFRC).

Onesimos Nesib's great-grandson, Pastor Barnabas Daniel Gammachis, has followed in his paternal great-grandfather's[13] footsteps and is pursuing his legacy as a pastor at the Mekane Yesus Church in London. His other great-grandson, Pastor Chala Gabisa Baro, is presently head pastor at the Ebenezer Oromo Evangelical Church in Minneapolis, Minnesota.

In the early years of his reign, Emperor Haile Selassie I was yet to face the unwinnable war against well-armed modern Italian forces. While the emperor was busy with his

---

[13] Please note that Ethiopian are named after their father (the father's name is the "last name"

reforms and modernization efforts, Italy was looking for the means to destroy Ethiopia's sovereignty in retaliation for Italy's humiliating defeat suffered at the battle of Adwa in 1894–1896. In the forty years since that defeat, Italy had made all the necessary preparations to wipe Ethiopians from their land and fulfill their initial plan of taking over the country. By 1935, Italy was fully ready for launching the planned war on Ethiopia, armed with modern weapons supported by aircraft carrying poisonous gas. By early September 1935, 200,000 men had already arrived in Ethiopia, with another 140,000 being processed to travel.

The emperor had placed his trust in the League of Nations, but they were no help. In early October 1935, the Italians launched the war against Ethiopia—a bloody invasion that Ethiopia was not prepared for. From October 1935 to the end of April 1936, Emperor Haile Selassie I and his army courageously waged this unwinnable war on the southern, eastern, and northern fronts until the Italians' intensive air attack with bombs and poisonous gas finally broke them. The emperor was forced by the Crown Council to leave the country in exile as a sign that Ethiopia would not submit to the foreign invader. The emperor, his family and ranked officials were taken by British war vessels and brought to England. [24]

> When Haile Selassie returned to Addis Ababa on April 30, he met with the council and was forced to accept its logic that as long as the sovereign was free and unbowed, Italian rule in Ethiopia could have no legitimacy.[24]

After five years in exile, the emperor finally secured the support of the British government to fight the Italian invader. He entered Gojam via Sudan on January 20, 1941, along with British Major General Charles Wingate, who trained

the army group called the Gideon Force. That army group
was composed of sixteen hundred exiles, patriots, and British
and Sudanese supporters. Already weakened and demoralized by the internal guerilla patriots, the Italian invaders
were defeated and surrendered with immense dignity and
ceremony, being allowed the honor of war.[25] Emperor Haile
Selassie victoriously entered Addis Ababa on May 5, 1941,
and addressed the Ethiopian people upon his arrival. Here is
an excerpt from his speech in which he addressed his nation:

> Today is the day on which we defeated our enemy.
> Therefore, when we say let us rejoice with our hearts,
> let not our rejoicing be in any other way but in the
> spirit of Christ. Do not return evil for evil. Do not
> indulge in the atrocities which the enemy has been
> practicing in his usual way, even to the last.
>
> Take care not to spoil the good name of Ethiopia
> by acts which are worthy of the enemy. We shall
> see that our enemies are disarmed and sent out the
> same way they came. As Saint George who killed
> the dragon is the patron saint of our army as well
> as of our allies, let us unite with our allies in ever-
> lasting friendship and amity in order to be able to
> stand against the godless and cruel dragon which has
> newly risen and which is oppressing mankind.[26]

Soon after his victorious return to Addis Ababa and the
restoration of his government, the emperor turned to the United
States and secured its support towards ensuring Ethiopia's
sovereignty and his future endeavors in education, agriculture, health care, transportation, foreign trade, development
projects, and other such ventures. The emperor's postwar
tasks included the additional burden of reconstructing his
war-trodden country. He wisely formed alliances with foreign
countries for help with the difficult task of nation building and

modernization, and the United States remained his favorite. Education was on the top of the emperor's priority list to transform the illiterate nation through educated manpower:

> To carry out modernization, Haile Sellassie was pushing forward to educate a devoted elite. He believed that the effect of education would transform his feudal state into a modern state.[27]

> The emperor's assessment did not appreciate that his country remained poor and backward even by African standards. He was not a relativist: he saw 240 medical facilities in 1955, whereas a quarter century earlier there had been 48. Tens of thousands of children were actually in school, compared with the meager few thousands of the 1931. Haile Sellassie was enough of a traditional figure that he could not grasp the reality of Ethiopia's problems as he witnessed and presided over changes that would have not been unimaginable to Menilek II, during whose reign he had been born, reared and educated. (p. 166)

By 1951, many schools had been opened, up to college level, including the Addis Ababa University College, which was upgraded to a university in 1961 and named after the emperor: Haile Selassie I University.

In 1950, the emperor invited Mr. Henry G. Bennet, who was then president of Oklahoma Agricultural and Mechanical College (presently Oklahoma State University) to discuss with him the possibility of establishing an agricultural college in Ethiopia. That connection resulted in securing the support of the United States towards establishing an agricultural college under the Point Four program. On June 16, 1954, the United States signed a technical-assistance agreement with Ethiopia through which Alemaya Agricultural College (presently Alemaya University), which was modeled under the American land-grant system, was established. Dr. Clyde R. Kindell of the United States played a remarkable role in giving Alemaya University a good start and laying a sustainable foundation. Dr. Kindell also served at Haile Selassie I University (presently Addis Ababa University) in Ethiopia for eight years, as the director of instruction and research at the Jimma Agricultural Technical School for two years, and as the president of Alemaya College of Agriculture and Mechanical Arts from 1961 to 1966. In 1967, after his return to the United States, he was named president of Murray State College. He held the position for twenty-seven years until he retired in 1994 and was inducted into the Oklahoma Higher Education Hall of Fame in 1998.

Training centers and colleges focusing on agriculture, public health, teacher training, polytechnic skills, and veterinary science were opened in the northern, eastern, and central (Showa) parts of Ethiopia. Some young Ethiopians were sponsored by imperial and foreign scholarships that were solicited for education abroad. The emperor also built a high school in Gulelle, Addis Ababa, specifically for the brightest male students from across the country. The school was named after the British army general Charles Wingate, who played a key role in the war that freed Ethiopia from the Italian invasion in early 1941. That boarding school provided a high-quality high-school education to the brightest male students in the country, such as Meles Zenawi, who later became prime minister of Ethiopia. Upon completion of their education, the students received awards from the emperor at his palace.

During Emperor Haile Selassie I's reign, education was free at all levels, and the quality of education was high. Colleges offered room and board as well as stipends. Students were well fed and well maintained, as I myself witnessed. The emperor himself paid regular visits to the university in Addis Ababa to ensure that the university students were well maintained and well fed. The Public Health College in Gondar, northern Ethiopia, a school that I attended, rendered quality education through American and Ethiopian instructors. The head of the school of nursing was an American woman. I will also never forget my American midwifery teacher, who equipped me with superior professional skills and professional ethics that helped me elicit change when I worked with Scandinavian missionaries. (The full story will be included in my next book.)

We students lived on campus and were served a variety of foods along with two or three side dishes. We had lamb every day except for Wednesdays and Fridays, which were fasting days. Our food was inspected once a week at the emperor's command. All students received excess food at each meal, which was then used to help the poor through the students' humanitarian program. We also received monthly stipends in cash and were provided with the use of buses that ran every ten minutes to transport us to downtown Gondar. During school break, the college always provided buses to transport students between Addis Ababa and Gondar and also covered expenses for students from the various regions. Evangelical Christian students, of which I was part, enjoyed fellowship after lunch every day. We called this time *berhan le hullu*, meaning "light for all" in Amharic.

From my exposure to American culture and leadership, it seems to me that Emperor Haile Selassie adopted a Western leadership style, although feudalism had long played a contradictory role in the life of the nation. I cannot speak for the politicians of the time, but in my personal experience, there was much freedom and respect for human rights—freedom of expression, freedom of assembly, freedom to bear arms. I can say that the spirit of democracy as found in the United States was there. Take, for example, the way the emperor responded to

61

the college students' strike at Public Health College in Gondar, northern Ethiopia, in 1971, an event in which I took part.

Although I did not know the reason for the strike, I felt I had to participate in it for fear of the student union, an organization that wielded a great deal of power at the time. The student union heads coordinated the demonstration with maximum freedom. The protest lasted for three days and was carried out without any threat or interference from the government's side. During the strike, we regularly ate our good-quality meals in the cafeteria as usual, lived on campus, and held our meetings in the student cafeteria without any fear of retaliation.

On the third day of the strike, the emperor sent mediators asking us, the student protestors, what we wanted. The student union held a meeting on the fourth evening and came up with two issues to be presented to the emperor: (1) the immediate and unconditional freeing of all political prisoners and (2) the construction of health centers in all regions of the country. The emperor satisfied the students' demands and resolved the dispute peacefully. He immediately released all political prisoners, but concerning the health centers, his response was that the centers could not be built overnight but would be accomplished over time.

Emperor Haile Selassie I is viewed by many as a reformer, advocate for equality, and a figurehead of African independence. On August 27, 1942, he abolished the legal basis for slavery throughout the empire and imposed severe penalties, including death, for slave trading.[28] He was so venerated that the Rastafaria movement arose in Jamaica, which worships Emperor Haile Selassie I as Jesus incarnate. Of course, we know that the emperor was merely human being and we should never worship him, but it does show the reach of his influence.

The emperor was exalted nationally and internationally as a global figure. Through him, Ethiopia became a charter member of the United Nations after World War II.[29] He was the first black to spend a night in the White House as the president's guest and made more official visits to the White House than any other head of state in the world.

One example of how he was honored by the United States is found in this excerpt from President Nixon's speech at a dinner reception in the White House on May 15, 1973. This visit, the emperor's last visit to the White house, took place just one year before he was ousted by the military:

> So tonight we honor him for what he has been to his country, to his continent, and to the world. We honor him also for what he means to history. What he means to history is something more than that of national leader or continental leader or world leader. What he means is a spirit—a spirit that in these days we sometimes think is lost, the spirit that does not give up when all the odds seem too difficult to overcome, the spirit that will not compromise when there is no compromise which would not destroy that in which he believed, the spirit that inspired us all in 1936, when we saw him standing tall and proud before the League of Nations talking for what all of the pragmatists, all of the realists said was a lost cause. But because he spoke so strongly and proudly and vigorously for what was said to be a lost cause, he was victorious, his nation was victorious. But what was more important, the cause of freedom, of strong men who refuse to be overcome by the odds and by the difficulties—that survived. What His Majesty leaves, that heritage, on the pages of the history books of the world means more than the leadership of a nation, or a continent, or, for that matter, of the world. And for

that moment of inspirational leadership we are all in his debt[14][30]

But did Emperor Haile Selassie I finish well? Unfortunately, the emperor suffered a very disgraceful end that terminated the world's oldest monarchy. He was resented by many of the elite social class that his reforms and new economic and educational policies had created. The opportunities that the feudal minority enjoyed because of his reforms ultimately worked against him and even against themselves.

Agitated by Russian Communist agents, university students demonstrated against his administration with the slogan "land to the tiller!" His opponents used the 1973 famine in the Wollo region to make the emperor look bad. He was removed from his palace by a military coup on September 12, 1974, and escorted by way of a small Volkswagen to the Fourth Army Division. Later he was moved to Jubuli Palace and held under home arrest, where it is believed he was assassinated on August 27, 1975. No one knew where he was buried until the current government, which overthrew the brutal military government in 1991, found the emperor's remains under a latrine on the palace grounds, according to a news program I watched in 1992.

---

[14] Toasts of President Richard Nixon and Emperor Haile Selassie I can be found at: http://www.presidency.ucsb.edu/ws/index.php?pid=2118#ixzz1wxTGZrlX. For the memorandum of conversation, please visit: http://2001-2009.state. gov/documents/organization/67407.pdf

4

Quandaries of Emperor Haile Selassie I's Reign

As I pointed out in the previous chapter, the unbelievable inequality between the monarchy's ruling class and their subjects, a condition that the emperor inherited from the old aristocracy, imposed persistent problems in the political, economic, religious, and social strata of the country. The autobiography of Mr. Emmanuel Abraham serves as firsthand evidence in these areas.

Emmanuel Abraham is an Oromo, born to Protestant parents on March 17, 1913, in western Wollega, Bodji subdistrict. Since early childhood, he has maintained his commitment to his Christian faith and moral values. He is the only imperial minister to avoid execution and who is still alive today. Although he was not related to the monarchy in any way, he was immersed in the monarchy's system from early life. In 1925, he became one of the first enrollees at the Tafari Makonnen School. Throughout the reign of Emperor Haile Selassie I (1931–1974), he served the imperial regime in various capacities, as director, ambassador, and minister. As a God-fearing and dedicated Christian, he sacrificed his scholarship opportunity, the opportunity that the imperial government had denied him in the past, and served the emperor with selfless dedication during the emperor's exile in London.

Mr. Emmanuel Abraham's personal qualities, professional standards, and deep commitment did not go unrecognized by the emperor. Since the emperor was governed by the crown, however, Mr. Emmanuel Abraham, because of his ethnic background and his commitment to moral and ethical values, faced several tribulations from the imperial administration. I will briefly point out the major problems that ignited the bloodiest revolution by which the centuries-old monarchy was finally brought to an end.

Feudalism

The fact that the feudal lords, including the gult and rist holders, retained power over land ownership prompted the student demonstrators' slogan "land for the tiller!" to become a reality. Just a few years before he was deposed, the emperor made an effort to introduce land reform. Unfortunately, his corrupt ministers, the Orthodox Church, the nobility, and the parliament, who all benefited from land ownership, resisted such a policy.

My father once told me a story he heard from a parliament member concerning the emperor's new land proclamation. According to the story, when the emperor's idea of land reform was opposed, the emperor raised his right hand and said, "Can I clap with one hand? I am alone and can't do anything." Unable to persuade them to follow his lead, the emperor nonetheless proclaimed a half acre of land to be given to all peasants. Although he was not a farmer, my father took advantage of that proclamation and acquired half an acre of farmland in a small village named Gedo Harangama in rural Wollega, Jarso Woreda, on which he planted a congregation and started a literacy school. Soon my father transferred the congregation to the Ethiopian Evangelical Church Mekane Yesus (EECMY), Nedjo Parish. The EECM eventually upgraded it to a church and a school for grades one through eight.

Because the emperor failed to treat the root cause of Ethiopia's problems—mainly feudalism and land issues—his provision was not sufficient to silence the younger political elites, mostly students, who craved a form of Russian Communism. Numerous political dissidents accused the emperor of being aloof to reform. The students whom he had pampered were used by lower-ranking military leaders in their efforts to depose the emperor. All reaped the consequences of their decisions. The emperor was not spared for trying to please his corrupt officials. Soon after he was removed from power by the military coup, members of the nobility and the royal family were all arrested, with the exception of Ras Imiru, who sympathized with the poor but didn't have the might to bring change. All imperial ministers, sixty-one ex-officials, and Prime Minister Akililu Habte were executed. One godly man alone survived, Mr. Emmanuel Abraham. He was still alive and strong when I met him in September of 2012 at a Sunday service in the Addis Ababa Mekane Yesus Church. He turned one hundred in March of 2013.

Corruption

Emperor Haile Selassie I's zeal for reform and moderniza-tion did not change the world's oldest monarchy's misuse of power and corruption. Instead, the nobility and feudal elites took advantage of the emperor's new economic policy by exploiting the economy and thus subjecting the vast majority of people to extreme poverty—poverty for which the country is known to date. As I indicated above, the nobles and the feudal lords enjoyed incredible wealth from exploiting the peasantry. Making matters worse, the emperor failed to get rid of or even to criticize and correct his corrupt leaders. He did not do what Proverbs 25:5 instructs: "Take away the wicked from before the king, and his throne will be established in righteousness."

The emperor was yet to learn the hard way that saying okay when it is not okay only brings failure. Let me give you a few examples. Ras Hailu of Gojam, for example, a man who accumulated incredible wealth from the new economy, shrewdly invested in real estate and dominated the region's economy. Together with his family, he was left alone until he was found to be a threat to the state. At last he was fined and finally put into jail. [31] However, the emperor did not take that kind of action against other corrupt leaders.

Although the emperor's efforts in elevating Ethiopia to modern standards through educated manpower were significant, the educated elites were assigned to function under the supervision of the corrupt, inefficient, and ignorant elites of the aristocracy. Take, for example, Germame Neway's coup attempt in 1960 that cost him his life. Germame was from a middle-class family of Menelik II's court and was one of Emperor Haile Selassie's educated elites. His master's paper at Columbia University in the United States was titled "The Impact of White Settlement Policy in Kenya" (Columbia University, 1954) In this paper, he exposed the suffering of the vast majority under aristocratic rule and revealed his passion to fuel change in his country.

Unfortunately for him, the emperor assigned him a post in the Ministry of Interior to work under the supervision of a most corrupt minister, Dej. (later Ras) Mesfin Seleshi. Harold G. Marcus calls him the "archetypical Ethiopian oligarch." While he was the governor of Kaffa from 1945 to 1955, Dej. Mesfin gained illegal ownership of huge prime tracts of coffee land in Kaffa and made a tremendous profit in a very corrupt way. He created enormous wealth for himself that he used to purchase more real estate, stocks in newly rising industries, and farmland in other parts of the country. [32]

The young educated elite Germame alerted the emperor to the necessity of ending corruption and misery, but the emperor listened instead to the corrupt aristocrats and recalled Germame. "Unable to criticize such a public idealism, Haile Selassie sent Germame to administer the pastoral Somalis of Jijiga" [33] Germame tried to model a wise and more democratic leadership there, but his actions were seen as an embarrassment to the provisional officers, resulting in his second recall by the emperor. Unable to achieve his goals, in 1960 he launched a failed coup attempt to overthrow the emperor and bring reform to the corrupt political system.[32]

The same thing happened to Mr. Emmanuel Abraham, but in a different manner. The man who did the emperor such a big favor during his time of greatest distress, as well as served the country with loyalty and diligence, suffered various plots devised by different officials to get rid of him simply because of his ethnic background, religious denomination and his stand against corruption. After being restored to power, the emperor invited him, in 1943, to work in the Ministry of Foreign Affairs in the post of director general, but he assigned over him a man from the nobility. Since the emperor favored Mr. Emmanuel Abraham, the officials could not just get rid of him, so they had to resort to intrigue to exclude him from their circle.

Mr. Emmanuel Abraham suffered even more after the emperor granted Prime Minister Aklilu Habte-Wold full authority to form his cabinet with the ministers he wished. Mr. Emmanuel Abraham did not fit into the prime minister's circle of corrupt relatives and friends whom he appointed as ministers. When opposition and intrigue against Mr. Emmanuel Abraham intensified, he was moved to other positions that were not preferred by the aristocratic elites. For example, he was appointed as the minister of transportation because it was considered a worthless post. When Mr. Emmanuel turned it into a most profitable institution, however, Prime Minister Aklilu Habte-Wold removed him and appointed his own relative to that position. Mr. Emmanuel Abraham quoted an Amharic proverb to express his situation of the unfavorable shifts: "Endayama tiraw endayibela gifaw" (meaning: Invite him, so he wouldn't complain; push him off so he shouldn't eat.[34]

Discrimination

Ethiopia has more than eighty tribes with 270 dialects who lived in harmony for many years in spite of their ethnic and religious differences. Originally Ethiopia was divided into the northern highlands and the southern highlands. The northern highlands included the northern regions, namely, Semien (presently Gondar), Gojam, Tigray, Eritrea, parts of Wollo, and northern Showa. The southern highlands covered the regions that submitted to northern imperial rule by warfare during the imperial expansion.

Discrimination began with territorial expansion to the south in the fourteenth century. Since that time, the monarchy's ruling class elite, the Amharas, assumed superiority over all the other tribes. The people of the conquered southern regions were discriminated against on the basis of their tribe, social class, and skills. Those with very dark skin, kinky hair, and thick lips were called *barya*, the Amharic word for "Negro," and were ostracized.

Although the Oromos were the largest tribe in Ethiopia (about 40 percent of the population) and possessed rich natural resources and the most fertile land in the country, they suffered the most discrimination in all aspects of life. They were put down, dehumanized, and treated as second-class citizens. As the Oromos sadly discovered, beauty and wealth often invite not only friends, but also enemies.

Those Oromos who did not speak Amharic or spoke it with heavy accents and those with Oromo names were ridiculed and called *Galla*. Out of desperation to gain equal access to opportunities, many Oromos chose to assimilate and changed their names to Amharic names or assumed baptismal names. Had it not been for the Western missionaries who built schools in the Oromia region, the Oromos would never have come close to matching the Amharas in educational achievement. I give as an example Mr. Emmanuel Abraham's experience.

Since Mr. Emmanuel Abraham's ethnic background and religious denomination were different from those in the monarchy line, the aristocratic elite brought several false accusations against him in an attempt to remove him from office, all the while pretending they were concerned for the country. When Mr. Emmanuel Abraham worked at the Ministry of Education in 1947, the emperor himself was the minister of education. The aristocratic elite made false reports to the emperor, accusing Mr. Emmanuel Abraham of educating only Gallas (Oromos were called Gallas at this time). The emperor was well aware of their plot against Mr. Emmanuel Abraham, so he went to the schools and conducted his own investigation. To document the evidence, he then ordered a survey of the tribal distribution of the students. Here are the findings: In April of 1947, 4,795 students attended schools in Addis Ababa. Out of those students, 3,055 were Amharas, and 1,740 were from other ethnic groups, of which 583 were Gallas. [35]

When the aristocrats' plot failed, Mr. Emmanuel Abraham's enemies raised the complaint that the increase in student population was outpacing the country's budget. Instead of correcting his corrupt officials, however, the emperor chose to play it safe and removed Mr. Emmanuel Abraham's from his post in 1947 on a paid leave of absence until he found him a diplomatic post two years later. [35] As a dedicated Christian, Mr. Emmanuel Abraham waited upon the emperor with due respect, obeying 1 Peter 2:17: "Honor all people. Love the brotherhood. Fear God. Honor the king."

The situation faced by the Oromos under the aristocracy gave rise to political conflict that the Oromo elite saw as colonization and thus struggled against to obtain their rights. God forbid that I judge authorities, but the emperor's failure to take action against his corrupt ministers and leaders brought forth God's justice:

> For I have told him that I will judge his house forever for the iniquity which he knows, because his sons made themselves vile, and he did not restrain them.
> — 1 Samuel 3:13

Religious discrimination also persisted, although the emperor declared religious freedom and equality by proclaiming "Haymanot yegil newu hager yegara newu" in Amharic (meaning, "religion is private; country is shared"). The position maintained by the Orthodox Church as the state religion meant that it assumed superiority over Protestant Christianity which they called, "mate haymanot" in Amharic meaning stranger religion. On several occasions, Orthodox clergies and believers persecuted evangelical Christians to the extent of committing violent crimes against evangelical believers, including but not limited to burning their churches and beating and murdering evangelical believers. Evangelical Christians were viewed as followers of a wrong religion. Even though the constitution of the present Ethiopian government (FDRE) declares separation of church and state and protects religious rights, the problem still persists. I will give examples in my discussion of FDRE government leadership in the pages to follow.

Gender Gap

Traditional law and the cultural heritage passed on from generation to generation ascribed to women a very low status in society. The monarchy's traditional law favored males in marriage, political, social, and economic life, obstructing women's entitlement to ownership, education, and the inheritance of assets and properties such as land. Traditionally, domestic duties were assigned to women and girls. The vast majority of Ethiopian women spend twelve to fourteen hours a day in unpaid and unrecognized physical labor, such as fetching water and firewood from distant places, farming the land, performing domestic duties, and taking care of children. As a result, Ethiopian women were overrepresented among the poor and the illiterate. Violence against women and girls also is common. Boys on the streets insult each other with words that denigrated the female gender and made girls embarrassed for being female. In the case of domestic violence, the assaulted wife often had to flee the assault while her abusive husband assumed authority and remained in the house. Let me share with you few of my own personal experience: One day, my husband physically assaulted me for holding meetings at my house with the poor women I was helping; whom he called illiterates. He scared off the women that way, and I run to the police station for the first time in our 14 years of marriage. However, it was unsafe for me to press charges against him. He physically assaulted me a number of times to cover up his immoral crimes and I had to flee while he stayed in the house.

Lessons Learned

Why did the reign of Emperor Haile Selassie I end the way it did, with the end of the centuries-old monarchy rule? What can we learn from this? Let's examine several factors.

First, the emperor's biggest mistake, in my opinion, was that he had one foot in the outdated monarchy rule that he inherited as heir to the throne and the other foot planted in the Western democratic leadership style. Oddly enough, he tried to sustain the old traditional monarchy style by adopting a modern democratic style. "He believed the Sovereign embodied tradition as the symbol of the nation. . . . He had constructed a central government totally reliant on the crown for policy and direction" [36]

Was it possible for the old and the new to work together in Emperor Haile Selassie I's modern leadership style? Consider the words of Jesus:

> Then He spoke a parable to them: "No one puts a piece from a new garment on an old one; otherwise the new makes a tear, and also the piece that was taken out of the new does not match the old. And no one puts new wine into old wineskins; or else the new wine will burst the wineskins and be spilled, and the wineskins will be ruined. But new wine must be put into new wineskins, and both are preserved. And no one, having drunk old wine, immediately desires new; for he says, 'The old is better.' "
>
> —Luke 5:36–38

This example from the Word of God came to pass with Emperor Haile Selassie I's regime. The new modern constitution that the emperor imposed on the old monarchy rule did not match with tradition. His new policy did not run parallel with the ancient aristocracy. The emperor should have learned from the United Kingdom during his five-year exile there and changed the form of Ethiopian government to a constitutional monarchy. Sadly, the emperor never considered that his outdated reform system might need to be updated. He had seen how the British constitutional monarchy worked and should have followed that route when he had the imperial constitution revised in 1955. He should have also learned from the United States, his most preferred ally, who established a constitution in the New World that was completely free from the old style. He should have at least adopted their policy of separation of church and state and revised his imperial constitution accordingly.

Second, Emperor Haile Selassie I betrayed Israel. The emperor expelled Israel from Ethiopia on October 23, 1973, and thereby severed Ethiopia's alliance with Israel [37] The emperor traced his ancestry to the Jewish King Solomon and even assumed the title the Conquering Tribe of the Lion of Judah. Nonetheless, he chose to sever the historical ties between Ethiopia and Israel when faced with threats from the Arab Islamic powers and Eritrea's guerillas, as well as from the Islamic domination in the United Nations and Organization of African Unity (OAU), presently African Union (AU)[37]

The emperor's official relations with the Jews of Palestine began in 1942 when an Israeli consulate opened in Addis Ababa; the following year, diplomatic and commercial alliances with the nation of Israel also began [38] Through the efforts of the Israeli leader David Ben Gurion, Israel also gained the support of President Dwight Eisenhower. [39] with which Ethiopia's alliance with Israel was strengthened and the emperor upgraded the Israeli consulate to an embassy in 1962. Eventually Ethiopia benefited greatly from the political, economic, social, and military relations between the two countries.[40]

However, severing relations with Israel did not prevent the problems the emperor hoped to avoid, but rather merely hastened his fall. Just eleven months after he expelled the Israelis from Ethiopia, he was overthrown by a military junta. Israel was the sole military adviser to Ethiopia and knew more about the lower-ranking Ethiopian military officials than their top leaders did; consequently, the withdrawal of the Israeli military advisers from the country resulted in the uprising of the dissatisfied lower-ranking military officials, who ousted the emperor. The very same Israel that had rescued Emperor Haile Selassie I from the 1960 coup could no longer come to his aid. When Germame Neway and his group attempted the coup in December 1960, the emperor was visiting Brazil. [32] However, the emperor's supporters alerted Israel, and Mr. Ben-Gurion ordered a plane to fly the emperor from Brazil to Asmara and rallied his forces to destroy the emperor's enemy[41]

Mr. Chanan Aynor, a former Israeli ambassador to Ethiopia, blamed the United States for the emperor's decision to sever ties with Israel, a decision made after the emperor's meeting with President Nixon in the spring of 1973. [42] It is true that Emperor Haile Selassie I met with President Nixon for seventy minutes in the White House on May 15, 1973 as mentioned above, and requested urgently needed support to avert the Somali threat to Ethiopia and to deal with the Eritrea problem as well as the political pressure from the Soviet Union and the Arabs. After he lost hope with Washington, the emperor formally severed relations with Israel on October 23, 1973, thus breaking Israel's periphery policy that linked Israel and Ethiopia.[43]

The emperor made a terrible decision when he gave greater importance to the Arabs' vote in the United Nations than he did to keeping his alliance with Israel. Contrary to the sovereign who claimed direct descent from King Solomon of Israel and who carried himself as the Conquering Lion of the Tribe of Judah, the atrocious atheistic president of Ethiopia, Mengistu Haile Mariam, cleverly maintained friendship with Israel. At the United Nations meeting in 1975, under Mengistu Haile Mariam's rule, Ethiopia abstained from voting for the Arab-sponsored "Zionism is racism" resolution. Upon his fall from power, Lieutenant Colonel Mengistu was flown peacefully with his family to his country of exile, where he still resides.

If the United States is to blame for the emperor's mistake, the blame should go back to 1954 because prevention is better than cure. I believe that the past and present problems could have been prevented if the United States had accepted the emperor's offer to expand relations with Ethiopia earlier. In the speech that the emperor delivered before Congress during his visit in May and June of 1954, he explained the opportunities that could be of mutual benefit to his country and the United States and welcomed America's ingenuity and technical skills towards investing in Ethiopia. Unfortunately, the United States remained aloof to his suggestions:

> He regarded Ethiopia as a land of opportunity, where American integrity and technical skills were welcomed. . . . He advised that his country's Christian tradition oriented Ethiopia toward the West. Haile Selassie reaffirmed Ethiopia's commitment to Western values and to the United States, a valued friend that had refused to recognize Italian sovereignty over Ethiopia. Yet neither the United States government nor American capitalism eagerly poured millions into Ethiopia.[44]

The United States was the emperor's favorite nation among Ethiopia's foreign relations. In that role, the United States could have brought change to the Ethiopian monarchy system by promoting good governance and democracy. In the founding of the Organization of African Unity (OAU), for example, the emperor referred to the United States as an inspirational role model. Given the emperor's loyalty to and trust in the United States, a good outcome could have been achieved if the relationship proposed by the emperor had been established. I am saying this from what I witnessed during my tour of China in 1997 through a course of study called Case Studies in International Business, Asia I. At this time, companies and businesses from Western countries, including the United States, Germany, Britain, Italy, the Netherlands, and Australia, were heavily investing in China to reap big profits from cheap labor. (By the way, we can see the evidence of their success from the "made in China" tag on our clothing and so many other things.) Hong Kong and Taiwan also invested there. A hardworking nation, China seized the opportunity to become who it is today.

Founded on August 15, 1991, the Beijing Economic and Technological Development Zone, which covers an area of eighty to a hundred square kilometers, was zoned for investment by the above-mentioned Western companies, including the Sino-American Factory. The residential area of the development zone was designed for the construction of apartments, villas, schools, and clinics, which were to be completed by the year 2000. It was expected to house a total population of 400,000–500,000.

The second example is the Waigaoqiao Free Trade Zone in Shanghai, which covers an area of 13.75 square kilometers and includes the Pudong development area and the Baoshan Iron and Steel (Group) Corporation. Located near the port of Shanghai, it combines free trade with bonded warehousing and other trade services with easy access. For example, 3M from Minnesota has a plant there. My group and I saw a man at Yuguan Garden wearing a Minnesota hat and soon discovered the man was the manager of 3M. Because of his wearing the Minnesota hat, we introduced ourselves and received the opportunity to tour the 3M plant in Shanghai.

Baoshan Iron and Steel Corporation near the port of Shanghai

Baoshan Iron and Steel Corporation near the port of Shanghai

China created the means for attracting investors whose ideologies and cultures differed from its own. Hong Kong reunited with mainland China on July 1, 1977 under the "One China, Two Systems" policy, which allowed Hong Kong to keep its capitalist policies while being governed by China's common law. With the ideological and religious ties it had with Western countries, I believe Ethiopia would have done better if the United States had accepted the emperor's idea and invested in Ethiopia.

Kum Lung Textile (Holding) Company Ltd.
(Hong Kong owned) in Shantou

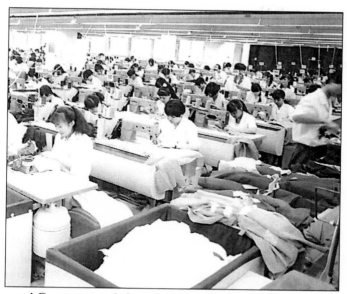

4 Garment workshops holding 1,500 machines with production capacity of 300,000 garments per month

So who is to blame for the emperor's decision that ended his government so disgracefully? Professor Haggai Erlich states that the Ethiopian people saw the emperor's expulsion of the Israelis as an indication that the emperor was becoming senile, because they considered his action a betrayal of their history and tradition [22] On October 6, 1973, when Israel came under surprise attack from a coalition of Arab states led by Egypt and Syria, Europeans dissociated from any country that supported Israel. They did so in fear of the Arabs' oil-embargo threat. Emperor Haile Selassie followed the flow and broke Ethiopia's long-time tie with Israel.

After the Soviet Union began sending arms to Syria and Egypt in the surprise attack against Israel, President Nixon decided to help Israel in order to prevent the beleaguered nation from going nuclear or being destroyed.[45] Only the United States, risking the Arabs' retaliation, stood with Israel through Operation Nickel Grass and provided the Israeli army with support in order to avert Israel's destruction. Because of the Arabs' oil-embargo threat, most of the European allies refused to even allow the United States to fly over their territory, let alone allow aircraft to land for refueling. However, Portugal did allow it, thus making the mission possible. With the help of the United States, Israel won the victory in a surprise counterattack, bringing that war to an end on October 25, 1973[46]

In order to punish the United States for helping Israel, the Arab members of the Organization of Petroleum Exporting Countries (OPEC) declared a complete oil embargo ("oil weapon") against the United States, banning gasoline exports to the nation and imposing restrictions on other countries that supported Israel[47] OPEC announced their decision on October 16, 1973. [48] as well as a cut in oil production. This decision led the nations of Europe and Japan to dissociate from the United States. The resultant oil crisis caused global damage that was particularly devastating in Third World countries with unstable economies.

The United States should have been praised for fulfilling its global responsibility in defending Israel's right to life, liberty, and the pursuit of happiness. Concerning Israel in particular, the Scriptures say this about that special land:

> I [God] will bless you and make your name great; and you shall be a blessing. I will bless those who bless you, and I will curse him who curses you.
> —Genesis 12:2–3

As can be seen from the past, all those powerful leaders who tried to harm Israel failed themselves and their nations. That tiny country, a mere dot on the earth, has been strategically placed by God as the center of planet earth, and it is important to Him that He keep His promises to Israel.

I learned this when I was still young. During the six-day Arab-Israeli war of 1967, I found this message, which I took at face value:

> Woe to those who go down to Egypt for help, and rely on horses, who trust in chariots because they are many, and in horsemen because they are very strong, but who do not look to the Holy One of Israel, nor seek the LORD! Yet He also is wise and will bring disaster, and will not call back His words, but will arise against the house of evildoers, and against the help of those who work iniquity. Now the Egyptians are men, and not God; and their horses are flesh, and not spirit. When the LORD stretches out His hand, both he who helps will fall, and he who is helped will fall down; they all will perish together.
>
> —Isaiah 31:1–3

Based on this fact, we can know that the price the United States has paid for serving God's purpose in defending Israel's existence will work out for the good of the nation: "And we know that all things work together for the good to those who love God, to those who are the called according to His purpose" (Rom. 8:28). First, Operation Nickel Grass provided an opportunity for the United States to discover its deficiency in American airlift capabilities. From that, the United States greatly expanded its aerial refueling capabilities, thus making long-distance flight operations standard.[49]

Second, the United States began developing alternatives, such as renewable energy, solar power, and wind power, to make the nation energy independent. It also maintained diplomatic efforts among its allies to establish and promote a consumers' union to control oil pricing [50] This persuades me to believe that the best of the blessings is yet to come for America. Beyond merely achieving energy independence, I believe the United States could become the world's largest petroleum supplier.

Third, from the very beginning, the emperor placed all his trust in worldly powers. He believed that membership in the League of Nations (presently the United Nations) was the only means to disentangle Ethiopia from the domination of Tripartite powers and worked vigorously towards having Ethiopia obtain that membership. [12] The main reason the emperor severed relations with Israel was that he feared Ethiopia would lose the Arab vote in the United Nations if he did not do so. His trust was in the United Nations and in the military. To make matters worse, the emperor, in his last year, mostly traveled abroad seeking help for Ethiopia, but in the process, he was alienated from what was going on at home. He was not aware of the great famine of Wollo[51] a fact that was used against him to undermine all his efforts and that cost him his reign and his life.

Fourth, Emperor Haile Selassie I's disgraceful ending was a test for the Ethiopian people and a lesson for all human beings. I say it was a test for the Ethiopians because of what happened after his death. I don't mean to imply that Emperor Haile Selassie I was a perfect leader; rather, I am giving my views based on what I witnessed.

"Honor all people. Love the brotherhood. Fear God. Honor the king," says 1 Peter 2:17. What we have seen so far proves that justice is served in God's government. However, the manner in which the emperor was deposed went against the culture and moral values that the Ethiopian people were known for. Those who received the light of education through the emperor's goodwill and dedication (Mr. Emmanuel Abraham's personal experience is an example) treated him like trash in his old age and in his time of greatest difficulty. This eventually brought a curse to the people of Ethiopia. Those who called him a despot soon found their real despot, as will be shown in my discussion of the Communist junta and Colonel Mengistu Haile Mariam's rule.

When the emperor surrendered to the military representatives who arrived at his palace to dethrone him, he behaved admirably. He stated that:

> All through his life, he had tried endlessly for the benefit of his country and his people, and that ones individual desires could not come ahead of the needs of the nation. The emperor's role was to lead in good times and bad, and to serve his people always and without fail. If it was determined that this was for the greater good of Ethiopia, then he would accept the decision and do what was required of him.[52]

In May of 1992, I watched the Ethiopian television news as they showed the emperor's remains that had been found under a toilet in the palace. I listened to the emperor's personal attendant saying that he told the emperor that he had been instructed not to come the next day (the day the emperor was to be murdered). Upon hearing this, the emperor wiped his tears with his fingers, and spreading his hands to the sky through the window, he said, "Ay Ethiopia! Bedlenish indehon, in Amharic (Oh, Ethiopia, if we have wronged you) The next day, the news was broadcast that the emperor had died from illness. The emperor's last words, which literally were a curse, reveal that he speculated they would murder him.

President Mengistu should have learned from China the value of respecting your leaders. My visit to see the embalmed body of Chairman Mao Zedong in his mausoleum located in Tiananmen Square in Beijing, as well as my visit to see the Terracotta Warriors in Xian, Shaanxi Province, revealed to me how the Chinese people respect their leaders. Although Chairman Mao signed in November 1956 the proposal that all central leaders be cremated after death, the Chinese people had his remains embalmed and put in a mausoleum that they built to house it. All visitors are required to follow strict rules, including dress codes, no talking, no smoking, and no photography. We had to leave everything in our possession, including our winter jackets, with the honor guards at the gate.

The same was true for Emperor Qin Shi Huang of the second century BC (reign, 221–207 BC). The Terracotta Warriors that were excavated in the 1970s consist of more than seven thousand life-sized pottery soldiers, horses, and chariots arranged in battle formation and armed with weapons designed to guard the deceased emperor. They represent the actual imperial guard of those days. The Chinese people did all this to safeguard their tyrant king's soul.

Terracotta warriors

Terracotta warriors in battle formation

An archer kneeling for shooting

Chariot

Chariot driver

President Mengistu and his group, however, humiliated and failed Emperor Haile Selassie I, who had played a major role in their rise to power. After their deaths, both Chairman Mao Zedong and Emperor Qin Shi Huang generated permanent wealth for their country, as their final resting places became major tourist attractions. Because of the manner in which the emperor's life ended, Ethiopia lost the opportunity that China is still benefiting from today. Ethiopians need to learn to balance and weigh the great things that history remembers their leaders for against the mistakes those leaders make as human beings—the very mistakes in which their subjects had a great stake.

A more recent example of the Chinese people's respect for leaders is seen in the 3.5- meter statue of Dr. Kwame Nkrumah of Ghana that stands in front of the newly built twenty-story African Union headquarters in Addis Ababa. This $200-million building was fully funded by the Chinese government as a gift to Africa and was inaugurated on January 28, 2012. By installing this statue, the Chinese government honored Dr. Nkrumah, a recipient of the Lenin Peace Prize, who was overthrown in a military coup while on a state visit to North Vietnam and China in 1996. However, Emperor Haile Selassie I, the core founder of the Organization of African Unity (OAU), was totally erased from the picture.

Emperor Haile Selassie I worked hard for Africa's independence and unity. He organized and hosted a conference in Addis Ababa on May 25, 1963, in which he brought together the thirty-two African heads of state and formed the OAU. Using his wisdom, the emperor motivated Casablanca and Monrovia to put aside their political differences and join the members who established the OAU. All thirty-two of the African founding members of the OAU unanimously voted the emperor "Father of African Unity" and elected him as the first president of the OAU.

If all forget the emperor, Dr. Nkrumah's statue itself remains a witness that history will remember him. The statue is Dr. Nkrumah's, but the features are those of Emperor Haile Selassie I. Dr. Nkrumah's statue stands with its right hand raised and its head also raised, looking into the heavens. Underneath the statue is an inscription of Emperor Haile Selassie I's statement on the founding of the OAU: "Ethiopia shall stretch forth her hands unto God. Africa must unite."

**Dr. Nkrumah's Statue at the AU
Headquarters in Addis Ababa**

5

The Emergence of Lieutenant Colonel Mengistu Haile Mariam (1977–1991)

The rise of the military junta with Major (later Lieutenant Colonel) Mengistu Haile Mariam and his Communist rule had its root in Prime Minister Aklilu Habte-Wold's leadership crisis that worsened the Eritrean civil war and facilitated the expulsion of Israel from Ethiopia in 1973. In the late sixties and early seventies, the Eritrean Liberation Front (ELF) grew stronger in its guerilla fight against Emperor Haile Selassie I's government, but the growing unrest in Eritrea was kept secret from the Ethiopian public.

I myself learned about it from an Eritrean friend of mine when I was a student at Public Health College in Gondar, northern Ethiopia. My friend's father was an army general, and she suffered from insomnia because of her fear that the ELF guerillas would kill her father. She told me that the ELF fighters were very careful when killing Ethiopian solders and were never identified. I witnessed that for myself in 1971 during my internship at Gorgora Training Health Center in Gondar, near Lake Tana. My Eritrean friend was also assigned there with me. There was an army camp near the health center, and two to three times a week, mourning took place for the soldiers killed by the ELF in Asmara.

Ras Asrate Kasa, Eritrea's *enderase* (regent) at the time, worked to resolve the Eritrean problem through peaceful negotiations with the Eritrean rebels as well as by using a commando force, primarily Christian Eritreans, who had been trained by the Israelis. Eventually Ras Asrate Kasa had ten to twelve Israeli advisers working closely with him to build and strengthen his commandos and police force. However, his rival, Prime Minister Aklilu Habte-Wold, strongly opposed Ethiopia's alliance with Israel and pressured the emperor to solve the Eritrean problem by declaring martial law in Eritrea and eliminating the ELF through harsh military action, as well as by appeasing the Eritreans' Arab allies. Ras Asrate Kasa tried to convince the emperor not to listen to Aklilu Habte-Wold, but the emperor ignored his advice and authorized major military campaigns in 1970. Mr. Emmanuel Abraham's accounts of his long-time experience working with the prime minister and the emperor detail the damage incurred by listening to the prime minister's advice.

The Israeli advisers' agreed with Ras Asrate Kasa on the guerilla counterinsurgency. The emperor's following of Prime Minister Aklilu Habte-Wold's advice, however, resulted in the killing of innocent civilians, driving them to seek protection from the ELF rebels. The harshest military campaign failed to defeat the insurgents and also resulted in the death of the commanding general. Eventually the prime minister convinced the emperor to recall Ras Asrate, declare martial law in Eritrea, and appoint a replacement for the commanding general who had been killed. Aklilu Habte-Wold's influence on the emperor resulted in diminishing Israel's influence [53]

While the Eritrean problem alone was a big enough problem for an emperor of advanced age, Emperor Haile Selassie I was also faced with multiple perplexing difficulties that surpassed even the fascist Italian war. First, Prime Minister Aklilu Habte-Wold, the technocrat whom the emperor raised above and favored over the monarchy elites, misled the emperor. On one hand, he pressured him to sever relations with Israel, and on the other hand, he advised him to solve Eritrea's problem through harsh military action, thus putting the emperor on the losing side.

Second, Libya asked the OAU (presently AU) during the meeting that was held in Addis Ababa in May of 1973 to persuade Ethiopia to break off relations with Israel. Third, the Arab members of the OAU threatened to move the OAU's headquarters from Addis Ababa to another capital, such as Cairo, even though the Egyptian president was a great threat to Israel and Ethiopia. As I pointed out above, the emperor turned to the United States to overcome all these threats. When that effort failed, Ethiopia formally broke off relations with Israel on October 23, 1973. That decision of the emperor marked the beginning of the end for the world's oldest monarchy.

Rather than serving the emperor's purpose, ending relations with Israel hastened Emperor Haile Selassie I's fall. This was because the withdrawal of the Israelis, his sole military advisers, paved the way for the Ethiopian military's dissatisfaction to explode in the form of a revolution. The top Ethiopian officers did not care or even know about the needs and problems of the lower-ranking military. According to Professor Haggai Erlich, the Israelis served as the only communication link between the lower- and higher-ranking soldiers. Their sudden departure left a vacuum, in that the top officers were not aware of the lower-ranking military officers' increased disaffection. The army complained of low pay, frequent delay in pay, lack of clean water, inadequate food, and scarce resources, but the upper-ranking officers ignored these complaints.

Just two months after the Israeli advisers' expulsion from Ethiopia, the revolution began with a military mutiny on January 12, 1974, in which the Territorial Army's Fourth Brigade at

Negele in Sidamo Province, southern Ethiopia, protested. They also took their commanding officers hostage in order to pressure the emperor to address the situation. The mutiny extended to other units in the military throughout the country. The Second Army Division in Asmara imprisoned its commanders and announced its support for the Negele mutineers.

The Arab oil embargo imposed in October 1973 hit hard Ethiopia's already unstable economy, adding fuel to the popular uprising against the regime. Various groups with different demands joined forces. All opposed an increase in fuel prices and taxation. Teachers and other employees asked for higher pay, employee benefits, and better working conditions. Students demanded land reform, political change, and appropriate response to famine. Finally, the groups demanded change in Prime Minister Aklilu Habte-Wold's cabinet and eventually his removal from office. Under pressure, Prime Minister Aklilu resigned from office on February 22, 1973.

Upon the recommendation of the Crown Council, the emperor appointed Lij Endalkachew Makonnen, a nobleman influential in the monarchy, as the new prime minister. Unfortunately, that change did not satisfy the military mutiny that was looking for a regime change. I don't think that the aged emperor knew what he was doing and who he was supposed to listen to at that critical moment. The situation grew so much worse after the newly appointed prime minister took office that his leadership lasted only until July 22 [54]On March 23, 1974, Colonel Alem-Zewde Tesemma established the Coordinating Committee of the Armed Forces, Police, and Territorial Army from the forty units of the Ethiopian military. That committee was officially announced as the *Derg*[15]

---

[15] "*Derg*" was a term used for the group that was first formed as the Coordinating Committee of the Armed Forces, Police, and Territorial Army during the military mutiny and remained the name for the socialist regime that ruled Ethiopia from 1974–1991

(Ge'ez word for "committee") on June 28, 1974, to maintain law and order during the nationwide military mutiny [55]

Each of the military units was expected to send three representatives, who were to be junior officers up to the rank of major. That was how the low-ranking military officers gained power under the leadership of Major Atnafu Abate, bringing Major Mengistu Haile Mariam into the picture. It was said that Major Mengistu was the least-known military officer, but was officially sent to represent the Third Division in the Derg because his commander, General Nega Tegene, recognized him as a troublemaker and wanted to get rid of him. General Nega Tegene never imagined that the man he got rid of alive would soon get rid of him dead by executing him in revenge. Major Mengistu Haile Mariam and Major Atnafu Abate were elected by the committee as chairman and vice chairman respectively.

The Derg's initial purpose was to study the grievances of various military units and investigate abuses by senior officers and staff as well as eliminate corruption in the military. In July 1973, the emperor made concessions to the Derg, empowering them to arrest military officers as well as government officials. Being granted that kind of power, the Derg soon imprisoned the resigned prime minister, Aklilu Habte-Wold, and his successor, Prime Minister Endalkache Makonnen, along with most of the cabinet, many of the higher-ranking military officers, and numerous regional governors. All of them were arrested on charges of corruption and other crimes. We will look at the details of the revolution in the following pages.

6

The Downfall of the World's Oldest Monarchy

September 11 is the Ethiopian New Year. On the morning of September 12, 1974, I turned on my radio to listen to the news and heard a shocking announcement that I had never imagined or expected. My father was with me for the Ethiopian New Year celebration. At the time, I was working for the Ethiopian Evangelical Church Mekane Yesus, Western Synod, in Wollega.

The radio announcement said, "His Majesty Haile Selassie I has been removed from the imperial throne and is being taken to the place prepared for him." The title *His Imperial Majesty* was omitted for the first time ever. The announcement was followed by voices screaming at the emperor, "*Leba! Leba! Tafari leba! Tafari leba!* Translated, this means, "Thief! Thief! Tafari thief!"

My father was shocked when he heard the news and started to yell repeatedly, "Does this emperor deserve this?" My father was a businessman who had often traveled to Addis Ababa in the late 1950s and was appreciative of the changes he saw take place during the emperor's reign, although he abhorred feudalism and its effect on the peasantry. According to what I heard later, the small group of young men stationed at the palace gate was actually a group of soldiers ordered by the Derg to appear in civilian dress in order to make the event look as if it were endorsed by civilians.

Two months later, I traveled to Addis Ababa to enroll in a pediatric nurse-practitioner course that was starting in January 1975. The course was a new program funded and organized by the Swedish International Development Agency (SIDA). The program director, a Swedish woman, favored me and arranged for me to stay at the nurses' residence in Princess Tsehai Hospital. Immediately after the Derg assumed power, the name of the hospital was changed to Armed Forces Hospital.

It happened that I arrived in Addis Ababa right when the turmoil started. Immediately after removing the emperor from his palace, the lower-ranking military group that overthrew him decreed itself the Provisional Military Administrative Council (Derg) and took control of the government on September 15, 1974. All imperial administrative structures, court systems, and the imperial constitution were abolished. In essence, the world's oldest monarchy was put in its coffin and buried.

Although there were no demonstrations or opposition in other parts of the country against Emperor Haile Selassie I, everyone in Addis Ababa seemed frustrated and curious. The failure of the patriarch of the Ethiopian Orthodox church to bless the emperor and the imperial family in his New Year's address sent a clear message that things were not going well. By tradition, the patriarch gave a New Year's address each year in which he blessed the emperor and his family. On September 11, 1974, however, for the first time in Ethiopian history, the patriarch of the Ethiopian Orthodox Church, Abuna[16] Theophilos, failed to do that in his address

---

[16] *"Abuna"* is a title given to a suffragan bishops of Ethiopia (bishop with epitomical and administrative role)

on national television and radio. The speech he delivered that day was like a parable as he compared Ethiopia to a ship in a stormy sea, navigating a new path towards the future. At the end of his speech, he wished success to the mission of the Coordinating Committee instead of blessing the emperor and his family. I don't think the patriarch realized that the success he wished for the mission would soon be a mission that would serve his own execution. We will discover the outcome of the patriarch's wish in the pages to follow.

Negative propaganda against the emperor and his regime continued to dominate the media. A film on the horrifying famine in Wollo where children, women, men, the elderly, and cattle were starving to death was shown continuously on Ethiopian television. After my arrival in Addis Ababa, I heard that the film was originally shown on the eve of the Ethiopian New Year, a day before the military coup took place. The Derg reedited the BBC film *The Hidden Famine* by Jonathan Dimbleby to make the emperor seem cruel and recklessly immersed in luxury while his people lived in incredible misery. The edited film included footage of extravagant palace banquets, ceremonies of the emperor's eightieth birthday, and the marriage of Prince Asrate Kasa's daughter, as well as footage of the emperor feeding meat to his dogs and pet leopards from silver platters held by liveried servants.

The Derg took advantage of Mr. Shimeles Adugna's good intention in showing them the film and used it in their plot against the emperor and his government. Emperor Haile Selassie I's government had established the Relief and Rehabilitation Commission (RRC) in 1973, just six months before the emperor's dethronement, and had begun working to address the famine problem under the leadership of Mr. Shimeles Adugna, who was commissioner at the time. Mr. Shimeles showed the above-mentioned BBC film to the imperial parliament and also to the Derg before they overthrew the emperor. Out of his compassionate heart and dedication, Mr.

Shimeles Adugna went above and beyond to address such a horrifying human misery. It was easy, however, for the Derg to use that timely film against the emperor and his regime on the eve of his dethronement. This tactic of fabricating evidence in a plot in order to achieve one's desire came from the monarchy's leadership in the first place and is still at work.

In an effort to gain acceptance, the Derg immediately appointed the popular military figure Lieutenant General Aman Michael Andom to serve as its new chairman and acting head of state. But the lieutenant general could not know that he would last only three months when he accepted the prestigious position. In order to gain legitimacy, the Derg created slogans that were in line with the political demands of radical students. Some of these were "Ethiopia first," "land for the tiller," and "equality and democracy to all." A song in Amharic said, *"Yale minim dem inkenwa yiwudem! Bekena menfes Ethyopia tikdem"*. This meant, "Without any blood, down with her wrong! Kindheartedly, Ethiopia first!" It was said that the song originated with the Ethiopian air force, and it was soon being broadcast continually over the radio and on television. The slogan "Ethiopia Tikdem" When translated, "Ethiopia first!" was everywhere in the city and followed every announcement on the Ethiopian radio and television. Customary signatures such as "Sincerely," "Yours faithfully," and "Respectfully" changed to *"Ethiopia tikdem"* ("Ethiopia first").

Freedom of press was banned immediately after the Derg government gained control over the media. Actually, Ethiopia quickly kissed freedom of expression good-bye and soon did the same with freedom of assembly, freedom to bear arms, and other basic freedoms. The media continued brainwashing the general public with libelous messages that totally destroyed the emperor's image, including but not limited to accusing him of the theft of billions of dollars from the Ethiopian people, abuse of power, etc. The above-mentioned film was continuously shown on the state-controlled Ethiopian television as proof.

Brainwashed by Russian Communism, the radical Marxist students were thrilled by the Derg's action against the emperor's long-lived regime. University students played a major role through their protest in February 1974 and served as a bridge for the Derg to topple the emperor and abolish the world's oldest monarchy. The Marxist propaganda lit the students on fire in their fight against feudalism. On October 11, 1974, students from Addis Ababa University and the Alemaya Agricultural College in Harar held demonstrations demanding land redistribution. Not knowing that they were paving the way for their own misery and death, the students cheered Colonel Mengistu as the new leader of Ethiopia. When the Derg government held a mass rally and parade on December 22, 1974, students were filled with emotion and shouted, "Viva Mengistu!" Indeed, they witnessed the crushing of their toothless lion (the Lion of Judah), the one who had pampered them, by the scavenging lion who would soon destroy them. Inspired by the changes at home, student activists who were abroad on imperial scholarships returned to Ethiopia in the summer of 1974 and early 1975 to join the Derg. Motivated by Marxist ideology, these students had formed political parties, including the Ethiopian People Revolutionary Party (EPRP) and the All Ethiopian Socialist Movement (MESON) while abroad.

7

The Revolution Heading Towards Its Bloodiest Form

The slogan "without any blood" did not last long. The line quoted in the previous chapter, "Without any blood, down with her wrong! Kindheartedly, Ethiopia first!" was soon condemned as too soft. The death slogan "Revolutionary motherland or death!" soon followed. On the evening of November 23, 1974, I heard from my room heavy gunfire directed toward General Aman Andom's residence. As mentioned earlier, I was residing in the nurses' residence of Princess Tsehai Hospital (presently Armed Forces Hospital) at the time, while completing my pediatric nurse-practitioner course. The next morning, November 24, we heard the shocking news from the state-controlled radio that the general had been executed, along with some of his supporters and sixty ex-officials of the imperial government who were arrested by the Derg. Their burial had already taken place.

Since the hospital compound was so close to General Aman's house, some fellow nurses and I ran to his residence after we heard the news that morning. There were numerous holes all over the walls. In fact, it looked like a spray of bullets had sprinkled the house on all sides. Among the executed ex-officials was General Isayas, a senior nurse's father who was taken from his deathbed in the hospital and executed. Former Major Mengistu's commander, General Nega, who had hated Mengistu as a troublemaker and sent him to join the Derg, was also one of the executed. How General Aman died remained secret. Some said that he died during the shootout at his house. Others said that he committed suicide. On November 28, Brigadier General Tafari Benti succeeded General Aman Andom as Ethiopia's head of state and chairman of the Derg, while Mengistu Haile Mariam and Atnafu Ababate were appointed as vice chairpersons and their ranks upgraded to lieutenant colonel.

On December 20, 1974, the Derg proclaimed socialism as Ethiopia's ideology and issued a document that targeted public ownership of the economy as well as granted equality for all cultural, ethnic, and religious groups. In the same month, Yekatit 66 Political School was established to train cadres with the aim of brainwashing the general public, whom the Derg called the "mass population" (*sefiw hizb* in Amharic) in the new political ideology. In February 1975, the Derg nationalized, without compensation, privately owned businesses, including banks, insurance companies, and all foreign-owned companies.

Wasting no time, the Derg cleverly created a unique program titled the Development Through Cooperation Campaign (Edget behibret zemecha in Amharic). The main purpose of the program was to implement the new revolution in rural Ethiopia. Through that program, university and high school students were dispatched, together with their teachers, to all rural areas of Ethiopia. The flip side of this action ensured that the Derg would clear the city of the potential hassles and crises that could arise from student demonstrations.

The new government said that any student who failed to participate in the campaign would be denied education and employment anywhere in Ethiopia. Schools in the city were closed, and the students and their teachers were deployed for two years. Approximately six thousand university students and fifty thousand secondary school students, along with their teachers, were sent to 437 rural sites and remote areas all over the country. In the belief that the Derg would truly serve as a transitional power for establishing a democratically elected civilian government, the students enthusiastically embarked on the *Zemecha*[17] in December of 1974. Their duties included providing literacy education, forming peasant associations, teaching hygiene, and constructing latrines, wells, and schools with the local dwellers. A literacy program named *Meserete Timihirt* in Amharic (Basic Education) was created to reach the entire Ethiopian population, both urban and rural, with literacy education.

On March 4, 1975, just a few months before the Zemecha students left, Proclamation 31 was issued by the Derg, nationalizing all rural land and granting each farming household up to ten hectares of land. The proclamation was broadcast through the state-controlled media. The nobility, the Orthodox Church, and the imperial family lost their estates and wealth as a result of that proclamation. It also established a farmers association, which was mandated to serve as a mass organization and governmental body.

Although the proclamation raised the Zemecha students' trust in the new government for fulfilling their demands, the situation was not easy on the ground. Many were faced with life-threatening opposition from landowners. The disturbing memory of a very handsome young man who lost his legs and arms during the campaign is forever burned into my memory. On the other hand, the Derg was growing repressive and was far from forming a just civilian government. Regardless, the students did a tremendous job in bringing literacy to the vast population of rural and urban Ethiopia.

---

[17] *"Zemecha"* is an Amharic word meaning military campaign

In May 1975, the Derg officially abolished the world's oldest monarchy and proclaimed Marxism-Leninism as Ethiopia's ideology. Soon after it gained full power, the Derg, under Colonel Mengistu's leadership, began working to change Ethiopia's mixed feudo-capitalist economy to a command economy of the Eastern Bloc style, while condemning the capitalist system of the Western countries, especially that of the United States. On July 26, 1975, Proclamation 47 was issued by the Derg, nationalizing urban land and houses, while allowing individual ownership of one house and up to five hundred square feet of urban land. The proclamation also established *Kebeles*[18] in Addis Ababa and five other urban cities of the regions.

The establishment of the Kebeles followed the pattern of the peasant associations and carried the name Urban Dwellers Association (*Yeketema Newariwoch Mahber* in Amharic). The kebeles of Addis Ababa consisted of 291 neighborhoods, each with three thousand to twelve thousand residents. In the beginning, the Kebeles were responsible for collecting rent from properties that were nationalized, establishing local judicial tribunals (*fird shengo* in Amharic), and providing social services such as literacy education (*Meserete Timihirt* in Amharic) and basic health care. In just a year, the Kebeles' services were extended to include the collection of local taxes as well as the registration of the residents' births, deaths, and marriages. *YeAbyot tibeka guwadoch* (neighborhood defense squads) were created and patrolled their communities both day and night. In some instances, those defense squads acted quite brutally, though against the government's knowledge and authorization.

By the end of 1975, all private businesses, industries, and properties were nationalized. As part of the Derg's

---

[18] "*Kebele*" is an urban administration (more or less equal to US precinct) that was started by the Derg

propaganda, mass ownership was declared, asserting that the *sefiw hizb* (mass population) were the owners. Rents for the nationalized houses were reduced, and two government structures were established to manage the newly nationalized urban land and houses: (1) The Urban Dwellers Associations, Kebeles, collected rent from houses renting for less than 199 birr per month. (2) The Urban Housing Administration (Yeketema Botawoch Astedader in Amharic) presently Government Housing Administration) collected rents on houses renting for more than 199 birr per month.

Other segments of society were also affected by the new economic system. The holdings of religious institutions were not spared, and the Ethiopian Evangelical Church Mekane Yesus's (EECMY) building was also nationalized. Farmers, too, were affected. All farmers were compelled to form farmers' associations in which all agricultural products were controlled and distributed by the government and were no longer available on the free market. By introducing a rationing system, the Derg had a tool for controlling the general public to promote its political agenda.

In 1981, the number of Kebeles had grown from 291 in the city of Addis Ababa to 1,260 Kebeles in 315 towns across the country. In April of 1981, the Derg issued Proclamation 25, granting those expanded Kebeles extensive power under a new administrative structure in which the general assembly of the kebele residents elected a policy committee, which in turn was authorized to appoint an executive committee, a judiciary, and a revolution defense committee. In the new Kebele structure, the Workers Party of Ethiopia (WPE) maintained supreme power over the Kebeles and could overturn their decisions.

Neighborhood defense squads were formed in all the Kebeles, both in the peasant associations and in the Urban Dwellers Associations. The defense squads patrolled the neighborhoods in their communities on day and night shifts.

105

During the Red Terror period, some of the squads took brutal actions outside the authorization of the government. For example, an employee of the Department of Defense Industries shot and killed teen-age twin brothers when he was on the defense squad. He was imprisoned and sentenced, but he was freed from jail together with all prisoners the night the TPLF-led rebels entered Addis Ababa on May 28, 1991. In general, the rise of the Derg marked Ethiopia's entrance into an era of incredible misery as can be seen in the following pages.

8

The Bloody Revolution under the Rule of the Communist Junta

I moved to Addis Ababa for good in January 1977 and took a job as the head of clinic at the Ministry of National Defense Department of Defense Industries, formerly Ammunition Factory). My employment there offered me the opportunity to learn more about the Ethiopian government under Colonel Mengistu Haile Mariam's rule. At the time, tension was escalating because of the internal conflict between the Derg members in their struggle for power. That ultimately resulted in the assassination of General Tafari Banti, the head of state and chairman of the Derg, in a shootout on February 3, 1977. It was said that fifty-eight other top Derg officers were also killed in the one-hour shootout.

The Derg now declared Colonel Mengistu its chairman and head of state. In that way, Colonel Mengistu gained absolute power as the leader of a totalitarian government. Although Colonel Mengistu managed to get rid of most of his rivals, serious threats were developing. He was soon to face opposition from his former supporters, the Marxist students, which led to the Red Terror and White Terror. The same famine that was used against Emperor Haile Selassie I's regime and the invasion by Somalia were also underway. He had yet to fight the unwinnable civil war with The Eritrean People's Liberation Front (EPLF) and the Tigray People's Liberation Front (TPLF).

In the month of February 1977, death knocked at every Ethiopian's door from different angles, both directly and indirectly. In that month, the Ethiopian People Revolutionary Party (EPRP), one of two revolutionary student political parties, revealed itself as the city's guerilla force and launched terrorist attacks against the Derg. The Derg called these attacks the "White Terror." EPRP's White Terror caused horrific damage that provoked the Derg to retaliate in the Red Terror. Hundreds and thousands of the younger generation lost their lives in the White Terror and the Red Terror. Others were officially recruited or drafted, only to die in the civil war.

EPRP and the All Ethiopian Socialist Movement (*Mellaw Ethiopia Socialist Niknake* MESON in Amharic) played major roles as both perpetrator and victim in the Terrors that claimed thousands of young lives. Both revolutionary groups, the Derg, and the student political reactionaries followed the same ideology, Marxism-Leninism, but they turned against each other in the end. In the beginning, however, MESON stood with the Derg, while EPRP resisted the Derg. Both MESON and EPRP propagandized against Christianity more than they did against the aristocracy.

EPRP's terrorist attack targeted Derg officials, public buildings, city buses, and supporters of the Derg such as *Abyot Seded* (Revolution Flame) and MESON. The EPRP was so well organized and skilled that its members drove by, shot to death targeted individuals, and escaped easily. When they started their reign of violent terror, it was said that the EPRP had already killed at least eight Derg members and many of their supporters, of whom my cousin, Hanna Geneti, was one. Since she had been an active member of MESON, Hanna was targeted by the EPRP and knew that she was in danger. In the months of late April and early May 1977, my heart was greatly troubled, fearing that the EPRP would kill my cousin before she turned in repentance to the God whom she denounced.

Several times I invited Hanna to my house to discuss the matter, but she refused. Finally, I sent her a message that I wanted to buy her whatever she needed for her graduation (she was among the graduating class of June 1977). She then came to my house on Saturday, May 14, 1977, and spent the night with me. I expressed my concern that the EPRP would kill her and advised her to leave the country immediately. She said she had a scholarship opportunity that she had previously ignored, but she promised me she would initiate the scholarship process on Monday, May 16. On Sunday morning, May 15, before she left my house, I asked her, "Have you acknowledged Jesus?" stressing my fear that the EPRB would kill her. She replied, "Did Judas Iscariot acknowledge Him?" Our conversation stopped there, and she left. On Monday morning, May 16, the EPRP murder squad shot and killed Hanna while she was entering her school compound. That incident showed me how our mercifully God pleads with His human creatures until their very last breath.

The EPRP's White Terror provoked the Derg into immediate counterattack on EPRP and all those the Derg considered its enemies. I watched on Ethiopian TV when Colonel Mengistu Haile Mariam made a speech at Revolution Square (formerly and presently, Meskel Square) in Addis Ababa in which he officially endorsed a savage campaign against the EPRP and other opponents. At the end of his speech, he screamed three statements: "The Ethiopian people will drain (in Amharic, *yafessewal*) the blood of counterrevolutionaries! . . . The Ethiopian people will drain the blood of terrorists! . . . The Ethiopian people will drain the blood of American imperialism!" He then smashed to the ground three bottles of what appeared to be blood—one bottle after each statement—as a demonstration of what the revolution would do to its enemies. The last slogan shouted during that speech was "Yankee, go home!" after which Western missionaries soon departed from Ethiopia.

It was said that Colonel Mengistu Haile Mariam's strong anti-American sentiment resulted from the racial discrimination he experienced while studying in the United States. He asserted that he associated that experience with the class discrimination he experienced in Ethiopia. According to Dr. Paulos Milkiya, after Colonel Mengistu Haile Mariam came to power, he emotionally expressed his sentiment at the Derg members' meeting at the headquarters of the Fourth Division in Addis Ababa:

> In this country, some aristocratic families automatically categorize persons with dark skin, thick lips, and kinky hair as "barias" [Amharic word for slave]; let it be clear to everybody that I shall soon make these ignoramuses stoop and grind corn.[56]

But I have a different opinion. I propose that Colonel Mengistu Haile Mariam's reaction against the United States resulted from Russian influence—as a condition for the support he obtained towards fighting the Somali invasion and to maintain the sovereignty of his country. For Colonel Mengistu and any Ethiopian, it was a matter of national sovereignty to do anything necessary to save Ethiopia, a nation with the fresh memory of the Italian invasion, from foreign attack.

Colonel Mengistu Haile Mariam's counterterrorism campaign slogan was "We will defeat White Terror with Red Terror!" Soon civilians were organized through their respective kebeles and received arms from the Derg to go door-to-door, disarm every Ethiopian, and track down EPRP members. Colonel Mengistu Haile Mariam's campaign against his enemies, whom he called "counterrevolutionaries" and "anarchists," also involved the assassination of Lieutenant Colonel Atnafu Ababte, the Derg's cochair, on November 13, 1977. It was said that by the end of November 1977, fifty three military officers had been executed, freeing Mengistu Haile Mariam from all rivals and clearing the way for him to seize indisputable power.

I found Colonel Mengistu Haile Mariam's brutality so hard to accept that I asked God who this man was. Here is the answer I received when I opened my Bible:

> Woe to Assyria, the rod of My anger and the staff in whose hand is My indignation. I will send him against an ungodly nation, and against the people of My wrath I will give him charge, to seize the spoil, to take the prey, and to tread them down like the mire of the streets.
>
> —Isaiah 10:5–6

That timely message from the Word of God helped me to realize that the worst was yet to come. In the following pages, we will see what more "the rod of God's anger" would do.

The Derg's campaigners continued hunting down EPRP suspects. Many youngsters who were suspected of being EPRP members and a few of their leaders were killed without any trial. In no time, MESON, Derg's supporter, became the Red Terror's next target. Many young people were taken from their homes during the night, others from the streets of Addis Ababa, and killed. Their corpses were thrown on the doorsteps of their parents' homes and in the streets of Addis Ababa. In some instances, parents were compelled to walk on their children's corpses, lest they themselves be executed. Parents were not allowed to bury or mourn for their children. The lucky ones were allowed to pay for the so-called wasted bullets by which their children were killed and received their corpses.

I was on maternity leave when the horrifying incidents were at their highest peak and did not see what was happening. Upon returning to my job in early April 1978, I viewed from a distance a dead body lying near Mexico Square in Addis Ababa. I did not want to go closer, in order to avoid forming a bad memory. I asked God why all this had been allowed and came across the following message when I opened my Bible. It was my first time to see this word in the Bible:

> For thus says the LORD: "Do not enter the house of mourning, nor go to lament or bemoan them; for I have taken away My peace from this people," says the LORD, "loving kindness and mercies. Both the great and the small shall die in this land. They shall not be buried; neither shall men lament for them, cut themselves, nor make themselves bald for them. Nor shall men break bread in mourning for them, to comfort them for the dead; nor shall men give them the cup of consolation to drink for their father or their mother."
> —Jeremiah 16:5–7

I was shocked to see this word in the Bible because it described exactly how the majority of Ethiopians responded to the loss of loved ones. They mourned and lamented for several days. Friends, relatives, neighbors, and social associations formed for such a purpose, called *edir*[19], comforted the family that mourned. It was also a long-standing practice to shave the hair, bang hard on the chest, and cut one's face.

Communism, the ideology followed in the terror campaigns, not only targeted Colonel Mengistu Hale Mariam's

[19] *"Edir"* is a traditional community association formed by its members to comfort mourners and assist each other during the mourning period. Edir members collect monthly edir association fees and deposit it in the edir's account to be given to mourners according to the assigned rate (rate varies depending on closeness of the deceased family member)

political rivals, but also evangelical Christians, especially those who were active in Christian outreaches. Many evangelical churches were closed, and Christian assembly was banned and controlled. The situation compelled churches to go underground, where they grew tremendously in spite of the severe persecution. Like many in the EPRP and MESON, many Christians were imprisoned, interrogated, tortured, and killed for refusing to denounce Christianity. Let me give you a few examples.

Misrake-Tsehai was a second-year college student when she was targeted because of her Christian faith. One day she was taken from her home, detained for twenty-four hours, and interrogated. Something even worse happened in a second incident. Armed men entered the room in which she was worshiping with a group of Christian students and watched the crowd until they finished worshiping. At the end, one of the students chose a song that said, "Victory is our Lord's, our God's / The enemy's roaring is nothing for Jesus / For He is in control." The men were so angered by the song that they took all the students to prison immediately and tortured them severely. The girl who had chosen the song received the worst torture. Misrake-Tsehai, one of those tortured, received lashes until her clothes were cut into pieces. She described her torture as minor compared to others in her group and thanked God for that. She is now serving the Lord as a marriage and family counselor.

Mulu Elala is the second example. One morning, Mulu Elala, a high school student at Yekatit 12 (formerly Menen High School) at Sidist Kilo in Addis Ababa, was riding bus 31 to school as usual. As she approached Arat Kilo, an internal voice spoke to her, saying repeatedly, "Mulu, return!". As she drew near St. Mary's Church in Amist Kilo, she decided to pray instead of going to school that day and got off at a bus stop across the street from the church and just a few meters from her school. She entered the church compound and spent the whole day there praying.

When she arrived home around 6:00 p.m., she found her parents dressed in black and mourning for her. With great relief, they told her they had thought she was one of the students executed at Yekatit 12 High School that day. In those days, those who lost their loved ones to execution heard the news from the media, and the whereabouts of their loved ones was considered none of their business. Mulu is now an evangelist in Germany.

The third example is Ato (Mr.) Erjabo, a Christian teacher from Shashamane, southern Ethiopia, who was imprisoned and tortured in an effort to force him to betray Jesus and relinquish his faith. When he gave me his testimony on the torture that he survived, he showed me the soles of his feet, which were as black as charcoal. They hung him upside down and flogged him, using electric cords as whips to beat his soles. At intervals, he was offered strong alcoholic beverages, which he had never tasted, but he refused. They continued beating him when he refused to drink.

As you may recall, the White Terror and Red Terror, as well as the torture and execution of Christians, were inflicted by the followers of Communism. In comparing evil with evil, I am inclined to believe that the Ethiopians were bound with moral and ethical values that, to some extent, softened their actions as torturers. For example, pregnant women were not tortured in Ethiopian prisons or executed. Rape was also not allowed.

From the stories I've heard of Christians tortured in Russia, I don't think that the Ethiopians dared to inflict the same awful forms of torture (in relation to God) that Richard Wurmbrand describes:

> . . . Christians tied to crosses for four days and nights. The crosses were placed on the floor and hundreds

of prisoners had to fulfill their daily necessities over the faces and bodies of the crucified ones. Then the crosses were erected again and the Communists jeered and mocked: "Look at your Christ. How beautiful he is. What fragrance he brings from heaven. . . ."

After being driven nearly insane with tortures, a priest was forced to consecrate excrement and urine and give Holy Communion to Christians in this form. This happened in the Russian prison of Pitesti. [57]

Richard Wurmbrand states that he told very little of what actually happened. Other things were too terrible and obscene to put into writing, he said. That is what our brothers in Christ went through and still go through now (p. 37). To me, the stories I read in his book are terrible enough. It is just unbelievable that any government would allow such crimes on its citizens—citizens who were created equal and endowed with the same rights as those who perform such terrible tortures upon them. As Richard Wurmbrand points out, Christians are still being persecuted, tortured, and even executed, although the form and the degree vary from country to country. For jihadist Islam, killing Christians is a holy act. Although Christianity is declining in Western countries, Islamic fundamentalists still consider the West as Christian and target its citizens. Who in the world is called by God and empowered by Him to intervene in such a horrible crime against humanity? I leave the answer to you.

9

The Predicament
of Socialism in Ethiopia

A fter defeating Somali's invading forces in early 1978
through the help of Russia and Cuba, Colonel Mengistu
gained control of the government leadership. But the insur-
gent guerrillas of the Eritrean Liberation Front (ELF) and
the Tigray People's Liberation Front (TPLF) grew stronger
against his government. In his speech at Asmara on January
25, 1982, Colonel Mengistu Haile Mariam declared the Red
Star Campaign (Keyy kokeb zemecha in Amharic) against
the EPLF. The campaign was meant to destroy, once and for
all, the EPLF whom he called the "separatists." My employment at the department of Defense Industries of the Ministry
of National Defense helped me obtain firsthand information
about the Red Star Campaign.

Ethiopia, under Colonel Mengistu Hale Mariam's direction, had purchased missiles from Russia and brought them to
Addis Ababa to be used for the Red Star Campaign. When the
missiles were tested in the Department of Defense Industries
before usage, it was discovered that they were missing
gunpowder, without which they could not be propelled. This
triggered a crisis because Colonel Mengistu had already

declared the campaign. Department of Defense Industries found a solution right away. A missile was modified with gunpowder found at the nation's ammunition depot located at Nefasilk, Debrezeyit Road, in Addis Ababa. When tested after modification, it flew five kilometers farther than the original product from Russia. After test-proving the modified missiles, the Department of Defense Industries ordered all its employees, including me, to work from 8:00 a.m. until 6:00 p.m. each day until enough missiles were modified. The employees regarded it as a national emergency and worked with passion. No one uttered a word about why Russia had sold the missiles to Ethiopia without gunpowder in the first place or why it did not replace the defective missiles.

Mr. Teshome Akililu, one of the department heads who used to come to my clinic office to chat with me during coffee break each day, stopped showing up during that period. One day I went to his workplace to see him and immediately noticed that he was not in good health. Since he was excessively overweight, working ten hours every day in a standing position had greatly affected his health. I advised him to go to the hospital and get checked, but he replied, "I won't allow my country to be defeated by its enemy—over my dead body!" Immediately after he said this, I went to the director general's office and reported to him that Mr. Teshome was in critical condition. The director general ordered his executive secretary to escort Mr. Teshome to the hospital immediately. He was admitted right away and passed away after three days in the hospital. Like Mr. Teshome, many others lost their lives in vain to the Red Star Campaign, as Colonel Mengistu did not win the war.

Shortly after the drama of the Russian missiles was handled, the Ministry of National Defense, under Colonel Mengistu's directive, entered into a contract with Czechoslovakia to develop munitions factories at five different sites under the Department of Defense Industries. These sites included

Shegole Meda/Gulele, Ambo/Homicho, Debrezeit, and Gafat (near Debrezeit). The aim was to cut Ethiopia's reliance on foreign arms supplies as well as to generate foreign currency through the export of munitions to other African countries. The implementation work was fully assigned to the Department of Defense Industries. Interestingly, the Department of Defense Industries also manufactured high-quality medical equipment, hospital beds, furniture, and more.

The arrangement with Czechoslovakia provoked another drama. Czechoslovakia wanted to send to Ethiopia twenty experts, who would be sponsored by the project to instruct and supervise the implementation of the project. After calculating the cost, management found that it was too expensive and reached an agreement on a cost-effective deal: two Czechoslovakian experts would be assigned to the Department of Defense Industries, and two hundred employees from the Department of Defense Industries would be sent to Czechoslovakia to receive the proposed training. The two Czechoslovakian men arrived in Addis Ababa and were provided with housing and a Mercedes car. They lived in an apartment building across the street from the Commercial School (presently College of Commerce) in Addis Ababa. One of them was in his forties, while the other was an older man who used hearing aids. The project covered all their expenses while in Ethiopia. I was yet to learn that their benefits included a large amount of life insurance.

One morning I was summoned to the director general's office, along with his executive secretary. Upon our arrival, we were informed that Mr. Kachina, the older Czechoslovakian expert, had not shown up for work for the last three days, and we were ordered to go to his apartment to check on him. We went to Mr. Kachina's apartment as ordered and had the building management open his apartment for us, since Mr. Kachina did not respond to our knocks. When we entered, we found the old man lying in his bed, with twenty codeine-phosphate tablets on his nightstand. We took him to the hospital right away, where he was examined thoroughly. Nothing abnormal was detected, except the hearing impairment that he had brought with him from his country. We took him back to the director general's office, along with his medical report.

Mr. Kachina took a piece of paper from his pocket, leaned over the director general's desk, and said, "Look how much you pay my family if I die," showing him a figure—in millions—that he had written on the piece of paper.

The director general yelled at him, "I will send you back to your country!" and told us to take him to the deputy director's office.

Mr. Kachina, in the same manner, leaned over the deputy's desk and repeated what he had said to the director general. The deputy asked Mr. Kachina what he wanted, and he replied, "Give me back my car."

The deputy replied in a very calm manner, "Listen, you killed a human being with that car, but you were not even charged or sentenced for that. We just changed your car to a Lada and gave it to you with a driver. You can go back to your country if you don't agree with our decision." Mr. Kachina replied that he did not want to go back to his country and accepted the decision.

Until that moment, I had known nothing about the entire ordeal. The issue was that one weekend the two experts had hit and killed a pedestrian in a car accident while driving their Mercedes to Ambo, 130 kilometers from Addis Ababa. Management replaced their Mercedes car with a Lada and banned them from driving the company's car, instead assigning a driver for them.

The immediate outcome of the munitions factories was a disaster. On June 3, 1991 (after the TPLF-led guerillas gained control of Addis Ababa on May 28, 1991), unidentified forces attempted to destroy the munitions factories. The new development at Shegole Meda and the nation's ammunition depot at Nefasilk (Debrezeit Road) in Addis Ababa were totally destroyed. The destruction caused by the bombing of the ammunition depot was like that of a very powerful tornado combined with an earthquake. It was 4:45 a.m. when I was awakened by the sound of the chain of explosions. Although our house was approximately twenty-five kilometers away, my entire family could not sleep from the explosions that shook our house. It was reported in the news that over a hundred people died and five thousand homes destroyed, leaving many residents homeless. I liken the incident to that of the September 11 attack on the Twin Towers in New York.

In spite of the tensions facing him from many angles, Colonel Mengistu continued working hard to consolidate his power. On December 18, 1979, he announced the establishment of the Commission for Organizing the Party of the Working People of Ethiopia (COPWE). The aim of COPWE was to pave the way towards establishing the Workers' Party that ruled the nation with an iron fist. Political organizations such as the All Ethiopian Youth Association, the Revolutionary Ethiopian Women's Association, the All Ethiopian Peasants' Association, and the Control Committee were formed. Many households in the country were organized into the government-controlled associations.

All women were required to become members of the Revolutionary Women's Association. I was denied a state ID for refusing to become a member, but I was not affected since I had God's favor on me. Privatization was condemned by labeling the employers of the nationalized private businesses and companies as "exploiters," "suppressors," etc., and creating enmity between the workers and private employers.

The Derg cadres who were trained at the Yekatit 66 training center brainwashed all Ethiopians into accepting Marxism-Leninism and spread propaganda about the Derg. Under the leadership of COPWE, political departments were established in all government organizations, and heads of political departments (cadres) were assigned. A training program called the Discussion Club (*Wuyiyit Kibeb* in Amharic) was established in all government institutions for the purpose of brainwashing. All employees of the Ministry of National Defense were required to take four hours of political training a week from the cadres, while all other government employees took two hours a week. After every *wuyiyit* (discussion) session, the Wuyiyit Kibeb participants were required to raise their left hands and loudly shout slogans such as "Down with feudalism!" "Down with bureaucratic capitalism!" "Down with imperialism!" "Revolutionary motherland or death!" and more. The Wuyiyit Kibeb meetings continued until I left the Ministry of National Defense in August 1983 after serving there for over seven years. As a Christian, I abhorred their ideology and considered their slogans as curses. They tried to intimidate me for not attending the Wuyiyit Kibeb, but God whom I trusted protected me.

Through its propaganda, the Derg's Communist regime asserted that the general public (*sefiw hizb*) was the king. But the truth is that all the new organizations served as powerful political tools that allowed the Derg to control everything. All previously formed associations quickly lost their authority. In my opinion, the slogan "land for the tiller" transformed tillers into Communist serfs (*gebar* in Amharic). I call them serfs because like feudal serfs, the peasants were obligated to farm for the families of the militia who were fighting in the civil war and to give contributions to their widows. Additionally, they now paid taxes at a higher rate than during Emperor Haile Selassie I's reign. They were also required to sell their products to the government (Agricultural Produce Marketing Corporation) at a lower price. The Ethiopian peasant associations were systematically converted into a government organ.

The government launched state farms and collectivized the peasant associations. The Agricultural Produce Marketing

Corporation (AMC), or *Ye Ersha Sebel Gebeya Dirijit* in Amharic), was established to control the marketing of agricultural products. AMC obtained agricultural products from the producers at a lower price and regulated the food markets by assigning quotas to the peasants and setting prices for the food products. Checkpoints were established at the provincial entrances and exits and at Addis Ababa's entry points to prevent peasants from smuggling their products into the cities. Coffee became subject to confiscation as a contraband item. As might be expected, food rationing followed the resultant food-shortage crisis, and people had to wait in long lines to purchase food. In an actual sense, the food rationing also furthered the government's power to force citizens to accept its ideology and serve its political interest.

The way things were during my years of service at the Ministry of National Defense Department of Defense Industries made me feel that we were being governed by two different governments. The formal administration, which was led by a director general (an army general) and his deputy (a colonel), served as a governing entity for the business and affairs of the organization, while the political department, which was led by a cadre, promoted the government's ideology. There were big differences between these two authorities. The formal administration was composed of well-disciplined and well-educated officers who displayed high professional and ethical standards, while the cadres were less educated, arrogant civilians who acted as though they were in control. In my opinion, the differences existed because the lower-ranking officers who came to power through military mutiny had to maintain power over the higher-ranking leadership officers through their cadres.

There were six cadres under the head of the political department. For the cadres from the lower social classes, which encompassed the majority of the Ethiopian population, serving the ruling party in that role brought a sense of great empowerment. As a result, they maintained loyalty to the ruling party, of which they were also a part.

Although I was well regarded and nothing bad happened to me, I felt that leaving the company would free me from the atmosphere I hated. Soon after I notified the director general of my intent to quit my job, I was hired by the Norwegian Save the Children (*Radda Barnen*) as the supervisor of community-health development. I was assigned to work at a village named Balle Gadula, located in the Bale region of southern Ethiopia. Even though living conditions were far below my standards in Addis Ababa, I was delighted to work for a Pentecostal Christian (my new boss). However, the problem I faced under his leadership led me to say, "It was better where it is worse." The atmosphere that I hated at my previous job was much better than this new one. One day, a senior employee asked me what our boss's religion was. When I replied that it was, "*Full Gospel*", he sputtered angrily and screamed, "Not even a quarter, let alone full".

That experience helped me understand Jesus' prayer in John 17:15 where He prayed, not that the Father would take us out of the world, but would keep us from the evil one. My new boss was such a very difficult person that the other employees petitioned against him. This was my first time to face that kind of a leader and situation. Although I refused to sign the petition, he reported to the headquarters that I had conspired with the other employees and encouraged them to petition against him. Taking his false report at face value, Radda Barnen handed me a letter terminating my employment. However, it worked out for my good. I had been planning to resign anyway, but I was waiting for God's will to be revealed to me.

It is scriptural that challenges bring forth opportunities that surpass the problems we face. When Radda Barnen discovered the truth and did not find my name on the employees' petition, they gave me three months' salary. Also, Dr. Jember, a Radda Barnen senior staff member, sympathized with me and helped me secure a better job opportunity. Unknown to me, the best was yet to come.

The most important thing in all this is that God opened a door for me with a purpose in mind. The experience taught me to discern God's will for my life, to identify my call, and to heed the high calling. Therefore, I did not blame and still do not blame the man who harmed me.

We all have a calling to be a witness for God by our life and our words, and this was a priceless opportunity for me to be one. As we can see from Jesus' disciples, we often look for temporary gain as human beings, but God sees the big picture:

> Therefore, when they had come together, they asked Him, saying, "Lord, will You at this time restore the kingdom to Israel?" And He said to them, "It is not for you to know times or seasons which the Father has put in His own authority. But you shall receive power when the Holy Spirit has come upon you; and you shall be witnesses to Me in Jerusalem, and in all Judea and Samaria, and to the end of the earth."
>
> —Acts 1:6–8

Radda Barnen opened the door for me to be a witness for Him by living out my faith. Nevertheless, I had to be processed and refined through it all for my eternal destiny.

During my employment at Radda Barnen, I was assigned to work with a development program focused on addressing the problems of recurrent drought among the Oromo resettlers at Balle Gadula. The resettlers were Islamic Oromo nomads who had fought in a civil war with the Derg in the late 1970s and surrendered. In spite of our religious and political differences, they were very open with me in disclosing their background. They told me their story of how they had received arms and training support from neighboring Somalia and fought against the heavily armed Derg military. They also told me how they had killed Mr. Baro Tumsa, an Oromo politician from a Christian family. From what I heard, he was a member of the Oromo Liberation Front (OLF), and no one had known his whereabouts, until now. The unity I witnessed among them was amazing. They were so loyal to one another that they never exposed or surrendered anyone from their group to the Derg cadres' investigations. In the following pages, I will share with you what I experienced in the areas of disaster relief and humanitarian aid.

10

Controversy Surrounding Humanitarian and Relief Aid

The rain failed to come during the usual rainy season of July and August in 1983. Predictably, a famine like the one of the early seventies was on its way again. As the saying goes, "What goes around comes around." As the Derg prepared for its tenth anniversary celebration in 1984, the famine was at its peak. As I mentioned in chapter 4, the emperor had been greatly criticized for his lavish eightieth birthday celebration while his people were starving to death. Similarly, the Derg was busy preparing for a very expensive celebration of its tenth-year anniversary while thousands of Ethiopians were starving to death. In fact, the scope of the 1983–84 famine far exceeded that of the 1973–74 famine. This time, six provinces suffered from a terrible drought, while only Wollo and part of Tigray were hit by the 1973–74 famine. Yet the Derg closed its ears to the cries of those caught in the famine and focused its attention on its anniversary celebration and the establishment of the Workers Party of Ethiopia (WPE). Congress Hall was built near Arat Kilo in Addis Ababa, ready to house the WPE.

A day before the Derg's celebration, the media was busy spreading propaganda on the achievement of Colonel

Mengistu whom they called "the determinant leader(*Koratu meri* in Amharic) and socialism, without any mention of the drought or famine. The media also praised Russia and Eastern Bloc friends, while bombarding the West for its imperialism. The four-day celebration gala included parades of military might (very long lines of tanks and weapons), lavish ceremonies, much pomp, and a banquet. All this was quite impressive to the Derg's Eastern Bloc allies. The intrigue behind all this was designed to scare the Derg's enemies by showing them its military might. It's too bad that Colonel Mengistu was an atheist and did not realize what the outcome would be: "Pride goes before destruction, a haughty spirit before a fall" (Proverbs 16:8).The heavy weaponry so openly flaunted was eventually captured by his enemies and used towards the fall of his own regime.

The long-planned anniversary achieved its intended purpose in establishing the Workers Party of Ethiopia (WPE). The WPE elected a central committee and formed a politburo that chose Colonel Mengistu as its general secretary, chairman of the Council of Ministers, and commander-in-chief of the armed forces. Colonel Mengistu delivered a very long acceptance speech describing his past achievements and his plans for the future. I was amazed at his arrogance when he stated in his speech, "We cut the budgets of those generals and pocked their buttocks with gun-knife (*sanja* in Amharic). Although the successful formation of the WPE accorded Colonel Mengistu full control of the central power, his cruelty would soon cost him the very power he grasped.

The famine alerts ignored during the WPE formation process could no longer remain a secret. The newly established politburo and Colonel Mengistu were forced to respond to the Relief and Rehabilitation Commission's (RCC) need to feed those affected by the famine.

Suppressed by Colonel Mengistu's agricultural and economic policy, which I highlighted in the previous pages, the country was unable to address the famine crisis by itself. It was inevitable that Colonel Mengistu would be forced to seek help from the Western countries that he had so blatantly criticized as imperialist. Under much pressure, his government finally allowed the previously banned Western media to film the famine in hopes of soliciting international support. In October, just one month after the WPE was formed, BBC television disseminated the famine footage worldwide. The newly formed politburo had to work hand in hand with the RRC to mobilize resources internationally and locally.

Nonetheless, Colonel Mengistu hated the West and placed his confidence in his Eastern Bloc allies for relief aid, but it did not go the way he thought it would. Fortunately, God had someone in store to rescue His creatures. Mr. Shimeles Adugna, RRC commissioner, used the wisdom that God granted him to cross political boundaries and solicited tremendous support from Western countries. Mr. Shimeles Adugna first tried to get help from the Eastern Bloc allies, but when they failed him, he turned his face to the West.

After seeing the televised crisis and hearing the moving plea of Mr. Shimeles Adugna, Western nations were compassionate enough to put aside their ideological differences and pour immense humanitarian aid and relief into the country. In addition to the abundant humanitarian aid and relief support from Western countries, a national program called Call of the Motherland (*Yenat Hager Tirri* in Amharic) was created to mobilize citizens. The government established a mandatory policy in which all employees were obligated to donate one month of their salary as well as provide famine victims with needed care and support. Each employee's financial contribution was spread over twelve months and cut from payroll each month.

My next career journey took me to an organization called the International Coordinating Committee for Welfare and Development Programs in Addis Ababa (ICC). That organization was strategically designed by the top Addis Ababa city-council officials to gain access to and exploit humanitarian and relief-aid supplies/funds. To that end, ICC formed under its umbrella a consortium of officially recognized international humanitarian-aid and governmental organizations, with the city council's higher official as executive committee member and social- affairs committee chair of the consortium.[20] The Christian Relief and Development Association (CRDA), an indigenous umbrella organization of NGOs and faith-based organizations in Ethiopia, was among the ICC members. Established in 1973 by thirteen faith-based and secular humanitarian organizations as a relief-coordinating agency, CRDA was a well-experienced, trustworthy organization and it was not even necessary to form ICC.

Using these organizations, ICC systematically maintained direct and indirect control of the funds that went to programs in the above-listed organizations.

ICC maintained direct control over humanitarian-aid organizations that were not members, including SKIP, the organization that hired me in 1985. SKIP was a program of Pestalozzi Children's Village in Zurich, Switzerland. I was interviewed at the ICC office, in the City Council in June 1985 by ICC member representatives and the chairman of Higher 21 Kebele 23. On August 2, I received the good news that I had been selected from thirty-one applicants and hired as a project officer to run the ICC/SKIP project at Higher 21

---

[20] ICC members include: the municipality of Addis Ababa, UNICEF, United Nations Food & Agricultural Organization (FAO), National Children's Commission, Addis Ababa Revolutionary Women's Association (REWA), Addis Ababa Schools' Office, Christian Relief and Development Association (CRDA), Red Cross Society (RCS), Norwegian Save the Children Federation (Radda Barnen, Ethiopia), Revolutionary Ethiopian Youth Association (REYA) Addis Ababa, Ethiopian Trade Union (ETU) Regional Office for Addis Ababa, and the Ministry of Labor and Social Affairs (Addis Ababa region).

Kebele 23 in Cherkos neighborhood, one of the poorest parts of Addis Ababa. ICC assigned the kebele chairman, who was married to a Swiss woman, to serve as the SKIP supervisor in order to serve their purposes.

My job title was attractive, but unfortunately, my actual job did not match it. The project had a day-care center with some twenty children and three day-care instructors who were not trained for the job. The project fund was depleted before meeting its intended purpose, so there was nothing more for me to do except to supervise the day-care center. On my own, I had the three day-care instructors trained, conducted a door-to-door survey to study the socioeconomic conditions of the target population, and launched a feasibility study on a foster-family program. However, my employer did nothing to help facilitate the program. I presented my concerns to my boss several times, but the response was always the same: "You do what we give you to do."

The project was to be evaluated by external evaluators from Switzerland before the end of 1986, but we did not even have a car for the evaluators to use, since the money allocated for the need was misused. However, since SKIP was partially funded by the Swiss government, the Swiss Embassy in Addis Ababa purchased a brand-new car for the evaluators to use during their evaluation work in Addis Ababa. Two evaluators soon arrived from Switzerland and conducted the evaluation as planned. Two pages of their evaluation reported on my work with SKIP, and they gave me an excellent review. But that did not prevent the ICC from attacking me for my stand against corruption.

After the evaluators left the country, SKIP decided that I should use the new car. Unfortunately, that decision exposed me to great danger because the government official who oversaw the ICC craved that car for two reasons. First, the car was only the second of its kind in the country; Comrade Colonel Teka Tulu, a member of the Central Committee, had the other. Second, in its effort to discourage Christians from going to church, the Derg had banned the driving of government and private cars on Sundays, while NGO cars, with their yellow plates, were allowed. As a strategy to gain access to my car, the city council assigned a driver to me, although I could drive myself and did not need one.

One Thursday morning, the official who oversaw the ICC called me to his office for the first time and asked me if I needed anything. I replied that the project was lying dormant because the ICC had not sent the donor agency the required progress report for releasing the project funds, and I needed that to happen. He promised that everything would be taken care of and encouraged me to ask for more. I was yet to discover that this first part of the conversation was designed to establish rapport with me.

The man continued his conversation, asking me if I needed the car for that weekend. I replied that I was too embarrassed to use the car on weekdays, let alone on weekends, because I did not have enough work. Nonetheless, he went on to say that he needed the car for that weekend and asked to use it. I told I would let him know and left. I went home, prayed about it, and told him the next day that he could use the car but should record the mileage in the logbook and buy fuel, since it was for his private use. It was very bold of me to say that.

This same official called me to his office the next month, this time on a Friday, and started his conversation the same way he had done before. Then he got to the point and asked to use the car that weekend. As I had done before, I replied that I would let him know and left. I prayed about it that evening, seeking God's guidance in dealing with a corrupt official, and received this answer from my Bible: "Better to be of a humble spirit with the lowly than to divide the spoil with the proud" (Proverbs 16:19).

Upon making sure that the answer from God was no, I boldly told the official that I could not lend him the car. The driver was shocked by my action and asked me, "Do you want to die?" I replied that I did whatever pleased God. My driver was so worried because no one ever dared to mess with the big guys, lest they be murdered. I was well aware that I would have to face the consequences of my decision, but I was not afraid. My faith in God made me bold enough to fear Him rather than man.

The official was so angered by my action that he had the ICC send me a letter the next week demanding that I hand over the car to them. My boldness only increased all the more, and I did not play it safe in my response. I wrote to the ICC and copied the Swiss Embassy, stating that the ICC was doing this because I had refused to give the car to the official for his personal use. I also stated that I was returning the car to the Swiss Embassy, the party who gave me the car in the first place, and advised the ICC to obtain the car from the Swiss Embassy if they still wanted it. I then took the car to the Swiss Embassy, together with my letter to the ICC, but the ambassador informed me that they could not take the car from me because the vehicle was from SKIP. If they took the car from a SKIP employee, he explained, they could be accused of perpetrating a human-rights offense, according to their country's laws.

I returned home with the car and parked it in my garage until the SKIP director and program coordinator for Ethiopia came from Switzerland to handle the issue. Three days after their arrival in Addis Ababa, the two men instructed me to meet them at the Ethiopian Hotel at 8:00 p.m. I suspected they were afraid to be seen with me in daylight, so they scheduled an evening meeting. I drove that troublesome car to the hotel to hand it over to them.

The first thing the director said to me was, "Agitu! You are boxing against a wall." I replied that the wicked are never protected by a wall and that I didn't want to be judged by God Almighty. I ended our conversation by telling the two men not to worry about me, but rather to worry about their project that had been stagnant for over four years.

Two days later, the ICC issued a letter firing me. A week later, ICC's coordinator (my boss) called me to his office, only to yell at me, saying, "The Swiss ambassador has such high regard for you that he sent a mediator on your behalf! Who do you think the Swiss ambassador is? We can kick him out of the country in twenty-four hours" (which they didn't do).

It took seven months until I got God's go-ahead to file a lawsuit against the ICC. It is a long story, but briefly, this is what happened. During that time, there was a labor court under the Ministry of Labor and Social Affairs (MOLSA) where petitioners were not required to have attorney representation. However, employees holding leadership positions were not authorized to use that court, so I hired an attorney to represent me in filing my lawsuit with the federal court.

Just when my documents were ready for court filing, the Lord spoke to me at our weekly underground fellowship that I should not use an attorney. Being confident that God was in control, I decided to take my case to MOLSA. My lawyer tried to prevent me from breaking my contract with him, but God gave me wisdom to overcome that obstacle. Since I was unfamiliar with the process, I wrote a letter to Mr. Shimeles Adugna, the minister of Labor and Social Affairs, briefly describing my situation. His secretary, Mrs. Tsega Legessie, accepted the letter from me and told me to return in three days. When I went back on my appointment day, Mrs. Tsega handed me the minister's response in a sealed envelope and told me to take it to Comrade Abba Saba, the executive director of the workers' labor court. When I asked her for the room number, she realized I thought his office was in the same building and directed me to a different location. I knew neither the process nor the location of the workers' labor court.

After reading the letter from the minister of MOLSA, the executive director instructed me to go ahead with my court filing and tell him which judge my case was referred to. After four months of battling, I finally won the case. Let me tell you how it happened.

One morning, before I left my house for my labor-court hearing, I received this word from the Bible:

> Say to him, "Be careful, keep calm and don't be afraid. Do not lose heart because of these two smoldering stubs of firewood—because of the fierce anger of Rezin and Aram and of the son of Remaliah."
>
> —Isaiah 7:4

Upon my arrival at court, I saw two men whom the ICC had brought to court as false witnesses against me. One of them was the Kebele chairman, who was also the SKIP project supervisor. I said in my heart, "These are the two smoldering stubs of firewood about whom I was warned this morning. I will not be afraid or lose heart."

After listening to the two men give false witness against me, I quoted to them, "Many seek the ruler's favor, but justice for man comes from the Lord" (Proverbs 29:26). Though Christianity was forbidden in my country at this time, I quoted the Bible, knowing that God is always great. At the end, the judge revealed that he worked with the sister of a city council official and the wife of the ICC coordinator (my former boss at ICC), and both had been nagging him every single day to render judgment against me. But he had been warned by his boss, Comrade Abba Saba, to make a just and timely decision in my case.

The situation made me realize that Mr. Shimeles Adugna, the minister of MOLSA, was well aware of what was going on at ICC and had recommended justice to be served regarding my case. I had never had any previous acquaintance with him.

My only contact was in the form of the letter that I addressed to him. I only knew his touching story that I mentioned in the previous chapter, how he was so emotional that he cried all the time he was soliciting support for the famine victims. But the God who knows everything guided me in the right direction. Because I listened to Him, I received His guidance and encouragement through the whole ordeal.

However, my case was not over yet. The court judgment ordered the ICC to pay my salary for the four months my case had been in court and to immediately restore me to my previous job. Unfortunately, the law did not allow the judgment to include the seven months between my firing date and court filing. When I presented the court's decision to the ICC coordinator, he looked at it and yelled at me, "You should be ashamed of yourself!"

Before he could go further, I replied, "Mr. Getahun, you are against me because you know whom you trusted, and I will be strong because I know whom I trust. We will find out who the winner will be." My boldness grew even more, and I spoke a proverb in Amharic, boasting of my trust in the Lord: *"Balebetwan yetamamench beg latea dej yadral"* meaning "a sheep that trusts her owner spends the night outside"). With that, I slammed his office door and left.

ICC filed an appeal, and I had to face a second-round court battle. Following the legal provisions, I went to the court that handled such cases because the law provided that I could resume my work during the appeal period. I went to the judge every working day for two months to have the court's decision executed according to the law of the land. Finally, he yelled at me, "Leave my office! Go away!" without even giving me a reason. It was very humiliating and more frustrating to me than ever before. It looked like that was the end of the matter, but I did not lose my trust in God, because the grace of God is greater than any difficulty.

Returning home, I prayed a special prayer in which I was reminded that Colonel Tesfaye Woldesellassie, who was the minister of Internal Affairs, heard such cases every Thursday. On Thursday morning, I went to Colonel Tesfaye's office with my plea. His office was in the building that the Derg had confiscated from the Ethiopian Evangelical Church Mekane Yesus (EECMY). It was 9:00 a.m. when I arrived, but there were so many people waiting that I did not get in until 4:55 p.m. I handed my plea to him and said, "I am before you because the action I took in the fear of the Lord worked against me, putting my children's lives at risk. I earnestly plead with you to examine my case and have me executed if you find me guilty, because my being alive means nothing if I cannot provide for my children." He read my letter and told me to check the status in three days.

In just one week, a court messenger delivered a notice to my house, summoning me to appear before the judge who had denied me the service I deserved. That was what he should have done before I submitted my plea to Colonel Tesfaye Wolde-Sellassie. But here comes the surprise victory! On our court date, the ICC coordinator and I stood before the judge. Picking up his phone, the very judge who had humiliated me earlier said angrily to the ICC coordinator, "Do you know where you are? I can call the police right now and have you jailed for six months if you fail to satisfy the court's judgment in favor of this woman."

The ICC coordinator bowed and responded, "Your Honor, she will go with me right now and start her work."

After we left the courtroom, I followed him to his office. He wrote me a check for one month's salary and told me to collect my paycheck at the end of each month until the appeal was settled, stating that it would be difficult to have me work in the office until then. Already demoralized by what had happened to the city-council official who was behind all this, the ICC coordinator did not have the heart to say or do anything except to fulfill the judge's order.

It was a good thing I waited for seven months until I received the go-ahead from the Almighty. What a good timing! The city-council official who oversaw the ICC and whom the other official trusted left Ethiopia just a week after I filed my lawsuit against the ICC. According to what I heard from the security officer who was assigned by the minister of Internal Affairs to follow up on my case, the official took a job with the South African Red Cross Society. Since he did that without the knowledge of Colonel Mengistu Haile Mariam, his employment was discontinued, and the official fled to Canada. The security officer also told me that the official was not supposed to do that, as a Central Committee member, and would be brought back for trial. As I opened my Bible during my time with God that evening, I came across this message: "Weep not for the dead, nor bemoan him; weep bitterly for him who goes away, for he shall return no more, nor see his native country" (Jeremiah 22:10). By that, I was assured that the government would not bring him back and have him tried in the country.

The ICC pressed forward with their appeal by assigning a lawyer from the city council to represent them. One day I told him that he could not win because I had Jesus as my lawyer, but he didn't understand what I meant. On the last hearing of the appeal, which took seven months, the judge warned the ICC that they would face the consequences for what they had done to me and gave us two weeks to reach a peaceful settlement before judgment would be made.

On the third day, the ICC sent three mediators to my home to reach a settlement with me before our final court date. They offered me two options: (1) to return to my previous job immediately or (2) to quit and receive a one-year salary and a recommendation letter. The one-year salary also included pay for the seven months that the previous judge had not ruled in my favor. I asked for three days to think about it. After thoughtful prayer during those three days, I decided to walk away with a one-year salary and begin my next chapter of life.

In the final analysis, I learned that the greater the challenges we face, the far greater the opportunities brought forth. Those difficult months gave me the opportunity to read my Bible more, fellowship with God more, and learn to know Him better, which in turn helped me gain clearer vision about my future endeavors. The same person who defamed me with the letter that fired me exalted me with a recommendation letter at the end[21]. Walking closely with God and listening to Him helped me to finish well that chapter of my life. The compensation that I received from the ICC was a tremendous help to move on to the next stage of my journey.

It was now time to pay attention to the nudging about my call that I had received while working for Radda Barnen. In 1989, after discerning God's will for many months, I received a clear vision to help displaced women and their families who lived in very poor conditions in my neighborhood, which was adjacent to Bole International Airport in Addis Ababa. I had yet to learn that the service would soon cross the ocean beyond my neighborhood. I asked my neighborhood kebele office if such a social group existed in the Kebele that that was known as a wealthy area in Addis Ababa.The Kebele staff told me about the families who had been displaced during the 1973 famine. A staff member was assigned to show me the temporary shelters in which these families lived.

Sadly, those "shelters" really could not be considered true shelters. Please don't even try to relate them to shelters in the United States. Each family had a four-by-four-foot room, covered with corrugated iron sheets and partitioned from other rooms by cartons. Though they were supposed to

---

[21] Please see appendix 1 and 2 for the fire-letter and letter of recommendation from ICC

be temporary shelters, they had been home to some families for fifteen years. Understandably, the roofs were old and leaked. Since everything went to the war front (*"Hullun neger wedetor ginbar!* Amharic for "everything to the war front!"), the government could not help those families it claimed to be helping.

Shelters

After examining the situation more closely, I got the idea to address the needs of those families through a holistic approach. Meeting their spiritual and physical needs through evangelism and self-sufficiency projects, I felt, would offer a lasting solution. The more familiar form of aid consisted mostly of handouts and Band-aid approaches that stamped "dependency" upon the minds of the poor. It was my determination to change that mind-set by promoting economic independence among these women.

That being my goal, I met with the women and discussed some options. Following that, we conducted a door-to-door survey and a needs assessment. Based on our findings and the women's recommendations, we decided to start three income-generating projects: (1) leatherworks/crafts, (2) sewing, and (3) food processing. I grouped the fifty-five women into three categories. The twenty-one women who had completed literacy classes and were able to read and write were assigned to leatherworks/crafts training. The twelve high school dropouts were assigned to pattern construction and sewing. The remaining twenty women were delegated to food processing.

We named our group the Women's Self-Reliance Association (WSRA), and three women were elected to serve as group leaders. We began working towards the initiation of the proposed projects, starting with investigating training and funding sources. I also concluded that conducting a marketing study was vital to achieving the best outcome in building the economic independence of the women. To that end, I visited leather factories and a large sewing factory in Addis Ababa. During my visits, I asked where their workers received their training and was told that those engaged in leatherwork received training at the Productivity Improvement Center of the Ethiopian Management Institute, while those involved in sewing took classes offered by the Handicraft and Small-Scale

Industries Development Agency (HASIDA). These were the only two skills-training centers in Addis Ababa.

My next step was visiting those two training centers and soliciting funding for the necessary training. A Swedish woman helped me to solicit our first funding from the Swedish International Development Agency (SIDA), which also resulted in opening a door of opportunity for me. The expert from the Inter-African Committee on Traditional Practices (IAC) in Ethiopia, through whom SIDA had reviewed our project proposal, called me from her office at the United Nations Economic Commission for Africa (UNECA) in Addis Ababa with the good news that our proposal had been approved for funding by SIDA. Additionally, IAC wanted to hire me immediately. My new employment and SIDA's support for the leatherwork and sewing projects came at the same time. The flour mill that SIDA had purchased for the food-processing project was already on its way from Denmark. The timing of it all was perfect. My job opportunity arrived right when my compensation from ICC was drying up. I gladly accepted my new job and continued to work with my women's group as a volunteer.

Since the cash grant was not enough to send the women to the training centers, I came up with the idea to have the trainers from the two government training centers provide on-site training during their spare time. The trainers accepted my idea and agreed to provide a two-hour training session on weekdays after work and six hours on Saturdays. The Kebele 20 (presently Kebele 02) administration in Bole allowed us to use their conference hall for free for the training sessions. The hall resembled a warehouse, with the roof and walls covered with corrugated iron sheets. We rented two sewing machines, purchased the needed hand tools and supplies, and began the training.

Leather crafts training in the conference hall

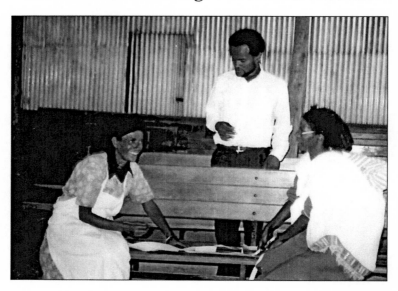

Though we managed to resolve the issue of training, we still needed to find a way to support the women who wanted to participate in the program, since they had no source of income. I turned to the Christian Relief and Development Association (CRDA) for humanitarian-aid assistance. Since the 1984 famine crisis was now over, the relief aid from Western nations was in surplus, and the CRDA had sufficient humanitarian aid available. Eventually I solicited enough support for my women's group. We used the relief and food assistance from the CRDA as remuneration for the hours spent by the women in hands-on training. Using initial handouts while working towards "hands up" achieved two things: (1) It addressed the immediate needs of the women and made it possible for them to commit their time to the training with high motivation and diligence. (2) It helped to build the women's dignity, self-worth, and self-reliance.

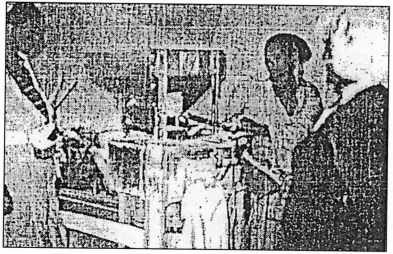

Milling and Food Processing

Pattern Construction and Sewing

Everything fit together like a puzzle and went well for the WSRA. I also did very well with my new job at the IAC, revamping the then-dying IAC national committee. The women also made me proud by completing their training in six months, with excellent results. We held a small graduation ceremony and invited a few people from the United Nations, the funding agencies, and concerned government institutions. We displayed the finished items that the women had produced during their training, including leather crafts such as sandals, ladies' bags, belts, coin holders, key chains, coasters, wallets, and other items from the leatherworks group, as well as handicrafts and clothes (mostly children's) from the sewing group. The items on display were sold at the event and generated unexpected income for the group.

Leather Workshop

Women in hands-on training

some samples of leather products

One morning in July 1990, just a few weeks after we held the above-mentioned event, a staff member of the United Nations Fund for Population Activities (UNFPA) came to my office in the UNECA Women's Center and said to me, "Your organization has been selected as a best practice model and will be visited in just three days by Dr. Nafis Sadik, undersecretary general of the United Nations and executive director of UNFPA in New York." He went on to state, "A few ministers and government officials have been invited, and Ethiopia Hotel has been scheduled to provide refreshments." He then urged me to begin preparing my draft speech on the WSRA. I asked if he meant my work at ECA, because WSRA was new and small. He assured me that it was WSRA, and rushed me to draft my speech, taking me to the UNFPA office to work on it.

My women's group and I were well prepared for the colorful and prestigious visit that took place on July 7, 1990. The Ethiopian Hotel served finger foods, coffee, tea, and soft drinks. We proudly displayed all the products that the WSRA women had made, as well as a blueprint of the WSRA's comprehensive plan. Through God's favor, my speech went very well, and the women sold most of the products displayed. Dr. Nafis Sadik paid for and ordered a pair of sandals, since we didn't have her size. That itself greatly boosted the women's morale.

My model to integrate maternal and child-health family planning into economic- development activities was commended, leading to the UNFPA's sponsorship of my study tour to Niamey, Niger. This is what Dr. Nafis commented during her visit: "This is a wonderful initiative of self-help by women to improve the life of their families. It deserves all our support."[22]

---

[22] Please see appendix 3 for visitors' comment

In December 1990, I visited the Ministry of Women's Affairs and Social Promotion in Niamey, Niger, through the UNFPA-sponsored study tour. The wonderful opportunities we had been blessed with thus far were a great encouragement to move forward. However, WSRA's situation and future was going to be different under the new government that was yet to come. You will find out all about that in the following pages.

11

The Fall of the Communist Junta and Succession of the New Government

While the Tigray People's Liberation Front (TPLF) and Eritirian People's Liberation Front (EPLF) were working to end Colonel Mengistu's rule, he was working towards strengthening his absolutism. A new constitution was drafted in 1986, establishing the *Biherawi Shengo* (National Assembly) and granting the Workers Party complete authority over the government's leadership. The new constitution provided the Shengo full authority to elect the head of state, or president, to a five-year term. From the Kebele structure that I described earlier, it is easy to see who had control over elections and voting.

On February 1, 1987, the Derg government held a referendum in which a draft of the constitution was approved. Upon adopting the new constitution, the Derg government dissolved itself and took a new name: the People's Democratic Republic of Ethiopia (PDRE), which was inaugurated on September 10, 1987. On the inaugural day, Colonel Mengistu Haile Mariam was sworn is as president. The new PDRE parliament consisted of 835 National Assembly (Shengo) members, the majority of them retained from the Derg leadership. From the way the PDRE ruled the country, it was not realistic to include the word *democratic* in the nation's new name. In my opinion, a good name was used to cover up bad deeds. There is an Amharic saying, "*Melke tifun besim yidegifu*", meaning "support the ugly with a name"), that describes the scenario quite well.

Grabbing all the power did not prevent President Mengistu from having to face the reality. Just two months after the new PDRE was inaugurated, the EPLF won a substantial victory over the army of the Ethiopian government. After his army faced this demoralizing defeat, President Mengistu sought Russia's help, but President Gorbachev declined to approve the request. President Mengistu then tried China, but that didn't work either. He flew to East Germany for the same, during which a failed military coup was attempted against him. President Mengistu responded to the coup attempt by killing many high-ranking generals and arresting several others. Already demoralized by the victory that the EPLF and TPLF had gained, President Mengistu's army was further weakened by his response to the coup attempt.

By April 1989, the EPLF had killed several Ethiopian solders in Eritrea and captured many tanks and munitions, with which it soon gained victory over the Ethiopian government. On the other side, the TPLF had grown stronger by bringing together antigovernment groups from different ethnicities, such as the Oromo Peoples' Democratic Organization (OPDO), the Ethiopian People's Democratic Movement (EPDM), and the Ethiopian Democratic Officers Revolutionary Movement (EDORM). Together these formed a coalition called the Ethiopian People Revolutionary Democratic Front (EPRDF). In March 1990, the EPRDF gained control of the Tigray region and large parts of Gondar, Wollo, and Shoa, while the EPLF controlled Eritrea, with the exception of Asmara,

Massawa, and Assab. Nonetheless, Derg cadres continued disseminating propaganda that Ethiopia would win the fight.

When I was in Gutenberg in February 1991, my host family said that Eritrea would control Port Asab soon, but I did not believe them because of the false propaganda that Ethiopians had been immersed in. The same week, I attended a Christian fellowship of Ethiopian immigrants (including Eritrean-born immigrants) and saw with my own eyes a video that showed how hard the TPLF-led guerillas were fighting and progressing towards victory. In the film, the former Prime Minister, Tamrat Layne, was weeping for his comrades who had lost their lives on Guna Mountain in Gondar. Eritrean immigrants in Sweden were receiving videotapes every week on the progress of the EPLF and TPLF. That made me realize the extent to which Ethiopians had been blinded by the Derg's false propaganda while the rest of the world knew the truth.

By May 1991, the TPLF-led coalition, EPRDF, controlled most of the northern parts of the country and was victoriously progressing towards Addis Ababa. Although he had boasted that he would fight until the last bullet, President Mengistu Haile Mariam was compelled by the circumstances to flee Ethiopia. On May 21, he fled to Zimbabwe, together with his family, and still resides there.

I was always curious concerning the direction Ethiopia's leadership would go, so I regularly listened to the BBC news. I once heard a BBC interview with a representative of EPRDF in which he was asked which ideology the group followed. The man replied that they followed Albanian Communism. Hearing that interview bothered me, since I could not see the difference between Albanian Communism and that of Russia.

In these next few pages, I will share with you my experiences and involvements from the time the EPRDF controlled Addis Ababa on July 28, 1991. During the week that Ethiopia was left with no government, there was no alternative for the Ethiopian people but to wait for whatever was coming.

Glory to God! All Addis Ababa dwellers, both Christians and Muslims, came together for a day of prayer and fasting, and the Lord answered. The first miracle dealt with the deposed Ethiopian government. Just after President Mengistu Haile Mariam fled the country, the army peacefully flocked into Addis Ababa, carrying their arms. They turned neither to the left nor to the right until they reached Jalmeda in Sidist Kilo, where they piled up their arms.

I believe the peaceful disarming was the result of the cease-fire negotiation that persuaded President Mengistu to flee the country. Those armies traveled on foot for many days to arrive in Addis Ababa. After fighting the unwinnable war against their own brothers, they were definitely hungry and thirsty. But they never looted nor committed any misdemeanor. While I strongly believe in God's protection and that He answered the nation's prayer in that regard, I also applaud the Ethiopian military for their commitment to their long-standing values and ethics.

After President Mengistu Haile Mariam fled the country, there was great fear, both nationally and internationally, that there would be a bloody transition of power. The airport was closed for five days, and sixteen thousand Ethiopian Jews were airlifted to Israel. Meanwhile, Ethiopians were left in fear and uncertainty about their future. Under such tension, the Ethiopian people waited with mixed feelings concerning the outcome of the London peace talks scheduled for May 27, 1991. Mr. Herman Cohen, US assistant secretary of state for African affairs, convened the peace talks in London between the rebels and the Ethiopian government, which was represented by Prime Minister Tesfaye Dinka. During the peace talks, a cease-fire agreement was reached by all parties, but Mr. Cohen nonetheless allowed the rebels to enter Addis Ababa. My fear of Albanian Communism left me after I sensed that the United States would have a stake in the new government.

On the evening of May 27, prisons in Addis Ababa were left unguarded, allowing all prisoners to be freed and rejoin their families. During that incident, I remembered a prayer I had prayed during our family prayer time just two months earlier. I had prayed that all prisoners would be released, but I did not even pay attention to why I prayed that. To tell you the truth, the prayer was not from me. I could not imagine that it would be just for criminals, especially murderers, to walk free.

On the evening of May 28, the EPRDF guerilla forces, which were composed of the TPLF-led coalition of antigovernment forces, finally assumed control of Addis Ababa. After seventeen years of struggle as a guerilla leader, the late prime minister of Ethiopia, Meles Zenawi and his group finally achieved their goal. Shootings could be heard that evening, but they were few. Since the Ethiopian military had already laid down its arms, the EPRDF fighters entered the city with little resistance.

The next day, I met a group of armed young men, who I believe had been assigned by the EPRDF to guard Bole International Airport. I started the conversation by telling them to thank God for helping them to gain such an amazing victory. As they only spoke Tigrigna, the language of Tigrian and Eritrean nationals, however, communication was difficult. They replied in their broken Amharic that it was their struggle that had given them victory. I went on to explain that if victory were dependent on might and strength, the Derg's army was stronger and mightier.

The EPRDF, under the leadership of Mr. Meles Zenawi, held its first multiparty national conference from July 1 to 5, 1991, in which the Transitional Government of Ethiopia (TGE) was established and a Council of Representatives was elected. Twenty-one local political groups, representatives from fifteen countries, and numerous international organizations were all in attendance. The newly established

TGE adopted a transitional charter that would last until election day in 1994. The eighty-seven-member Council of Representatives confirmed Mr. Meles Zenawi as TGE's transitional president.

The council was given the authority to establish a commission to draft a constitution. Ethiopia was restructured into nine ethnic-based federated states, and the new constitution was ratified by the constitutional assembly. The TGE appointed an independent judiciary as well as made political and economic reforms that attracted Western countries and donors. Through certain legal provisions, President Meles officially terminated press censorship.

In spite of the challenges, remarkable changes were made by the TGE while preparing for the 1994 election. For example, the Derg's command-market economy was replaced by a free-market economy through the TGE's new policies. Once freed, the market works for itself, and that happened with the new free-market economic policy.

The TGE administration saw no need to reinvent the wheel, but sustained itself on the structures left behind by the fallen President Mengistu government. The Kebeles continued their services just as before, including the collection of rents and local taxes as well as the registration of births, deaths, and marriages. The Kebeles in Addis Ababa collected rent from homes renting for 199 birr or less per month.

After armed conflict erupted between the EPRDF and Oromo members of the new Council of Representatives, an encampment accord was signed between the EPRDF and the OLF. A National Electoral Commission (NEC) composed of ten multiethnic members selected from the Council of Representatives was founded. Local administrations with multiethnic political representation were also established. Because of the ethnic conflicts that intensified while preparing for the 1993 election, many members of the Council of Representatives, including the OLF, the Islamic

Front for the Liberation of Oromia (IFLO), the All-Amhara People's Organization (AAPO), the Ethiopian Democratic Action Group (EDAG), and the Gideo People's Democratic Organization (GPDO), withdrew from the election.

At last, the OLF decamped, igniting a civil war that was controlled quickly, and finally withdrew from the TGE's eighty-seven-member Council of Representatives. In 1993, the TGE made appointments to the country's first independent judiciary. On April 27, 1993, Eritrea declared independence from Ethiopia following a referendum supported by the cooperative relationship between the two new transitional governments (Ethiopian and Eritrean). In August 1995, President Meles Zenawi was elected prime minister of the new Federal Democratic Republic of Ethiopia (FDRE).

Now, let me return to my WSRA story. The TGE's newly established Kebele administration discovered my successful women's NGO operating in their conference hall. New Kebele leaders had been elected, but the secretarial staff had not changed. The men who were initially elected as chair and vice chair of the new kebele both declined the positions. Eventually a Tigre young man, whose chairmanship would later prove disastrous to me and to my group, assumed the leadership position. He was from a lower social class and was less-educated, but the fact that he was a Tigre was enough for him to take advantage of the new TPLF-led government.

My journey with the WSRA also brought to my attention a story of a terrible crime involving relief aid that was even worse than what I had experienced with the ICC. In 1993, I gave a ride to a UNICEF expert who was conducting a site visit with my women's NGO. The expert had to inspect a new day care for licensing and requested that I take her there prior to going to my NGO for the site visit. When we arrived at the day-care site, we met the owner, and she was dressed in black. She looked so depressed that we asked her what had happened. She replied that she was still grieving the loss of her husband, a businessman who had been murdered in October 1992. She shared with us the horrifying story of her husband's murder, and this is what she told us:

One day the woman's husband received a call from an RRC official to collect some sugar he had purchased and to bring the cash payment for it. Her husband went to the main commercial bank, withdrew the money from his business account, and gave it to the RRC official as usual. Before picking up the sugar, however, he was invited to a dinner that afternoon at 5:00 p.m. Attired in his white Ethiopian national dress, he left his home for the dinner, never to return. The search for the woman's missing husband continued for two days, and his corpse was finally discovered in a forest near Kidane-Mihiret Church at Entoto in Addis Ababa. To add to the woman's misery, her mother died of a heart attack soon after her son-in-law died. Her father-in-law died few weeks later.

I was shocked by what I heard. I don't know how long the sugar business with the RRC had been going on. The house they lived in was one of the big nationalized homes; it was evident that it had been obtained at a cheaper rent through favoritism from government officials. At least the wife benefited from the big government-owned house through the kindergarten she started in it.

After a thorough investigation, the RRC official and those involved in the corruption were arrested, but one of the RRC officials and the person who murdered her husband disappeared soon after they were bailed out of jail. The woman decided to forgive and move on and still does not know what happened to those criminals. Presently she is a very successful businesswoman in Addis Ababa who owns a kindergarten, schools and a new hospital building.

In the pages to follow, I will brief you on my assignment from God to participate in political affairs. I am doing so because some Christians who saw me on TV gossiped that I was involved in politics, which, according to their beliefs, I was not supposed to do as a Christian. Here's how it happened.

My study tour in Niger was instrumental in establishing the Ministry of Women's Affairs in Ethiopia. As I mentioned earlier, I was sponsored by UNFPA and visited the Ministry of Women's Affairs and Social Promotion in Niger in December 1990. Using my Niger experience, I lobbied the Transitional Government of Ethiopia (TGE) to establish the Ministry of Women's Affairs. On September 12, 1991, just a little over three months after the EPRDF took power, I submitted to Prime Minister Tamirat Layne my petition, along with my study-tour report, recommending the establishment of the Ministry of Women's Affairs in Ethiopia, following Niger's model.[23]

In January 1992, I was officially notified that an office for women's affairs had been established within the Prime Minister's office in the way I had proposed in my letter to the Prime Minister. I was then invited to meet with the new Women's Affairs head (later, minister of Women's Affairs), Mrs. Tadelech Hailemikael. We met for three hours, and she listened to my long testimony of how God had given me the vision and led me through it all. She then told me that my document had reached them at a time when they didn't know what to do with the Revolutionary Ethiopian Women's Association (REWA). Mrs. Tadelech Hailemikael continued the conversation by telling me that my testimony made her realize how her own mother's faith and advice had sustained her during those terrible years. She went on to tell me her full story.

Mrs. Tadelech Hailemikael's husband was the founder and leader of the Ethiopian People's Revolutionary Party (EPRP), having started the organization while he was a student in Paris.

---

[23] Please see appendix 4 for letter to the prime minister petitioning MOWA's establishment

He was killed in the Red Terror campaign, and MrsTadelech Hailemikael was jailed. When taken to prison, she did not know that she was pregnant. She completed her pregnancy in prison and gave birth to her baby girl there. While her pregnancy saved her from being tortured and executed, the brutality of the Derg still required the innocent baby to remain in prison with her mother. I could not contain myself while listening to her story and was soon in tears.

Mrs. Tadelech Hailemikael was released after four years in prison. Soon after her release, however, she was taken from her home again and put back into jail, with her captors informing her that she had been released by mistake. When she was jailed the second time, her mother advised her to acknowledge God's protection and guard her heart. Mrs. Tadelech remembered that those who had been released from jail with her and not taken back to jail had been killed. After spending another eight years in prison, Mrs. Tadelech was freed when all the prisoners escaped on May 28, 1991, the night the EPRDF fighters entered Addis Ababa.

Although she had been separated from society and was behind bars for twelve years and eight months, Mrs. Tadelech did a very good job in establishing the Ministry of Women's Affairs. Under her leadership, women's groups from various governmental and nongovernmental organizations, private businesses, and different sectors of society in Ethiopia came together to form a forum to draft the National Policy on Ethiopian Women. Through her, I was privileged to be one of the fifteen women who designed the policy in 1992. The policy was adopted and published in 1993. Following that, Mrs. Tadelech secured three seats for women on the constitutional commission that was formed in 1993 as well as coordinated women's participation in the drafting of the country's federal constitution, which was adopted in 1994, thereby ensuring protection for women's and children's rights. Finally, the Women's Affairs Office within the prime minister's office eventually became a separate Ministry of Women's Affairs of Ethiopia, with Mrs. Tadelech as its minister.

My participation in the drafting of the federal constitution was outside that of the Women's Affairs Office. When the TGE was having the draft amended by the general public, I had the opportunity to make a contribution that I feel good about to this day. The TGE held a one-day workshop for religious leaders and NGO leaders on the draft constitution's separation-of-church-and-state section. When the presenter opened the floor for questions and comments, I suggested that the statement "no religion is superior over any other religion" be included in the constitution. As I did so, providing evidence of brutal actions against evangelical Christians by the Orthodox Church, the presenter stated that I was accurate in my statement.

The other area of my contribution was in the Relief and Rehabilitation Commission. In May 1993, I participated in a study sponsored by the United Nations Development Program (UNDP) called the Development Program for Displaced Persons, Refugees, and Returnees in Central America (PRODERE). Two government representatives and one NGO representative were selected from seven African countries and sponsored by UNDP to participate in the one-month study tour of the region. After returning from the study tour, I forwarded recommendations to the TGE to adopt PRODRE's approach to the national context of Ethiopia and work in partnership with NGOs towards addressing the needs of the country's displaced population.

Since the WSRA was starting from a scratch, our needs were immense as we embarked on full-fledged production activities, but God supplied those needs. Through divine guidance, I traveled to London on my own expense and secured eleven table-model sewing machines from Tools for Self-Reliance. After conducting a site visit, the self-help fund of the United States Embassy in Addis Ababa also found our project "excellent" and funded the purchase of two industrial sewing machines and some hand tools.[24]

The US Embassy's support was so timely and meant a lot because the two industrial sewing machines and the two flour mills that UNICEF had purchased for the WSRA vanished at Port Asab in Eritrea when the EPLF controlled the port in 1991. The embassy's support came while we were waiting for UNICEF's reorder to arrive. The Dutch Embassy also gave us a generous grant. In fact, the Dutch Embassy funded WSRA twice.

UNICEF's donation also arrived. The Addis Ababa Region 14 Administration Economic Development Sector gave WSRA land at a prime location—just a mile from Bole International Airport—for the construction of a comprehensive center including a workshop, a supermarket, and a day-care facility. A separate parcel from the Kebele's holding was also allocated to WSRA for the planned Maternal and Child Health (MCH) clinic. We secured pre-project funds from UNFA toward the MCH clinic, but we didn't get it because the government did not allow direct funding from the UN to NGOs. The Swedish Save the Children (Radda Barnen) also gave WSRA a generous grant to start the first phase of construction. With this kind of success, the kebele offered to rent WSRA three rooms in their office building for 350 birr per month, but there was a hidden agenda behind it.

Success followed success, and the organization gained recognition as a best practice model. The WSRA was given the opportunity to participate in the International Trade Fair Expo that was held in October 1993. A 15,000-birr fee for the booth was waived. The WSRA made even more sales at other international trade fairs and at international events like UN conferences. Five UN agencies in Addis Ababa—UNDP, UNESCO, UNFPA, UNHCR, and UNICEF studied NGOs

---

[24] Please see appendix 3 for visitors' comment

in Addis Ababa and found WSRA one of the eleven best indigenous NGOs in Ethiopia.

The UN report was submitted to the Relief and Rehabilitation Commission (RRC) NGOs' desk, a government authority that oversaw NGOs and had been recommending the WSRA to international donors. The UN evaluation opened the door for the WSRA to access international donors. For example, Plan International conducted a site visit with the WSRA and provided the funding to turn the temporary shelters into permanent homes and to construct roads in the neighborhood. However, the RRC leadership directed them to the northern part of the country, asserting that there were more NGOs Addis Ababa than in the North.

Fueled by the wonderful success we had achieved thus far, I thought we would face no opposition down the road, but only approval. However, that was not the reality. As I mentioned earlier, soon after assuming power, some leaders started strategizing how to use their power to serve their personal interests. The new Kebele 20 chairman, and a Woreda[25] 17 official, took advantage of the TPLF-led TGE's new government and destroyed WSRA while it was still in its early stages.

I was very naive about the new kebele administration's hidden agenda when I moved into their office space. I did not even realize the illegality of the fee that the WSRA had agreed to pay in rent. It was illegal for any Kebele in Addis Ababa to charge over 199 birr per month in rent, but the WSRA signed a lease agreement with the Kebele 20 administration for 350 birr per month.

On the other hand, I did hear two complaints that made me skeptical of the Kebele administration, one from a businesswoman in my neighborhood and one from Kebele 20

---

[25] *"Wereda"* Amharic term also spelled *"Woreda*) is a third-level administrative divisions (the smallest unit of local government) of Ethiopia composed of a number of Kebles (wards) or neighborhood associations

security guard. The businesswoman had formerly brought commodities from Dubai and delivered it to shops in Markato on wholesale. She and few other retailers eventually had to return their licenses because the stores would not buy from them any longer. New retailers were clearing their commodities through Ethiopian customs duty-free in the name of "transit to Eritrea" and thus were supplying the stores at cheaper rates. The security guard's complaint was the kebele chairman's corruption in relation to the food-aid he had shipped to Tigrai at night.

The unforeseen second problem was associated with an aid supply of used clothing that was solicited from the Netherlands in 1993 and cleared from Ethiopian customs. After the container arrived, customs officials told us that a new policy required a tax to be levied on used clothing and asked us to pay forty thousand birr. We submitted our plea, seeking exemption as a young and poor NGO and stating that the policy had been put in force after the donation arrived. Additionally, we had not even known about the tax. However, our request was denied.

Forty thousand birr was a lot of money for the WSRA to pay, so I held a meeting with the women to get their input. After going through the list of donated items, they determined it would be worth borrowing money to pay the tax in order to get the shipment. Based on their decision, we borrowed the money, paid customs, and had the donated items cleared.

The third and the worst problem arose from my own foolishness. In August 1993, Kebele 20 held a community meeting chaired by the above mentioned leading officer from Woreda 17. The purpose of the meeting was to evaluate the Wereda 17 leaders. Unaware that it would work against me and my group, I commented on areas where she (the leading officer) could improve. In retaliation, they immediately began attacking me and the WSRA. What foolishness it was for me to even go to an evaluation meeting that only pretended good governance!

Their attack plan became public at a Kebele community gathering held on Sunday, October 10, 1993, to discuss the government's land-lease policy. During that gathering, the Wereda 17 officer announced that the Kebele would take over the WSRA because it had been found corrupt by an investigative committee. Participants of the community gathering asked for a court verdict, with which the Kebele was authorized to take such action. But that didn't matter to the Wereda 17 official. Since she was a TPLF member, she had no need for real evidence because her fabricated evidence would be trusted.

The next day, three men who claimed they had been assigned by Kebele 20 leadership to investigate WSRA came to our workshop and asked me to hand over WSRA's belongings. One of the three men, Melese Hagos, was a criminal who had escaped from prison when the EPRDF army entered Addis Ababa on May 28, 1991. I replied that they had no legal authorization to interfere because WSRA was their tenant, and any concern they had should go through the Ministry of Labor and Social Affairs (MOLSA), a government authority with whom WSRA had signed a ten-year operational agreement. We immediately reported the issue to MOLSA. In response, MOLSA established an inquiry committee from four different government organizations to investigate the issue and notified the Kebele about it.

Although they were supposed to wait for the results of the inquiry committee, the Kebele leadership continued to perpetrate many unlawful acts against our group. For example, Melese Hagos was given a room facing our workshop so that he could work against our group full-time. The Kebele locked the door to our workshop, and the women were ordered to use the front door of the building instead. There the women were checked by Kebele security guards upon entry and exit. I was also summoned by a letter signed by the Kebele 20 chairman to appear at the Kebele's office. Additionally, they shut down our milling and food-processing workshop, which was housed on the premises of the Kebele adjacent to the plot of land allocated for the WSRA. A technician whom we brought into our workshop to fix some of our sewing machines was prohibited from removing a machine that needed to be fixed in his own workshop. At that point, the Kebele notified us that we were prohibited from removing any property of the WSRA from Kebele premises.

When surveyors deployed by Region 14 Administration (the city council) arrived at the site to erect boundary demarcation stones on the plot of land given to the WSRA, the Kebele sent armed guards to scare them away. Following that incident, our construction workers were stopped by the Kebele's armed guards while doing the foundation work.

The Wereda 17 official rejected our construction permit in front of the team she formed against us. On October 22, 1993, we submitted a letter to the Region 14 Administration Office, the permit-issuing division, notifying them of the issue and asking for their intervention.[26] An official from the sector (Oromo by ethnicity) scheduled a meeting at Woreda 17, (The Wereda officer's workplace) with the Wereda 17 officer. WSRA women's group representatives, WSRA board members, and I were also in attendance. Although the Region 14 Administration official represented a higher authority that oversaw all Weredas in Addis Ababa, and was supposed to have us meet in his office, he brought a large file from the city council's archives to prove to the Woreda 17 official the authenticity of our permits. He also showed her our original certificate of title, site inspection report, our extensive correspondence with their sector, and documentation proving our legitimacy for the land permit. (That plot

---

[26] Please see Appendix 5 for letter to Region 14 Administration Office

of land holds registration under an NGO to date). He did all this to convince the Wereda 17 official to agree to a decision to resume the construction work immediately. However, she (The Wereda 17 official) told us to wait until she spoke with certain concerned persons, and that left us stuck for an indefinite period of time.

The next month, two of our women were attempting to take out their products for display at the International Trade Fair Expo, but were prevented by the Kebele's armed guards from doing so. At that point, we submitted our petition to Bole Wereda police and managed to have our products released for participation in the International Trade Fair Expo. The illegal perpetration from the Kebele went on and on.

In submitting our complaints, we followed the proper chain of command. We submitted them first to Wereda 17 administration, although we were aware that the Wereda 17 official had more power there. When we did not receive a response, we submitted our petition to the president (mayor) of Region 14 administration (Addis Ababa), listing the Kebele's illegal acts and requesting his administration's intervention, but again we received no response.[27] Later we heard that the Woreda 17 official was angry when we submitted our petition to Region 14's president and that our letter never reached him.

Finally, the WSRA's board decided to file our dispute with the Zone 3 Economic Development Sector, who determined that the Wereda's and the Kebele's misuse of power should be brought to justice. Eventually, the zone official referred us to the prosecutor's office in region 14, instructing us to file a criminal lawsuit against the perpetrators. Upon reviewing our case, the prosecutor's office ordered the Bole Wereda police station to examine our case.

We submitted seven witnesses from Kebele 20, who were heard by the police on our case. When summoned by

---

[27] Please see appendix 6 for WSRA's complaint to the mayor

the police detective, the Wereda 17 official resisted being investigated, asserting that she was a TPLF member and had the right not to be sued. But the police chief convinced her that they were instructed only to notify authorities before arresting a TPLF member, so she also would be investigated. After the investigation was completed, I was summoned to the police station, where they had me hear the witnesses' words and view the police report before submitting it to the prosecuting attorney's office.

The Kebele 20 chairman, and Melese Hagos, the criminal who was appointed by Kebele 20 to work against the WSRA full-time, were summoned by the chief of the prosecuting office to appear before him on December 21, 1993. I was also summoned to appear, representing WSRA, and was present. After hearing their views, the chief explained that he could order their immediate arrest, based on the crime they had committed against the WSRA and against me, but he would give them one chance to correct their mistakes, since they represented the community. In speaking about me, he said to them, "You made her bow her head in humiliation among the community she serves." He concluded by ordering them to immediately dissolve the investigating committee they had illegally formed and to await the outcome of the legal evaluating committee formed by MOLSA.

Instead of fulfilling the prosecuting office's order, the two men, with the backing of the Wereda 17 officer, intensified their conspiracy against us. The next day, they gathered the WSRA women in my absence, gave them false reports that I stole their aid money, and agitated them to file a lawsuit against me, promising the Kebele's backing. They threatened to arrest those women who refused to do so, further dividing the women and causing the group that accepted the Kebele's plot to stigmatize those who were against it. They forced the women to sign a petition to cooperate with the very inquiry committee that the prosecuting office had ordered them to dissolve. With the fresh memory of the Kebele's brutality during the Derg regime, most of the women signed the petition. Two of the women who refused to sign the petition were arrested.

We submitted our final letter to the prosecuting office on January 27, 1994, documenting how the prosecuting office's deliberations of December 21, 1993, had made things worse for us.[28] I don't know if it was merely coincidence or that his fairness in handling our case worked against him, but after a month, the chief we had been working with was no longer there. We had been going to the prosecuting office twice a week to check on the status of our case. Finally, after two months, the new chief showed us legal provision against crimes involving the abuse of power and informed us that he was transferring our case to the Supreme Court because of the level of the crime. At that point, our last option was to wait for the outcome of MOLSA's inquiry committee while the court was processing our case.

In spite of all the difficulties with their imposed uncertainties, we did not relinquish our faith in the justice system. We were not asking for any kind of favor, but rather for truth and justice to prevail. After several months of hard work, the inquiry committee formed by MOLSA issued its final report. The six-page report not only documented the facts, but also criticized the kebele for their demoralizing and damaging conspiracy against us.

As we waited for the court's decision, we continued with our initial plan of empowering the women. We secured funding from the Canadian International Development Agency (CIDA) and deposited money in the WSRA women's cooperative bank account to cover their operating costs for a year. We handed over to the women's group the machines,

---

[28] Please see appendix 7 for final letter to the prosecuting attorney dated January 27, 1994

the hand tools, and the flour mills, as well as transferred to them the workshop that we leased from the kebele. We did this to ensure that the women would function independently in cooperatives.

Just a few months after the majority of the women petitioned against me, the women held a meeting and asked me for forgiveness. I realized from their action that they were suffering from guilt. Holding grudges was against my values, so I never held anything against any of those poor women whom I was called to serve. One of the group leaders said something that was particularly moving: "We treated you like a piece of meat thrown to hyenas." Despite the apology, the group maintained their relationship with the kebele administration. I left Ethiopia in August 1994 with the WSRA issue still pending.

My hope in relating all this to you is that seeing a different continent's realities will encourage you not to take your opportunity for granted and thereby inspire you to do your part in making the world a better place. In the following pages, I will give a brief summary of my personal experience in the United States.

12

Experiencing Differences in Making a Difference

As I mentioned earlier, my children and I arrived in Minnesota in August 1994. We made that big move only because it was the will of God for us. (The full story will be covered in my future writings.) Since I enjoyed a decent life in Ethiopia and my children attended one of the best private schools in Addis Ababa, I had never wished to live outside the country.

When I received a call to serve God, I was confused about how to serve Him as a professional so, I applied for enrollment in the Moody Bible Institute (MBI). However, as a condition for my admission, the institute required that my husband join the family. That was not God's will, however, and it didn't work out that way.

Four years had passed since I first heard back from MBI when I came to the United States in the summer of 1993 on my way home from a study tour in Central America. During my short stay in the States, I went by the admissions office at Moody Bible Institute to find out why my process had been delayed for such a long time. They informed me that they had never received an application for my husband and gave me new applications for both of us to fill out for the 1994 fall semester. While MBI was processing our applications, my family received an invitation to go to Minneapolis. My children and I accepted the invitation and arrived in Minneapolis on August 24, 1994, but my husband stayed behind because he did not want to go.

In front of Moody Bible institute
(Agitu in the middle, Moody's students on the left)

Upon our arrival at the airport, my new friend, Kathleen Moore, whom we had hosted at our home in Addis Ababa the previous year, met us. A crowd of people was with her, all awaiting our arrival. Kathleen had moved to a friend's house so my children and I could stay at her house and have enough room. She also took a one-week leave to help us during our first week in the country. Overwhelmed by her kindness, I remarked that I felt better when I gave than when I received and that I didn't feel comfortable that she was going the extra mile to do so much for us. Kathleen replied, "It is time for you to learn to receive, because others, too, feel equally good when they give." That helped me realize how God had it all planned according to His way.

I summoned my courage and applied for admission to Metropolitan State University in St. Paul, Minnesota. Since I already had my TOEFL test score, I was able to meet the application deadline for the spring semester. This was another confirmation to me that I was in God's will.

I hated to burden Kathleen, so in the month of October, my children and I moved to Riverside Plaza Apartments. I had learned that many immigrants from different parts of the world lived there, and the Brian Coyle Community Center, right across the street from the apartments, served those immigrants.

Back in Ethiopia, the Women's Self-Reliance Association (WSRA) was still in jeopardy. Prior to my trip to the States, I had applied for a United Nations grant to fund the salaries of the executive director and an administrative assistant. I traveled to Nairobi in November 1994 to check the status of the grant application and then relayed the good news to the WSRA board of directors that our application had been approved and we had secured salaries for an executive director and an administrative assistant. I had never been paid by the WSRA, so it was a big thing to secure such a generous grant. Additionally, the grant included good benefits, such as full medical insurance, for the incoming executive director and her family through the UN/ECA clinic. I left the responsibility of WSRA in the hands of its seven-member board of directors, who held prestigious employment positions (two of them in the UN), and returned to Minneapolis. Soon after my return, I received an acceptance letter from the admissions office at Metropolitan State University.

Shortly after moving to Riverside Plaza, I began to familiarize myself with my new neighborhood. In the process, an incident occurred that confirmed God had indeed placed me there for a purpose. One day a man called me on the phone and told me about a woman in Riverside Plaza who was suffering domestic abuse. He gave me her name and apartment number so I could help her. Amazingly, I had known this woman and her husband prior to moving to the United States. What a small world! I went to her apartment that evening and knocked on the door, but she wouldn't open it; her husband had threatened her against doing so, and she was afraid. I knocked several more times, but she still would not open the door. Then I called her name, announcing my own name loudly, and she finally opened the door for me. I went in, and she told me her terrible story.

After listening to the sad story, I immediately returned to my apartment to figure out how to help her. I was new to the country myself and did not know anything, but I looked up some resources in the yellow pages and placed a call to First Call for Help that evening. They gave me a few referrals, and I decided to call the International Institute of Minnesota first thing in the morning. Thank God for that decision! I called the exact right place.

The International Institute of Minnesota immediately placed the victim with the Lutheran Social Service Housing Services and began processing her green card under the Violence Against Women Act (VAWA), which had been enacted in 1994. As one of the first beneficiaries of VAWA, the woman received her green card in a very short time. For those of you who do not know what VAWA is all about, it is a federal provision that frees immigrant women who are victims of violence from needing an immigration petition from their US citizen spouse. Thanks to VAWA, such a victim can get her green card without her husband's petition, provided that they are legally married. God bless America abundantly!

When I realized that I had ended up in that neighborhood to serve God's purpose and that I had much to contribute, I met with Mr. Mike Wayne at the Brian Coyle Community Center and explained my vision to him. After listening to my story, Mr. Wayne instructed me on how to set up a nonprofit to serve immigrants and referred me to the Dorsey & Whitney law firm for their help in having it incorporated on a pro bono basis. Following Mr. Wayne's instruction, I scheduled an appointment with Mr. John Somers, attorney-at-law at Dorsey & Whitney, and met with him in his office for over two hours. During our meeting, I explained to him my experience with the WSRA in Ethiopia and requested his help in establishing a similar nonprofit organization for refugee/immigrant women and their families. I gave him copies of the WSRA's bylaws and relevant documents.

Mr. Somers had me sign a representation form right away and promised to have the new nonprofit incorporated as well as to serve as its registered agent. We agreed on the assumed name of the new nonprofit: International Self-Reliance Agency Women, Inc. (ISAW). I left his office indebted by the confidence he was placing in me, a stranger. Above all, I was grateful that God was blessing me with wonderful Americans who put the needs of others first and demonstrated good citizenship in action. I then went to my school and signed an agreement to use the nonprofit organization for my internship work at the university.

My children and I lived in Riverside Plaza Apartments for only five months. Then we moved to a duplex in south Minneapolis, about five miles from the Brian Coyle Community Center. I began my internship work with the center by forming a core group of ten refugee women that would meet once a week, and I also did a needs-assessment survey. Mr. Wayne helped in writing a grant proposal, and with it we secured our first grant from the Minneapolis Foundation. By then, Mr. Somers had the nonprofit incorporated.

During our first six months of operation, Straitgate Church provided us with office space in their church basement. In a few months, we secured additional grants from the McKnight Foundation and the Catholic Charities Christian Sharing

Fund. Both donors funded ISAW for three consecutive years. As soon as we received the first grants, we leased a small office in the Cedar Riverside People's Center, located on the corner of Riverside and Twentieth Avenues.

Soon after we moved into our office, a generous state-grant opportunity knocked at our door. A few days earlier, I had enjoyed the privilege of being one of three speakers at International Women's Day, an event organized by the Minnesota Advocates for Human Rights. On Monday, the next working day, a grant-application package from the Minnesota Center for Crime Victim Services (MCCVS) was delivered to our office. It just so happened that one of the participants at the Women's Day event was a woman from the MCCVS, and she sent us the packet with a note enclosed in the application, stating, "I was moved by your speech." In turn, I myself was moved by the compassion demonstrated by the Americans who had crossed my path thus far.

When we received the packet, there were only two weeks remaining to meet the application deadline, but we made it with the help of God. Fellow Americans, you may think that those entrusted with your tax money are careless or extravagant; I assure you, they are not. I am saying this from what I have experienced in over a decade here in this country and while in Ethiopia prior to moving to the States. The first grant review was conducted in a closed session in the presence of all competitors and was very strenuous. After we received the grant, managing the money was not easy, but the experience was very educational. The grant specialists were meticulous in conducting desk audits and reviewing quarterly financial status reports, midyear reports, and year-end progress reports. Since government grants are outcome oriented, they released the grant money on a quarterly basis, only after reviewing the previous quarter's report and tracking down where each penny went.

ISAW secured grants from different sources which enabled us to move to a spacious office near our previous location and start additional programs such as computer training and a resource bank. The resource bank provided our target population with linkage to resources that match their identified needs. Work-study students from the University of Minnesota whom I assigned for this task researched and compiled data of available resources (Hard copy and soft copy) with which we established the resource bank. Just two months after we moved to the new location, ISAW obtained Special Consultative Status with the Economic and Social Council of the United Nations in New York.[29]

ISAW Computer Training

---

[29] Please see Appendix 8 for WSRA's special consultative status with UN Economic and Social Counsel

Resource Bank

My academic internship at Metro State University and Brian Coyle Community Center turned out to be a great success, touching many lives and making a great difference. The stories of the women served by ISAW are too numerous and too long to be covered in this book. Without exaggeration, I can say that each woman's story could make a book by itself. But let me share just one such story with you.

One day in 1999, one of our participants came into our office and was silent for about five minutes. I paid no attention to her until she handed me a note she had written. When I read it, I was amazed at how well she expressed herself. Here is what the note said:

It was one of the toughest and most sorrowful times in my life. God used a friend who got me ISAW's telephone number. Guess who answered the phone? It was my angel (Agitu). She instantly came to my rescue. She would call me from time to time with words of courage. Agitu has helped me in so many ways, even

175

financially, just to put food on my table for me and my little girl. She just loves me. She loves people. She has helped me with my educational opportunity. I think of her as a mother because she treats me like a daughter. Sometimes I want to express my feelings about how much I appreciate all her effort and support, just to keep thanking her, but she would likely say, "It is God who helps me." She doesn't want to accept any credit for helping strangers (abused women) from different countries and cultures. Blessed is the day I spoke with Agitu. She has done wonderful things in my life, and my self-esteem is growing gradually. Thank God for our new Mother Teresa, Agitu Wodajo. Thank you, and may God bless you and your family. Amen.

Fola Afolabi

Many expressed their experience with ISAW as "life saving and life changing," and all this happened because of those wonderful Americans and their system of government that is built on a well-crafted and well-framed constitution—a system in which human values and human aspirations are highly valued and acknowledged . . . a system that made this country a land of opportunity . . . you add the rest.

Here I want to make clear that I am not trying to say that the American government is perfect, for I am well aware that Americans are also human beings. The wrong deeds that take place in the rest of the world happen in America as well. In fact, you will find more misuse and abuse of freedom where there is much freedom. Rather, I am trying to express, from personal experience, the importance of good governance and godly values in making good citizenship possible. This is a trademark of American culture.

The difference I experienced here in the United States from what I experienced in Ethiopia was remarkable. In the United States, I was recognized and encouraged for helping immigrant women and their families, while in Ethiopia I was persecuted by a few selfish individuals for serving the least of their own citizens. The first thing I learned from this was the importance of the rule of law, but just as important, I learned that America is all about people.

While I was still on a student visa at Metropolitan State University and working with my nonprofit organization through my internship, I wrote to First Lady Hilary Clinton, sharing my views about the necessity of having the Illegal Immigration Reform and Immigration Responsibility Act reviewed and revised before it was signed into law by President Clinton. I was encouraged to do so by the eighth item in a summary of comments on the Beijing Platform for Action, which stated, "Continue to speak on behalf of human rights of all people." I received a kind reply from the First Lady, informing me that my letter had been forwarded to the president's Interagency Council for Women.

Here comes the big difference: I received a response directly from the president of the United States. You may laugh at me when you read this, but without even looking at the signature and the White House stationery, I could tell by the wording that it was from the president. I never imagined I would get a letter from him, so I took it to my instructor and asked, "Who is this man with this kind of authority?" Pointing at his signature, she replied, "The president of the United States—good for you! Can't you read?" What a cultural difference! It was never like that back in Ethiopia. A person like me could never expect to even see the head of state passing by, let alone have access to him. (Note: I was not and am not a politician, nor do I belong to any political group.)

The story doesn't stop here. I forwarded the case to the late Senator Wellstone and returned my focus to my post-graduate course work. Senator Wellstone sent me three letters updating me on the progress before he even got one response back from me. In his fourth letter, he commented, "I haven't heard back from you. Did you get any response from the White House?"

One thing I want to stress here is the effect of isolation and fear on immigrants. President Clinton had a solution to that when he signed in to law the Illegal Immigration Reform and Immigration Responsibility Act (IIRIRA). All illegal immigrants were granted amnesty to adjust their immigration status under Section 245-I through employment or family petition. I did my best to spread the good news to the illegal immigrants in the Twin Cities metro area. I organized a workshop to educate them on that one-time wonderful opportunity, and I secured four volunteer immigration attorneys to provide detailed information on the law's provisions and one-on-consultation on the process.

Although we sent out invitations ahead of time and did our best to attract and motivate illegal immigrants, the turnout was not great. A number of Vietnamese immigrants took advantage of the opportunity and attended the workshop, but very few of the rest of the diverse immigrant population showed up. My women's nonprofit organization (ISAW) did petition on behalf of one woman, and I witnessed that the law indeed worked for the few who took advantage of it. However, many people lost a golden opportunity, while those who did not have a relative or an employer petitioner fell through the cracks.

Among the things that make America different is the approval and encouragement its citizens give to those interested in making a difference. For example, Metropolitan State University recognized my efforts and gave me several awards, including the Internship Award and the Outstanding Service to Women Award for the contributions I made through my internship work. As a community-centered educational institution, the university highly valued its students' contributions to their communities. My tour of China was also funded by a unanimous donor through the University of St. Thomas.

Next in line to credit me for my services to others were the Bush Foundation and Professor John Bryson of the Humphrey School of Public Affairs. After reviewing my credentials, Professor John Bryson interrupted his vacation, came to his office and issued me a letter of acceptance to their new Master's of Public Affairs program that was designed for mid-career professionals. By so doing, he made it possible for me to meet the deadline for the Bush Leadership grant. I feel I was given these approvals and awards because Americans considered my service to others as though I did it to them. In that way, they truly imitated Jesus:

And the King will answer and say to them, "Assuredly, I say to you, inasmuch as you did it to one of the least of these My brethren, you did it to Me."
—Matthew 25:40

13

Risking the Unknowns in Making a Difference

You may be wondering how the WSRA back in Ethiopia was doing. I did not abandon it or give up on it. Upon the recommendation of the former RRC NGO desk official who knew the WSRA very well and did not want it to fail, it was reregistered as an international NGO by the Ethiopian Ministry of Justice in 2001. We went through a lengthy process to have WSRA reregistered under the same name with the International Self-Reliance Agency for Women (ISAW) in Minneapolis. Since that time, I had been doing constant follow-up.

According to the updates I received, the Kebele had notified the women in 1998 that they were not current with their rent and banned them from entering the workshop. The milling and food processing workshop at the other location also remained closed. In the meantime, the Supreme Court summoned the Woreda 17 official; the Kebele 20 chairman; and Melese Hagos, their agent. The Kebele 20 chairman appeared on the court date, but the Woreda 17 official did not; and Melese Hagos was deceased. The judge set another court date, with a court order to have the Woreda official escorted by the police to the court proceeding. When the WSRA representative arrived for the hearing, the case was not on the list for the scheduled court date. The representative checked with the court and was told that they could not find the file.

When I returned to Ethiopia in 2005, I asked the court's records office for the WSRA case file. The woman in the court's records office boldly asked me to pay her to look for the file, stating that she would need extra time to do so, but I did not pay her. I guess she was just trying to take advantage of her ethnic background. When she said she could not locate the file, I went to the Ministry of Justice and notified an official about the situation. Soon after I returned to the States, I was informed that the Woreda 17 official and Kebele 20 chairman had again been summoned, but neither appeared.

When I was in Ethiopia in 2006, I was summoned by the director of the department in the Ministry of Justice that oversaw NGOs to meet with him concerning the WSRA. He pulled out two files he had in front of him. One file was for the Women's Self-Reliance Association (WSRA), and the other was for the International Self-Reliance Agency for Women (ISAW). He informed me that we could not have two organizations serving the same mission and instructed me to dissolve one of them.

I tried to refresh his memory of the long process we had gone through in 1999 to have the WSRA reregistered under ISAW's name, in which case the WSRA had been cancelled. Nonetheless, he ordered us to have both the old founding members of the WSRA and the ISAW board of directors to sign a petition and dissolve one of the two. In compliance with his request, I circulated the petition to the WSRA founding members as well as obtained ISAW board approval. With that, we had ISAW Ethiopia closed, and the WSRA continued its registration with the Ministry of Justice. Though WSRA's activity remained dormant, its registration was active. However, the worst was yet to come.

In 2007, I returned to Ethiopia with a new adoption agency that I believed would enable me to help the WSRA survive and thrive. With a strong belief that going back with the adoption agency was the best option, I registered Better Future Adoption Services, Inc. (BFAS) with the Ethiopian Ministry of Justice in June 2007. The government's requirement that all adoption agencies conduct development work in order to sustain their licenses appealed to me as the best way to help Ethiopia's vulnerable women and children. In 2008, I handed over the International Self-Reliance Agency, Inc. (ISAW) to its board of directors and took off for Ethiopia with my new adoption agency.

Even after I submitted my resignation, the ISAW board members pleaded with me to reconsider my decision, but I did not listen. I felt I had secured enough funding (the state funding that had been ongoing since 1996 and two other sources) to help my successor until she adjusted to her new role. Consequently, I did not feel bad about leaving. One thing I would like to mention, though, is what I realized later on: I had developed adult "spiritual attention deficiency syndrome," as I call it. From being stretched so thin between grant writing and the overall management of ISAW's programs, I was not seeking divine guidance. My ability to discern and build wisdom was slowly eroding, but I did not even realize it.

Although there were some difficulties, the first two years with BFAS went very well. Since BFAS was the most efficient and least expensive adoption agency, many prospective parents switched to us. Running an adoption program, however, proved to be the most difficult task I had ever performed. Nonetheless, the problems and the resulting trauma were the jolts I needed to take up the assignment the Lord had given me so long ago—writing this book.

The first problem began with a false accusation by an adoptive parent from Minnesota. She filed a complaint with the Minnesota Department of Human Services Licensing Division, alleging that the agency had withheld information concerning her adoptive child's HIV risk. In reality, the child had received a DNA/PCR HIV test before being referred to her adoptive family and before they accepted the referral. The US Embassy in Addis Ababa also did its own DNA/PCR HIV test before they issued her a visa. In response to the complaint, which we were unaware of at the time, two specialists from the Minnesota Department of Human Services Licensing Division walked into the BFAS office on the morning of June 24, 2009, and conducted a thorough investigation of the alleged case. The investigation was finalized on July 16, 2009, stating that no violation had occurred.[30] Although the allegation was found to be false, the adoptive parent was all over the Internet posting libelous and defamatory statements against the agency and me. She probably did so in fear of retaliation against the false accusation.

The second problem that BFAS faced was a bigger one. It began in April 2009 after I hired a certain government official as BFAS's country representative. The man accepted the new job on his ninety-day preretirement leave. I was impressed that he was retiring as the head of the prime minister's office for human resources and training, and his project proposal on a child-welfare NGO appealed to me, so I hired him. Beyond that, the tremendous help he provided in a most difficult adoption from Gambella made me trust him even more. However, my heart was uneasy when I handed over to him the responsibility for the agency and returned to the States.

In May 2009, just ten days after I returned to the States, I received the bad news from the representative that BFAS nannies and their driver had been detained at the Shashamane police station, located southeast of Addis Ababa, for investigation. Our seven children with pending court dates in Addis

---

[30] Please see appendix 9 for DHS's report

Ababa had been temporarily placed under the care of an orphanage in Shashamane.

I called an emergency board meeting, and we decided that I needed to go back to Ethiopia to handle the situation. The board also revoked the country representative's power of attorney and appointed Abebe Tigabu as deputy director of BFAS. Before hiring him, we investigated his background by checking his referrals, and interviewed him personally.

I left for Addis Ababa on August 7. My lastborn son withdrew from college and accompanied me on the trip at his own expense. We arrived in Addis Ababa on Friday, August 8, and received the good news that the court had set the nannies and driver free with a "not guilty" verdict. Additionally, an adoption hearing in federal court in Addis Ababa had been scheduled for August 11 for three of the seven children, and three more would be cleared the same week before court closed in August (Ethiopian courts are normally closed in August and September of each year). The seventh child's adoption hearing was scheduled for October.

The next day, I asked the outgoing country representative for a report on the entire situation. Upon reviewing the report, I noticed that the financial section didn't seem right. In addition, the receipts provided for most of the expenses were not acceptable, and there was no receipt at all for the big chunk of money supposedly paid to the orphanage in Shashamanne. I demanded official receipts and a financial report from the accountant, who disclosed that the BFAS driver, Techane Nigusu (also known as Baisa and Tefaye) owed 25,000 birr for "work advance." I was shocked to discover that the agency was not following the financial policy that had been developed by a professional at a high cost. The driver was issued a written notice to pay the money he owed and suspended until he did so. I was yet to learn that the new deputy director was also using the "work advance" system to obtain money he needed for personal use.

After a few days, the new deputy director produced a receipt from the orphanage, but it lacked the orphanage's seal and was not acceptable. By now, I highly doubted that the new deputy director was dependable. While all this was going on, the driver threatened to cause harm in retaliation that his salary was held and stole my car (BFAS did not own a car, so they were using my car at the time). I didn't even know that he had a key to my car. I reported the theft to the police, and two officers were dispatched to locate the driver and my car. One of the policemen called me that night and said they had found my car parked by the BFAS office.

In the meantime, the adoptions for six of the children were finalized, and we were all filled with joy. Two of those families brought their adoptive children home in September (just one month after I was back in Addis Ababa), and the other four families arrived in Addis Ababa in the last week of October to take their children home.

My son and I were scheduled to fly back to the United States on November 3, 2009. Around 10:00 a.m. that morning, three undercover policemen, who were led by a criminal (the BFAS driver whom I reported to the police for the car theft), arrived at the guest house to arrest me and take me to the police station. Before coming to the guesthouse to arrest me, they arrested the BFAS accountant.

My son was outside where he saw the policemen arrive at the guesthouse being led by the driver whom I reported to the police for car-theft earlier, and he confronted them. I was inside working on a project and did not know what was happening until one of the adoptive families who witnessed the assault from the 2nd floor knocked on my door and told me about it. Three men had assaulted my son, handcuffed him, and taken him away in a taxi. Immediately after hearing the shocking story, I began to cry.

I soon received a phone call from a police detective, summoning me to appear immediately at the Bole police station. I called a friend to accompany me, and he came right over and took me there. Upon my arrival at the station, I saw my son outside the building, screaming, and a policeman was trying to appease him. I felt at peace, seeing the policeman doing that, though I was still bitter about the unbelievable crime against humanity that had already been committed against my son. My son then told me that one of the policemen who arrested him had slapped his left ear hard after handcuffing him. Another policeman, he said, assaulted him after he was taken to the police station.

The detective took me inside and began interviewing me about my adoption work. He asked me where one of the seven children was, mentioning her by name. I replied that she had gone home with her adoptive parents in September. He asked, "Through Kiya Orphanage?" to which I replied no and then told him the whole story. As I spoke, he listened carefully and wrote down everything I said. I concluded my story by saying, "And that is why I am here," meaning Ethiopia.

I could tell he was saddened. Then he said, "That is why we have you here, too," and showed me the documents that the driver had fabricated. They claimed that I had trafficked the children and had them adopted with false documents through Kiya Orphanage.

The Ethiopian government's antiterrorist policy provided protection for anyone who reported a crime. The driver took advantage of the policy and used false document towards filing criminal charges against me and the accountant in order for him to get away with the 25,000 birr that he owed BFAS. The police arrested us without even questioning the validity of the report.

After completing his interview with me, the policeman interviewed the BFAS accountant. The criminal charge against her was that she had paid three mothers for putting up their children for illegal adoption through BFAS. The driver used three false witnesses against her in his criminal report. Finally, we were released at 6:30 p.m. and left the police station.

My son was waiting for me outside. He was in a great deal of pain from the slap to his left ear. I started crying because of the harm inflicted on him, but he tried to comfort me by telling me to thank God that nothing worse had happened. When we arrived at the guest house, we learned that the adoptive families had fled to the Gion Hotel. We packed hastily and left for our trip back to the United States.

Immediately after we returned home from Ethiopia, my son saw a doctor and was diagnosed with a perforated eardrum. The doctor initiated a treatment, giving us hope that his eardrum would heal. I e-mailed the Ethiopian embassy details of the crimes inflicted against us, requesting that justice prevail over injustice. I tried to see the police commissioner when I went back, but he never had the time. The driver, protected through Ethiopia's antiterrorist policy, was not held accountable for the crimes he committed, nor could we press charges against him.

While the trauma should have been more than enough to remind me of my second awakening call, I still did not pay attention. Instead of ending the adoption work and discerning God's will for me, I pressed forward in the hope that truth always wins and things would work out. On January 22, I returned to Ethiopia to try to straighten things out. Updating the US Embassy's adoption unit about the entire situation was at the top of my priority list. Upon my request, the embassy scheduled a meeting for February 9, 2010. I took Abebe Tigabu, the new deputy director, with me to the meeting.

The US Embassy consular section chief, the adoption unit chief and the adoption-unit staff were in attendance and took notes at our meeting. I provided a detailed report on the Shashamane incident and the police actions perpetrated against us because of false allegations. My intention was to alert the embassy to the unknowns surrounding Ethiopian adoptions. Although I was open and honest with the report I gave, I admired the embassy's leadership for not taking my report at face value. If all US embassies around the world were as cautious as they were, their safety and service quality would be guaranteed.

Just one week after our meeting, the BFAS was put under scrutiny by the US Embassy. During this time, our processing time for adoptions rose from two weeks to two months so that there could be a thorough investigation of every BFAS adoption. The notice we received from them on February 18 shows you how meticulous they were.[31]

Below is a brief summary of the Ethiopian adoption process, just to show you what the US Embassy examined before approving adoptive families' visa petitions:

According to Ethiopian law, a child had to come from an orphanage in order for that child to qualify for adoption. Here was the legal process for placing a child with an adoptive family:

---

[31] Please see appendix 10 for Us embassy's notice to BFAS

Abandoned Child

- An abandoned child *had* to be picked up by a police officer. The officer then took that child to the local Women, Children, and Youth Affairs bureau in order for them to fill out a child-study form and authorize the child's admittance to an orphanage.
- The police had to wait two months from the day the child was admitted to the orphanage before issuing a paper officially relinquishing the child to the orphanage. This was to allow adequate time to search for the child's birth parents. The orphanage was required to distribute flyers in search of the birth parents during these two months.

Child with Birth Parents

- In the absence of biological parents, immediate relatives of the child could act as birth parents. These could be a grandmother, grandfather, uncle, aunt, brother, sister, niece, or nephew.
- Birth parents applied to the Kebele/Wereda (local administration), requesting their letter of support to relinquish the child to an orphanage. The child did not meet orphan criteria if both parents were alive, unless they had a fatal health condition such as HIV/AIDS.
- Upon receiving the birth parents' petition, the Kebele scheduled an appointment for the birth parents to start the legal relinquishment process in the Kebele/Woreda court (local court).
- Birth parents brought three witnesses to the Kebele/Wereda court to attest to the death of the child's parents or a health condition incapacitating the child's biological parents, and to attest to the birth parents' inability to raise the child. A death certificate was required for deceased parents.

189

- Birth parents obtained a court decree that they submitted to their local Ministry of Women, Children, and Youth Affairs (MOWCYA) bureau for approval of the child's relinquishment to an orphanage.
- The local MOWCYA bureau, after receiving the Kebele/ Woreda court decree and relinquishment documents (birth parents' petition, witnesses' affidavits), filled out the child-study form and provided the birth parents with a letter of support addressed to the orphanage that the child was being relinquished to.
- Birth parents took the child to the orphanage, along with the kebele/woreda court decree and relinquishment documents, and the child-study form and letter of support from the MOWCYA bureau.
- Both in cases of abandonment as well as in cases of relinquishment, the orphanage assumed full custody of the child and could put the child up for adoption if it was licensed to do so.

The Adoption Process

- The orphanage referred the child to an adoption agency by providing the agency with the child's dossier, which included the initial birth parents' petition filed with the kebele/woreda, the kebele/woreda court decree, witnesses' affidavits, police paper (if abandoned), child-study form, letter of support from the MOWCYA bureau addressed to the orphanage, and MOWCYA's recommendation to put the child up for adoption.
- The adoption agency provided the adoptive family with child-referral information. The BFAS referral included the child's photograph, medical report, HIV test result (DNA/PCR), child-study form, and child-referral acceptance form.

- After the particular adoptive family officially accepted the child referral, the orphanage represented the child and signed the contract of adoption with the adoption agency that represented the adoptive family.
- The adoption agency then processed the adoptive family's dossier, which was authenticated by the Ministry of Foreign Affairs, translated into Amharic, and then authenticated by the Ministry of Justice. It was then filed with the court, together with the child's dossier, and a court date was set for the adoption hearing.

The Adoption Court Process

- Upon receipt of the child's and the adoptive parents' dossiers, the court issued a summons to MOWCYA asking for their recommendation (positive or negative) on the adoption. This recommendation was also sent to the orphanage representing the child and the agency representing the adoptive parents.
- The adoption agency submitted to the federal MOWCYA the adoptive parents' dossier and the child's dossier, together with the court summons to MOWCYA to send their recommendations for the adoption court hearing.
- The orphanage summoned the child's birth parents to appear in court for the adoption hearing and to legally relinquish the child.
- On the court date, a representative from the orphanage appeared in court along with the child's birth parents (or documentation of legal relinquishment in abandonment cases). On behalf of the adoptive parents, a representative of the adoption agency appeared (since 2011 the adoptive parents also appeared), along with MOWCYA's sealed recommendation. During the hearing, the judge would ask the birth parents if they realized that Ethiopian

191

adoptions were final and that they could no longer claim or see their child.

- After court approval, the adoption agency received a letter of support from MOWCYA to obtain a birth certificate and passport for the child.
- The adoption agency received the court decree, and the child's dossier was translated into English. This was then submitted to the US Embassy, along with the child's birth certificate, passport, US Embassy–authorized medical report, and a letter from MOWCYA confirming the child's adoption approval.
- After receiving all the required documents, the US Embassy conducted an investigation of the orphan status prior to inviting the adoptive parents for their visa interview.

In their scrutiny, the US Embassy's adoption unit investigated not only BFAS, but also its partnering orphanage and the Shashamane incident. They started their investigation with the cases that we had already submitted to the embassy and that were scheduled for visa interviews in March. Their first task was to examine the children's orphanages in Addis Ababa. Then they traveled to the children's birthplaces, Awasa, Hosaena, and Jimma, and conducted a thorough investigation of the birth parents, the relinquishment process, and documentation on file at the children's orphanages. They found everything in order but did not stop there.

The chief of the adoption unit went to court with each child's file and interviewed the judge who approved those adoptions. The chief of the adoption unit did so without even letting us know she was doing that. In March, we were notified that our cases were cut and dry, and the scrutiny was lifted. Eventually the March embassy appointments for our BFAS families were honored.

While the embassy's investigation was going on, I was busy doing housekeeping with BFAS, not knowing that it would ultimately destroy the organization. Like the BFAS driver, the deputy director soon took advantage of the antiterrorism policy and used his profession as a lawyer to twist the Shashamane case, which had closed on a "not guilty" verdict a year earlier, into a fabrication of allegations to cover up his own wrongdoing and unethical practices.

Since the financial issue with deputy director was still pending when I left for the States in early November, I asked the BFAS accountant to provide me with a financial report. She gave me the report in memo form and expense forms, showing that the deputy director had signed for unauthorized use,19,800 birr in just seven weeks. We contracted an external auditor to have BFAS audited.

The situation grew worse soon after I returned to the States in May. At that point, I realized that Abebe was too much to handle. His skill and manipulation in the misuse of funds was beyond reach. Eventually I hired a Christian country representative, and contracted a legal adviser while Abebe retained his position as deputy director. When our legal consultant asked him to settle up with what he owed BFAS funds, the deputy director replied that he must be paid 120,000 birr if he was to be terminated before his employment contract ended. Finally the new country representative issued a letter firing him and filed a lawsuit against him.

After speaking with our legal consultant, the deputy director had continued to work full-time (still paid by BFAS) while plotting to destroy us and walk free. By the time he received his termination letter, he was ready with carefully fabricated, well-orchestrated evidence that he filed in a false report with the Ministry of Women's Affairs (presently the Ministry of Women, Children, and Youth Affairs, or MOWCYA). He alleged that BFAS was involved in child trafficking and was using falsified documents to place children for adoption.

The Deputy director engaged in a great deal of administrative malpractice and unethical activities against BFAS. He also knew how to obstruct justice. Here is one of the intrigues he used to achieve his goal: He falsely set up a family as needy, wrote up a solicitation letter and endorsed financial assistance for them (Please see Appendix 12 B). Then he later used that as the basis for false allegations in which he blackmailed and eventually destroyed BFAS. He also used Sendek, which he said was his friend's newspaper, to write an article in which he accused the agency of giving to this same family money for assistance. The name of the child's father who signed the application for assistance was Ermiyas. But in the newspaper, the name of the child's father was reported as Tesfaye. Yet, this particular intrigue is first on the list of reasons with which the CSA board upheld the revocation of BFAS's license.

Upon his first court appearance for the BFAS lawsuit filed against him, the deputy director vowed to have BFAS shut down before his second court appearance. He cleverly managed to use MOWCYA towards achieving his avowed goal and did indeed walk free. He accomplished this by blackmailing BFAS and covering up his own wrongdoing and unethical practices while pretending to be a concerned citizen and lawyer. Government officers were easily manipulated to advance the deputy director's plot. The former adoption processing officer and the former Children's Rights and Safety Enforcement directorate director of MOWCYA, accepted Abebe Tigabu's false report and allegations at face value and caused great damage that ultimately led to the suspension of BFAS's license.

Later we learned that immediately after the adoptive mother of a child who was denied final processing after his adoption court approval left her office in October 2010, the

Children's Right and Safety Enforcement directorate director ordered MOWCYA's attorney to write to the Charities and Societies Agency (CSA), a government authority that oversaw NGOs in Ethiopia, to take administrative action against BFAS.[32] BFAS was not copied on that letter and never even knew of its existence until BFAS sued MOWCYA and obtained the documents on their first court appearance.

For two months, BFAS's country representative wrestled in vain with endless bureaucratic red tape between the Children's Rights and Safety Enforcement directorate director's and the State/deputy Minister's offices at MOWCYA. I flew back to Ethiopia in December 2010 in hopes of having those vulnerable children join their adoptive families. The country representative and I met with the new MOWCYA Minister to explain the facts and provide her with evidence proving that the allegations against BFAS were false. Although our meeting went well, we did not get any response. I am not sure if that was their policy, but BFAS never received a response to the many pleas and petitions we submitted to the government institutions involved.

As a result, BFAS submitted a complaint to the adoption judge. In response, the judge summoned the Children's Rights and Safety Enforcement directorate director, but the junior adoption-processing officer, appeared before the judge and responded that BFAS had been submitted to CSA as well as to the police and MOWCYA was awaiting the result. Since we received no response to any of our letters, we filed a lawsuit against the two MOWCYA Officers, MOWCYA itself and BFAS's deputy director.[33]

Soon after we filed our complaint with the adoption judge, and the lawsuit following that, MOWCYA pressured

---

[32] Please see appendix 11 for letter to CSA from MOWCYA's attorney

[33] Please see appendix 12 for lawsuit filed against MOWCYA's officers, MOWCYA and Abebe Tigabu

the Director General of CSA to revoke our license based on the deputy director's false allegations that BFAS had trafficked seven children from Shashamane to Addis Ababa and was engaged in illegal adoptions. Since they had been doing all this behind our back, we knew nothing until the defendants brought to court the allegations they had filed with CSA. By the time we found out, and before the second court hearing on the lawsuit we filed, the CSA Director General had already suspended our license. In his letter, he indicated that the grounds for his action was that BFAS had allegedly misused its license after its re-registration by trafficking seven children from Shashamane to Addis Ababa through fraudulent documents and falsifying documents of children with biological parents.

In addition to the evidences we submitted proving that the allegations against BFAS were baseless, it was unconstitutional to criminalize BFAS retroactively. As Article 22 of the Ethiopian constitution, titled "Prohibition of Retroactive Criminal Law," clearly stated:

1. No person shall be held guilty of any penal offense on account of an act which, at the time of commission or omission leading to the charge, was not defined by law as an offense. Nor shall a penalty be imposed on any person which is greater than the maximum penalty which was applicable for that offense at the time it was committed.
2. Notwithstanding the provisions of sub-Article I of this Article, a law promulgated subsequent to the commission of the offense shall apply if it favors the accused.

We also provided the CSA director general documentation proving that the deputy director himself had processed the adoptions of the said seven children through MOWCYA in compliance with their guidelines and had represented them for their adoption-court approval and US Embassy visa process by which the children joined their adoptive parents in 2009 before BFAS was reregistered. After reviewing all the evidence, the director general found it convincing enough to prove the allegations under which our license had been suspended were unfounded and false. He promised to help but also said that he needed to work with MOWCYA in righting the wrong and having BFAS's license reinstated, since the demand for the revocation had come from them.

BFAS also submitted its appeal to the CSA board, according to CSA Proclamation 104:3. Although the appeal was addressed to the board, we had to submit it to the director general's secretary because he was the one who presented NGO appeals to the board.

Coming back to the root cause of the ordeal, the deputy director did not even have to wait for the final revocation of BFAS's license to walk free at his third court appearance. Although he had not been copied on the letter, he was able to access the initial revocation letter and use it towards his premeditated purpose. He presented to the judge the initial revocation letter with which he backed his argument that BFAS had been shut down and can't sue him. With that, the judge passed a judgment in his favor. I don't think she (the judge) was aware of the provisions of CSA's Proclamation, Article 104:4, "A charity in an appeal process shall be deemed not canceled until final decision is rendered by the concerned authority".

Since the CSA secretary assured us repeatedly that the director general was diligently working with MOWCYA on our case, which he himself reaffirmed, we were left dangling between the two entities. He also told us that the US Embassy had submitted a letter against BFAS (he didn't disclose the content of the letter), but he said he would continue to work with MOWCYA anyway to right the wrong.

When the BFAS country representative and I went to MOWCYA the next day to follow up on our case, a concerned official there asked us, "Are you okay with the US Embassy?" I replied yes, boasting that the United States was different in that its privacy act prohibited the release of information without the knowledge or consent of the concerned party. Although I was confident about the US Embassy, the country representative pressured me that we needed to find out for ourselves, since both CSA and MOWCYA had given us similar information.

We thus made an appointment with the embassy and were scheduled for a February 4 meeting with the consular section chief and the adoption-unit staff who had documented my report on the Shashamane issue on February 9, 2010, and the new adoption-unit chief. Unfortunately, that meeting did not go well from the start. The meeting began with an unexpected interrogation from the adoption-unit chief, who did not even give me a chance to speak. From that, I sensed an atmosphere based on assumptions and misinformation, which triggered a tense and not so cordial discussion that resulted in my misunderstanding of the roles the CSA and the embassy were playing in this particular case.

The adoption-unit chief never took a breath in his interrogation, so the consular section chief and the adoption-unit staff did not say a word until I interrupted and asked about the letter that the embassy had written to CSA and MOWCYA. They replied they were not aware of any letter, and the adoption-unit chief quickly said, "But we have to give them a report of our findings."

In the past, whenever we were unaware of an issue, a discrepancy, or a flaw in the work of our organization, the problem was immediately brought to our attention by the US Embassy's adoption unit. However, it was not so with this new adoption-unit chief at the US Embassy in Addis Ababa. From what I understand about the role of a diplomat, the chief should have investigated, verified, and questioned the validity of those allegations and determined the root cause of the travesty. As Gary Wills writes:

> An important recommendation for any diplomat is trustworthiness. Yet his very job seems to undermine trust in him. If he is only a tool of his principal, he seems little better than a spy. If he "goes native" in the place he is sent to, the home office will consider him a liability. (Gary Wills, p. 70)

On February 9, 2011, some adoptive parents informed us that the Amharic and English translations of the letter by which BFAS's license was suspended were posted on the US State Department's website announcing that BFAS's license was revoked. At that time, our license had not been revoked, only suspended. According to CSA Proclamation Article 104:4, this should not have happened:

> Any charity or society in the process appeal, where it is in relation to registration or cancelation, shall be deemed not registered or canceled until final decision is rendered by the concerned authority. (Article 104, Claims and Appeals)

Nonetheless, *CBS News* grubbed the information from the US State Department's website and immediately disseminated it all over the world. The rest of the world media thought they had unearthed an interesting news story about an adoption agency involved in child trafficking and quickly did their part in scattering the story. In December 2011, we (BFAS) received an e-mail from a journalist named Kathryn Joyce stating that she is a journalist working on a story for *Newsweek International* about adoption in Ethiopia and hoped to speak to someone at BFAS about the accusations made against the agency by the Ethiopian government and the revocation of its license.[34] That email excited me with the thought that *Newsweek International* would bring the truth to light.

With much excitement, I called her myself. She said she had already interviewed Abebe and wanted to do the same with me. Following our first telephone conversation, I e-mailed to her numerous documentations, including auditors' reports showing the figure for which BFAS had sued Abebe Tigabu. I continued pursuing her by phone, pushing her to take the true story to the media as quickly as possible.

In April 2012, she conducted another long telephone interview with me. At the end of the interview, she remarked, "But Abebe said he paid bribes." By these words, she made clear that she trusted Abebe over me. She apparently did not know it was illegal to give or receive bribes in Ethiopia and that the defamation Abebe was using to cover his illegal activities would only make it worse for him. At the end of our telephone conversation, I asked her how soon *Newsweek International* would disseminate our story. To my surprise, however, she replied that she was writing a book on adoption in Ethiopia. Until that point, it had been my belief that she was writing a news article for *Newsweek International*.

Taken aback, I asked her to allow me to review the story she wrote before having it published. What could I expect from her book when she clearly chose to side with Abebe Tigabu regardless of the documentation I provided showing his real image? Abebe Tigabu had represented the adoptive parents in court for their adoption approvals as well as accompanied them to the US Embassy for their visa appointments. How could this man's words be trusted when he contradicted his own work by alleging that those children had been fraudulently processed? The BFAS driver was the

---

[34] Please see appendix 13 for the email from Kathryn Joyce

first to use the charges of "child trafficking" and "falsification of documents" to walk free from his theft by falsely criminalizing the innocent. Second on the list was Abebe Tigabu. I did not know who might be third, fourth, and so on.

I wish the media would formulate their reports from an evidence-based investigation of both sides. When I say "evidence-based," I am stressing that it should be correct and true evidence, not fabricated lies. The quality of food that we consume matters a great deal to our physical health and fitness. Likewise, the quality of information that we consume affects our mental, social, and psychological well-being, which is even more important than physical health. It's like comparing a nutritionally deficient sugary food with a healthy organic food, when it comes to the consumption of information.

In addition to the court verdict, the very definition for child trafficking should have given anyone a clue to the irrelevancy of the allegations:

> This note is based on engagements among international agencies in 2006 and 2007. Under international law, child trafficking is a crime involving the movement of children for the purpose of their exploitation. Child trafficking is essentially slavery, and that has been around for centuries. It is common in the third world, where young girls, for example, are forced into prostitution in the third world and even in Western countries. Child trafficking concerns the business of removing children from their homes and families, transporting them elsewhere, whether elsewhere within the country or overseas, to be put to use by others, usually to make money. (Terre des Hommes Foundation)

As six of the so-called trafficked children ranged in age from two months to two years old (the other child was four years old), and no financial gain was involved, I don't know how these children fit the above-cited definition.

Just before I submitted this manuscript to my publisher, someone forwarded to me a blog site for Kathryn Joyce.[70] I discovered that she has actually written a book titled *Child Catchers: Rescue Child Trafficking and the New Gospel of Adoption* in which she uses the story she wrote about us to attack evangelicals. To uncover the real truth, take a look at this excerpt from her blog and then at my actual e-mail communications with the adoptive mother in the story.[35] As can be seen from our email communications, I have never seen the adoptive child's birth mother. In marketing her book through this blog, Kathryn Joyce acknowledges her different funding sources and that "support for the reporting in this piece came from *Pulitzer Center on Crisis Reporting*". See for yourself the "dark underbelly" the blogger refers to. First, here is the blog excerpt:

The Child Catchers: Evangelicals and the Fake-Orphan Racket, April 24, 2013, 8:26 p.m.—By Kathryn Joyce

In her shocking new book, Kathryn Joyce uncovers how conservative Christians have come to dominate the international adoption circuit—and its dark underbelly. When Hawkins called BFAS to present this information, she reached Agitu Wodajo directly. Despite the many reassurances Hawkins had received in the past that the girl was abandoned, she said Wodajo replied without hesitation that yes, she had met the girl's mother herself.

---

[35] Please see appendix 14 for email communications with the adoptive parent in the story

I want to give you a snapshot of what the evangelicals really stand for, as far as I know. When I first started working with BFAS, I asked the executive director of an adoption agency why she had selected such a difficult career when her master's degree could earn her a much easier one. She replied, "Yes, it has given me gray hair, but I can't tell you the satisfaction I get from seeing these children have loving and caring parents." I received the same answer from adoptive parents who went the extra mile to open their homes and hearts to vulnerable children.

As can be seen from the adoption process I explained earlier, Ethiopian birth parents have full control over the information by which their children are relinquished to an orphanage. Out of desperation to give their children a better future, many birth parents will do anything, and adoption agencies and orphanages have no control over that.

Child abandonment in Ethiopia extends beyond the normal definition of abandonment resulting from cultural, social, and economic reasons. For example, young Ethiopian women who work at other people's home as servants sometimes are raped by an adult male in the house, such as the head of the household, a son, a guard, etc. If the girl becomes pregnant, she will be kicked out and face unspeakable life-altering situations. Through no fault of her own, she will be ostracized and lose social acceptance. Such girls have nowhere to go and no one to turn to. They cannot find work or a place to stay, both while pregnant and after the birth of their children. Their only alternative, it seems, is to commit suicide or throw the newborn baby into a pit or latrine.

Some girls decide to abandon their babies in front of an orphanage or a well-to-do family's home, on the streets, or in the health institutions where they gave birth. In the eastern and southern parts of the country, newborn babies are commonly abandoned during the night. Blessed are the compassionate who sacrifice so much to come to the rescue of these children and young girls.

From the very beginning, the revocation of BFAS's license did not follow the guidelines of the CSA proclamation concerning charities and societies. BFAS did not receive prior notice, verbal or written. Article 92:1a of the proclamation said that any charity or society that failed to comply with the agency's order within the time set by the agency could by suspended until it came into compliance.

Despite the evidence we had and without the chance we deserved by law to present our case to the CSA board during their meeting in April (in other words, without any due process and without our defense), a decision to revoke BFAS's license was made in our absence.

Just a month before he presented our appeal to the CSA board, the Director General of CSA accepted from the Children's Right Enforcement and Safety directorate director at MOWCYA, documentation against BFAS, that she had modified and sent directly to him in March 2011. MOWCYA's minister was copied on these documents through a cover letter, but BFAS was not. These documents were submitted to the CSA board in April 2012 as supportive evidence against our appeal. With this, the board upheld the revocation of BFAS's license. Consequently, BFAS became one of the NGOs whose licenses were revoked in the same time period, including organizations such as Samaritan's Purse, Mobility without Barrier Foundation-Ethiopia (MWBF-E), the Ethiopian Women Lawyers' Association (EWLA), and the Human Rights Council (HRC) of Ethiopia. [58] [59]

Although I was unaware of the circumstances of the four above-mentioned organizations, I knew the evidence submitted to the CSA board against BFAS could not avoid exposing their fraudulence. In the initial revocation letter, for example, BFAS's license was suspended for allegedly trafficking seven children from Shashamane to Addis Ababa and for the illegal processing of abandoned children. In the final revocation letter, however, grounds for upholding the initial decision was based on a study conducted through the children's rights and safety enforcement directorate director that yielded conflicting information.

In the final revocation letter, BFAS was first accused of processing the adoption of a child who had parents and of paying the parents not to disclose the case. Second, the letter said that when BFAS was refused processing of five children by the court in Addis Ababa, it transferred the children to an orphanage at Asasa in Aris zone. Furthermore, the children's rights and safety enforcement directorate director stated that ten families had filed complaints with the police on the where-abouts of their children, for which a court warrant was issued to BFAS officers. Third, BFAS was accused of financing two orphanages to illegally process its adoption cases.

The inaccuracies and inconsistencies between the initial letter and the final letter upholding the revocation should have been convincing enough to reveal the truth.[36] However, the validity of the evidence did not seem to matter, since CSA's proclamation did not give provision for foreign NGOs to appeal the decision in federal court.

At this stage in my writing, I remembered the Samaritan's Purse's case and was curious how the license of such a globally respected humanitarian organization had been revoked. Thus I initiated a search on Google. Several sources reported that based on press interviews with the director general of CSA, the license of Samaritan's Purse was revoked because the organization had employed fourteen American nationals who worked in Ethiopia for three years without work permits and had also failed to pay employee taxes to Ethiopia in an amount over seven million Ethiopian birr. In its appeal to the CSA board, Samaritan's Purse asserted that the alleged

---

[36] Please see appendix 15 for CSA's initial and final revocation letter

fourteen Americans were student volunteers. Nonetheless, their license was revoked after more than a decade of dedicated service addressing the physical and spiritual needs of the needy and transforming the lives of many. [59]

It was really too bad that foreign NGOs could not appeal beyond the CSA board. Samaritan's Purse was highly regarded all over the world. Why not in Ethiopia? In my analysis of the entire situation, I eventually realized that I had faced more than enough tribulation in my work with WSRA and should have learned from the past. I had seen the result of WSRA's lawsuit against the Woreda and Kebele officials, and now I learned the hard way that it was wrong of me to agree with suing MOWCYA.

During my Google search of the Samaritan's Purse situation, I also came across information on the revocation of the license for the Ethiopian Women Lawyers Association (EWLA). Established in 1995, the EWLA was the first of its kind and the only women's NGO dedicated to women's rights advocacy in Ethiopia. [59] I mention EWLA's situation to alert not only foreign entities, but also Ethiopian nationals who put their trust in foreign intervention on how good intentions can bear bad consequences. I am doing this from the concern I have for the Ethiopian people and from the lessons I learned from my vast involvement in addressing the needs of vulnerable women and children in Ethiopia.

The circumstances of such an ancient country as Ethiopia and the situation of women in it are very different from other nations, as I pointed out in chapter 4. When it comes to women and girls in Ethiopia, long-standing traditional law and the cultural heritage of the nation relegated the status of women as subordinate to men in social, political, and economic life. For centuries, Ethiopian men owned women's services and persons. To make a long story short, Ethiopian women could not afford to lose EWLA. As an overcomer (I use *overcomer* rather than the word *survivor*) of domestic violence who has seen it all, I understand what EWLA's advocacy meant for those women who were less fortunate than others. EWLA played a remarkable role in bringing change to Ethiopian family law. Let me give you one example.

In years past, any woman who dared to file for divorce on the grounds of adultery had to bring witnesses to court for proof of evidence. The judge would ask the witnesses,"Did you see them in the form of thread and needle? *"Kirrenna merfe honew agnetehachewal?"*in Amharic. In other words, he would ask, "Did you see them having sex?" Who in the world would do such a thing in public? But now, according to the revised Ethiopian family law, divorce in Ethiopia is "no fault."

In 2001, EWLA's license was suspended by the Ministry of Justice, a government authority that oversaw NGOs at that time, alleging that EWLA was engaged in activities different from those it was mandated to perform by law. While the Ethiopian government's situation was understandable, it was also evident that Ethiopian women and girls could not afford to lose EWLA. The Human Rights Watch reached out with a letter to the late Prime Minister Meles Zenawi, dated October 17, 2001. I would like to quote the first and last paragraphs of their letter:

> We are writing to express our deep concern regarding the recent suspension from operation of the Ethiopian Women Lawyers Association (EWLA), a leading local nongovernmental women's rights organization. ... We urge you to ensure that the Ethiopian Women Lawyers Association and other human rights organizations in Ethiopia enjoy their rights to pursue their objectives freely without any arbitrary interference by the government. [60]

The intervention of the Human Rights Watch worked well, and EWLA's license was reinstated. Unfortunately, EWLA was caught in a different trap a few years after their license was reinstated, which, I believe, contributed to the establishment of the Charities and Societies Agency (CSA), the new government authority that oversees NGOs. On Ethiopian television, the Ethiopian government accused the EWLA of giving the US Embassy in Addis Ababa false reports that damaged Ethiopia's reputation. The government claimed that reports from the US State Department and the Human Rights Watch (HRW) that accused Ethiopia of violating human rights were based on these unfounded charges. According to media sources, it was rumored that Mahder Pawlos, executive director of EWLA, would face imprisonment, and thus she fled the country in 2009. [61].

Established in February 2009 with a brand-new proclamation, CSA made it a requirement that all charities operating in Ethiopia reregister under CSA. Section 1:2/2 of the proclamation required Ethiopian NGOs to generate 90 percent of their income from Ethiopia. I found it hard to understand how this new policy could work in a poor country where organized volunteerism and philanthropy have not been a common practice. This greatly hurt EWLA because, according to media sources, [59] they already had around 12 million birr raised from abroad deposited in their account when the CSA was established. In 2010, the CSA revoked EWLA's license and confiscated 8.6 million birr from their account, alleging that EWLA had violated CSA's code that limits Ethiopian charities' foreign funding to 10 percent of their income. EWLA appealed based indicating that they had raised the 12 million birr from international sources during the grace period before the CSA proclamation was in effect, but their appeal was denied. [59] .

In my opinion, foreign entities (including the Diaspora) should know their limitations and circumstances of the particular country when intervening in any foreign country's affairs and keep the safety and well-being of that nation's subjects in mind. You can see from the BFAS story how irresponsible, selfish individuals can use the system for self-benefit and how others will try to take advantage of the slightest mistakes. Ethiopian charities, like any organization, need to be very cautious for the sake of those they serve rather than rely on wrong expectations, including trust in foreign intervention.

14

The Effects of the Remnants Brought Forward

I will begin this chapter by doing a little accounting of the government leaderships that I have discussed so far. Before I proceed, though, I urge you to understand that I am neither an accountant nor an economist, so you will have to accept my points as a layperson's view. I also want to stress that the focus of this book is on the importance of good governance in making the world a better place, and the issues addressed in this book are in support of that. In my accounting of the government leaderships addressed in previous chapters, I will use the phrase *remnants brought forward* for the usual accounting term *balance brought forward*. In so doing, I cannot avoid repeating some of what I discussed in the preceding chapters.

In accounting, a company finishes its accounting year and then determines its *closing balance*, which is the last balance in its account. It is the amount remaining in an account, positive or negative, at the end of an accounting period or fiscal year. The *balance brought forward* is the closing balance that is taken from the previous period and moved forward to begin the new one. In other words, it connects the two periods, the previous period and the new period, because the ending balance of the previous period becomes the opening balance for the new one.

In chapter 3 of this book, we saw what Emperor Haile Selassie I inherited from his predecessors as a descendant of the world's oldest monarchy and how that affected his government, ultimately leading to the end of monarchy rule. Although the emperor was a reformer and brought incredible changes to Ethiopia, the linkage between his new government and the previous government invited the revolution that ended his regime. The two governments that succeeded Emperor Haile Selassie I's regime, the People's Democratic Republic of Ethiopia (PDRE) and the present Federal Democratic Republic of Ethiopia (FDRE), formed their new governments on completely new ideology. However, they could not form a radically new system free from the residue of the old monarchy system.

The Founding Fathers of the New World were able to establish a completely different form of government because they fled to a new country and started with a clean slate. From my evaluation, the secret behind the Founding Fathers' success in establishing the most powerful nation on earth is found in Acts 4:32:

> Now the multitude of those who believed were of one heart and one soul; neither did anyone say that any of the things he possessed was his own, but they had all things in common.

This is not to say that the ideology of the early settlers was socialism, that "they had all things in common." With one heart and one accord, those men learned from the tyrannical rule of the past and said no to mixing even a drop of the old with the new. The old government's system emphasized the divine right of kings and used religion to retain absolute power, but the new system with its new laws said each man was king of his own private property. The new did not assume kingship in order to gain lordship over all the land or to own land. As a result, property rights were instituted, entitling the people to land ownership and lordship over their own land.

Although that is what made America the most successful nation on earth, the situation was not the same in Ethiopia. This was a country that tried to sustain the new on the old, even when trying to make reforms, and the old always persisted. While I believe that much research would be required for a broad and precise coverage of the issues, the table below provides a brief summary of how the major problems that Emperor Haile Selassie I inherited from his predecessors filtered down to his successors.

I. Government's Ideology

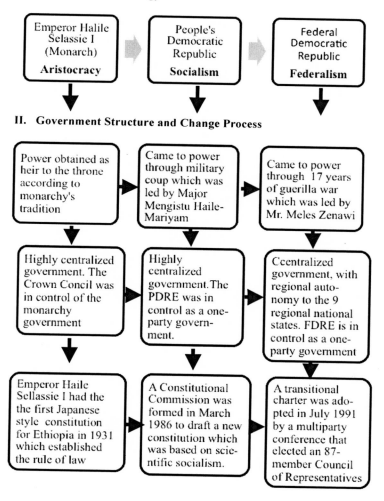

| Emperor Halile Selassie I (Monarch) **Aristocracy** | People's Democratic Republic **Socialism** | Federal Democratic Republic **Federalism** |

II. Government Structure and Change Process

| Power obtained as heir to the throne according to monarchy's tradition | Came to power through military coup which was led by Major Mengistu Haile-Mariyam | Came to power through 17 years of guerilla war which was led by Mr. Meles Zenawi |

| Highly centralized government. The Crown Concil was in control of the monarchy government | Highly centralized government. The PDRE was in control as a one-party government. | Ccentralized government, with regional auto-nomy to the 9 regional national states. FDRE is in control as a one-party government |

| Emperor Haile Sellassie I had the the first Japanese style constitution for Ethiopia in 1931 which established the rule of law | A Constitutional Commission was formed in March 1986 to draft a new constitution which was based on scie-ntific socialism. | A transitional charter was ado-pted in July 1991 by a multiparty conference that elected an 87-member Council of Representatives |

Government Structure and Change Process

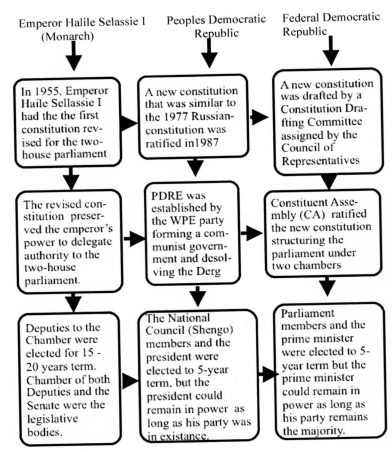

Emperor Halile Selassie I (Monarch)   Peoples Democratic Republic   Federal Democratic Republic

In 1955, Emperor Haile Sellassie I had the the first constitution revised for the two-house parliament

A new constitution that was similar to the 1977 Russian-constitution was ratified in1987

A new constitution was drafted by a Constitution Drafting Committee assigned by the Council of Representatives

The revised constitution preserved the emperor's power to delegate authority to the two-house parliament.

PDRE was established by the WPE party forming a communist government and desolving the Derg

Constituent Assembly (CA) ratified the new constitution structuring the parliament under two chambers

Deputies to the Chamber were elected for 15 - 20 years term. Chamber of both Deputies and the Senate were the legislative bodies.

The National Council (Shengo) members and the president were elected to 5-year term, but the president could remain in power as long as his party was in existance.

Parliament members and the prime minister were elected to 5-year term but the prime minister could remain in power as long as his party remains the majority.

Government Structure and Change Process

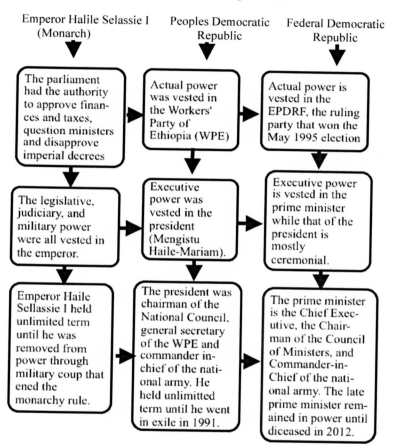

Emperor Halile Selassie I (Monarch)

Peoples Democratic Republic

Federal Democratic Republic

The parliament had the authority to approve finances and taxes, question ministers and disapprove imperial decrees

Actual power was vested in the Workers' Party of Ethiopia (WPE)

Actual power is vested in the EPDRF, the ruling party that won the May 1995 election

The legislative, judiciary, and military power were all vested in the emperor.

Executive power was vested in the president (Mengistu Haile-Mariam).

Executive power is vested in the prime minister while that of the president is mostly ceremonial.

Emperor Haile Sellassie I held unlimited term until he was removed from power through military coup that ened the monarchy rule.

The president was chairman of the National Council, general secretary of the WPE and commander in-chief of the national army. He held unlimitted term until he went in exile in 1991.

The prime minister is the Chief Executive, the Chairman of the Council of Ministers, and Commander-in-Chief of the national army. The late prime minister remained in power until diceased in 2012.

III. Land Ownership

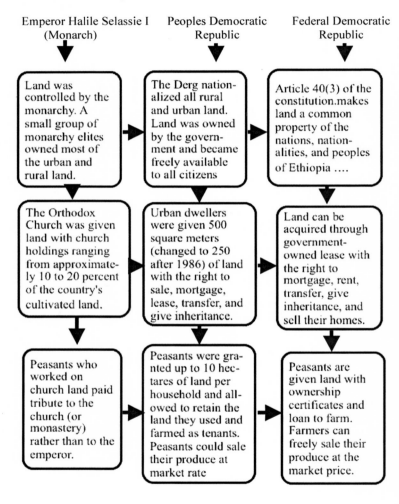

Emperor Halile Selassie I
(Monarch)

Peoples Democratic
Republic

Federal Democratic
Republic

Land was controlled by the monarchy. A small group of monarchy elites owned most of the urban and rural land.

The Derg nationalized all rural and urban land. Land was owned by the government and became freely available to all citizens

Article 40(3) of the constitution.makes land a common property of the nations, nationalities, and peoples of Ethiopia ....

The Orthodox Church was given land with church holdings ranging from approximately 10 to 20 percent of the country's cultivated land.

Urban dwellers were given 500 square meters (changed to 250 after 1986) of land with the right to sale, mortgage, lease, transfer, and give inheritance.

Land can be acquired through government-owned lease with the right to mortgage, rent, transfer, give inheritance, and sell their homes.

Peasants who worked on church land paid tribute to the church (or monastery) rather than to the emperor.

Peasants were granted up to 10 hectares of land per household and allowed to retain the land they used and farmed as tenants. Peasants could sale their produce at market rate

Peasants are given land with ownership certificates and loan to farm. Farmers can freely sale their produce at the market price.

Land Ownership

Emperor Halile Selassie I (Monarch)	Peoples Democratic Republic	Federal Democratic Republic
Land privately owned by monarchy elites and feudal lords in the south could be sold to investors of coffee plantations	The Derg converted in to state farms, the nationalized commercial farms owned by the state and monarchy elites	All nationalized urban and rural houses, land, and commercial properties are owned by the government and are subject to sale and lease by the state.
Worthy followers and loyal servants were given land in the form of rist, with the right to use, lease, transfer, and give inheritance to family members. Monarchy elites and government officials were privileged through land ownership.	Political-party members, cadres, and their favorites were able to obtain land or property according to their choice. Higher government officials were provided housing benefits from nationalized homes.	Political-party members and cadres were able to take advantage. Higher officials get government housing and benefits. Parliament members from the 9 nations and nationalities are given government housing.
Peasants of the southern provinces (65–80 percent) became serfs to feudal lords and shared up to 50 percent of their agricultural produce with them.[64]	In 1979, peasants came under the control of the Derg through a collectivization policy and were required to sell their produce to Derg for less than market price.	Small-holder farmers are given land with ownership certificates and loans to farm. Farmers can freely sale their produce at the market price.

IV. Ethnic Discrimination

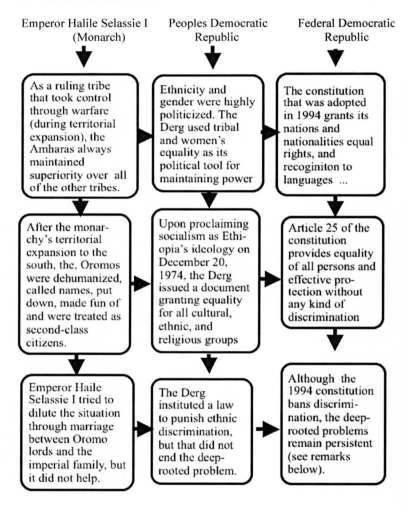

Emperor Halile Selassie I (Monarch)	Peoples Democratic Republic	Federal Democratic Republic
As a ruling tribe that took control through warfare (during territorial expansion), the Amharas always maintained superiority over all of the other tribes.	Ethnicity and gender were highly politicized. The Derg used tribal and women's equality as its political tool for maintaining power	The constitution that was adopted in 1994 grants its nations and nationalities equal rights, and recoginiton to languages ...
After the monarchy's territorial expansion to the south, the, Oromos were dehumanized, called names, put down, made fun of and were treated as second-class citizens.	Upon proclaiming socialism as Ethiopia's ideology on December 20, 1974, the Derg issued a document granting equality for all cultural, ethnic, and religious groups	Article 25 of the constitution provides equality of all persons and effective protection without any kind of discrimination
Emperor Haile Selassie I tried to dilute the situation through marriage between Oromo lords and the imperial family, but it did not help.	The Derg instituted a law to punish ethnic discrimination, but that did not end the deep-rooted problem.	Although the 1994 constitution bans discrimination, the deep-rooted problems remain persistent (see remarks below).

Ethnic Discrimination

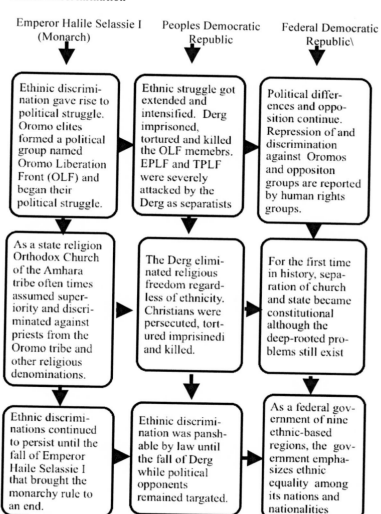

Emperor Halile Selassie I (Monarch)

Peoples Democratic Republic

Federal Democratic Republic\

Ethinic discrimination gave rise to political struggle. Oromo elites formed a political group named Oromo Liberation Front (OLF) and began their political struggle.

Ethnic struggle got extended and intensified. Derg imprisoned, tortured and killed the OLF memebrs. EPLF and TPLF were severely attacked by the Derg as separatists

Political differences and opposition continue. Repression of and discrimination against Oromos and oppositon groups are reported by human rights groups.

As a state religion Orthodox Church of the Amhara tribe often times assumed superiority and discriminated against priests from the Oromo tribe and other religious denominations.

The Derg eliminated religious freedom regardless of ethnicity. Christians were persecuted, tortured imprisinedi and killed.

For the first time in history, separation of church and state became constitutional although the deep-rooted problems still exist

Ethnic discriminations continued to persist until the fall of Emperor Haile Selassie I that brought the monarchy rule to an end.

Ethnic discrimination was panshable by law until the fall of Derg while political opponents remained targated.

As a federal government of nine ethnic-based regions, the government emphasizes ethnic equality among its nations and nationalities

219

Summary Notes on the Effects of the Remnants Brought Forward

Land Ownership

Land ownership remained critical to the Ethiopian government because of its economic and political importance. Emperor Amde Tsion's fight for territorial expansion to the south in the fourteenth century was aimed at gaining control over the fertile land of the south. His strategies to achieve his goal were shrewdness, cleverness, and military power. Giving rewards in return for assistance was part of his cleverness in gaining power, and it worked better than mere military might. For example, Emperor Amde Tsion gave loyalists gult rights (land) in return for service. Emperor Menelik II paid large tributes to Emperor Yohannes in return for autonomy over Showa, which earned him the throne and made his territorial expansion successful. Abba Jifar paid Emperor Menilek II tributes and tax revenue in return for autonomy, and on and on it goes. The tributes always came from exploitation of the conquered south.

The Orthodox Church was also awarded land privilege in return for Christianizing the non-Christians, whom they called "heathens," and for teaching subjects to submit to the divine rights of kings. That leadership culture did not disappear with the abolishment of the monarchy, but rather changed to different forms by using whatever language and ways suited the time or the regime.

During Emperor Haile Selassie's reign, land-tenure patterns erected serious barriers to agricultural production and exerted negative influences on urban development. This was due to the fact that powerful monarchy elites lowered and evaded land taxes, thus causing the state to lose revenue that could have been used towards promoting the country's development and progress. Absentee landlords who owned land in the south also lived in the cities, but never cared about urban improvements and development.[62] Those monarchy elites who took advantage of the economic policy and became wealthier finally grew so strong that none of the emperor's attempted land reform was possible:

> Speaking on the occasion of the submission of a draft legislation to parliament to reform some features of the land tenure system, the emperor expressed the need to replace the customary land tenure system with a modern and formal land tenure institution: "The intent of the draft legislation is to define the rights, duties and responsibilities of tenants and landlords, to ensure a fair and equitable share of returns for both parties, to provide the required governmental assistance if and when both parties wish to have a written agreement of document specifying their obligation, and to provide an incentive for sustained increase in the income of both parties by establishing on a legal basis the traditional and customary system."[63]

Although the Derg made the "land to the tiller" slogan a reality through its radical land reform of 1975, it switched gears a few years later and became a controller of and competitor with the very tiller it freed from tenancy. The Derg forced the farmers to sell their produce to the government at a price lower than that of the market price, while at the same time expanding state farms, which took most of the country's agricultural resources. State farms received more than 90 million birr in direct subsidies alone in two to three years during the early 1980s. Expanding state farms at the expense of the peasants, however, did not meet the intended purpose of reversing the decline and boosting food production [64]

The FDRE's constitution greatly improved the land-ownership situation, especially for peasants. Subarticle 4 of the constitution gives Ethiopian farmers the right to obtain land without payment and provides for protection against eviction from their property. Similarly, Subarticle 5 grants Ethiopian pastoralists the right to free land for grazing and farming as well as protection from displacement. From the way I see it, the provisions of these two subarticles are tantamount to private ownership of land since they guarantee full right to permanent land tenure, including the right to use, transfer, sublease, mortgage, or use the land as collateral.

Those who favor private ownership criticize FDRE for constitutional land ownership by the state. Although I know from experience how it feels and what it means to own property, for several reasons I find it difficult to take a stand on this issue when it comes to Ethiopian peasants. Ethiopian peasants have been using the old-style plow method of farming in subsistence agriculture for centuries. Thus they lack the resources and technical skills to be on their own. They need governmental support and backing until they attain self-sufficiency. The support that the government currently provides through land registration and certification guarantees tenure security. The package that comes with it, such as loan and technical support as well as the liberty to sell their produce at market value, promotes efficiency and further empowers farmers to become self-reliant. On the other hand, issues associated with good governance and corruption make it difficult to have confidence in the applicability of the constitution. Research is required to study who benefits the most out of the current policy.

From my experience as a homeowner, both in Ethiopia and in the United States, I find it confusing to understand how government ownership of land and a land-lease system works in Ethiopia. It seems to me this means a property has two owners, with the government owning the land and the homeowner owning the construction. I suppose the land-lease fee could be considered tantamount to a property tax, but would I feel secure if the co-owner of my property was not even a fixed entity? I would be concerned that the situation might change with a shift in government position, policy, or bureaucracy.

From my analysis of ownership and property rights in the United States, I have come to the conclusion that the government of Ethiopia does not benefit as much from a land-lease system as it would from private ownership. In the United States, private ownership is of mutual benefit to the owner and to the government. A property owner, either residential or commercial, maintains, improves, develops, and makes profitable his investment, and the government ensures good governance and the rule of law which make situations conducive for every person to succeed. The government benefits as well from the collection of property taxes, mortgage taxes, and sales taxes on home improvement, maintenance, development, etc.

Religious Discrimination

After the fall of the monarchy, religious discrimination assumed various forms. Protestant/evangelical Christians were severely persecuted by the Derg government for more than a decade. Many evangelical Christians and religious leaders were arrested, tortured, and killed. Several church buildings were closed. Religious education was removed from school curriculum, and Bible schools were closed.

All that changed immediately after the Derg was overthrown by the EPRDF in 1991. Under the new government, Christians were granted religious freedom to worship freely, evangelize, build churches, and perform all other religious activities. However, persecution of evangelical Christians continues to raise its head, although legislation bans all kinds of discrimination and guarantees religious equality. Article 25 of the constitution states:

> All persons are equal before the law and are entitled without any discrimination to the equal protection of the law. The law shall guarantee to the persons equal and effective protection without discrimination on grounds of race, color, sex, language, religion, political or other opinion, national or social origin, wealth, birth, or other status.

Just as the Oromos were called *Galla* in the past, Protestant Christians have been given the name *P'ent'e*, from the word *Pentecostal*. They are also called *tsere Mariam* (anti-Mary) and still face persecution from some Orthodox clergies and local followers. Since Orthodox Christians are in the majority, oftentimes persecution is not reported.

On some occasions, Orthodox parents kick out from their homes children who convert to Protestant/evangelical Christianity. There have been instances where Protestant/evangelical churches have been burnt down and evangelical Christians murdered. The dead bodies of evangelical Christians have sometimes been taken out of their graves and left in the open field to be eaten by hyenas. Since the Orthodox Church still owns most graveyards, evangelical Christians have few options for burying their dead.

Let me share with you three examples to show you the type of persecution faced by evangelical Christians in Ethiopia. The first story is the story of a woman named Ayantu Hunde from Bethel MekaneYesus in Gulelle, Addis Ababa. This woman started a Protestant (Mekane Yesus) congregation ten miles from Addis Ababa in Sululta, Gidda Woreda, in the Showa region of the national regional state of Oromia. Followers of Orthodox Christianity immediately began persecuting the group of evangelical believers by looting, throwing stones at their property, beating them, and even shooting them. The corpse of an old woman named Workie Woldegiorgs was removed from her grave and thrown outside. Her family reburied it, but it was removed a second time and finally eaten by hyenas. The persecution intensified when a man named Mengistu was shot, and eight families fled the area.

The second example involved a farmer who owned a minibus and a grain-grinding mill but lost them in the persecution. His minibus was thrown into a ditch and his grain-grinding mill set afire. The criminals were brought to justice and sentenced. A court verdict ordered the criminals to pay for the victim's belongings. Since they could not afford to satisfy the judgment, they asked the man for forgiveness, assuring him they would respect his constitutional right to preach the gospel. As a born-again Christian, the man who lost his minibus and grain-grinding mill forgave them in return for the freedom to preach the gospel without persecution. According to the 2007 national census, 94.34 percent of Sabata inhabitants practiced Ethiopian Orthodox Christianity, while 2.76 percent were Protestant, and 2.07 percent were Muslim. The number of Protestants reaching 2.76 percent could be the result of this legal protection.

The third example was a crime committed against a woman evangelist from Mekane Yesus Seminary in Makanisa, Addis Ababa. While she was ministering to students at the

Mekane Yesus Seminary in Afaan Oromo (Oromo language), an officer outrageously screamed at her not to preach in that language and forcefully kicked her in her lower abdomen. The woman, being two months pregnant at the time, fainted and was immediately taken to the hospital. However, the pregnancy ended in miscarriage, and the woman remained unconscious in the hospital for two weeks.

Angry students petitioned against the criminal offense. The man who assaulted the young woman unsuccessfully tried to take advantage of "no arrest" protection as a member of the ruling political party. Unfortunately, the man disappeared after being bailed out of jail.

Corruption

Out of 176 countries on the 2012 Corruption Perceptions Index of Transparency International, Ethiopia ranks 113, with "1" being the best, with a corruption perception index of 33.[65] Presently the government of Ethiopia is vigorously fighting against corruption under the leadership of Ethiopia's Prime Minister Haile-Mariam Desalegn, and the story is being reported through many media outlets. The government launched its biggest crackdown against corruption on May 1, 2013, when authorities arrested more than fifty people, including government officials, businessmen, a minister, and both the director general and his deputy of the Revenue and Customs Authority. Other officials were apprehended on suspicion of tax evasion.

Mr. Alemayehu Atomsa, the President of Oromia Regional State of Ethiopia, actually started cleaning corruption from his administration immediately after he took office in September 2010. Crackdown on corruption was carried out throughout Oromiya in which several corrupt administrators and those involved were arrested. Others lost their political-party membership. Just few months later, Mr. Alemayehu Atomsa became seriously ill and was in a foreign hospital from 2011 to early 2012. He is still suffering ill health. According to media sources, he is presently in foreign hospital for treatment. It is encouraging to see that these two great leaders have the courage to live-out their faith and do what is morally and ethically right, but their task is not an easy one.

I am not sure how the government would be able to discover corruption committed in a less obvious, more careful manner. Corruption among FDRE officials and their associates has followed the pattern of the monarchy elites and feudal lords. I am amazed that corrupt officials do not seem to learn from the experience of corrupt monarchy elites and feudal lords that the reverse can be true of the saying *"Sishom yalbelabet sishar yikochewal"* meaning "one who doesn't eat when appointed will regret when deposed"). *IPS News* posted that these arrests have highlighted how corruption has insinuated itself into the higher levels of officialdom. This is what they were told by Mr. Berhanu Assefa of the Federal Ethics and Anti-Corruption Commission of Ethiopia:

> Corruption is a serious problem we are facing. We now see that corruption is occurring in higher places than we had previously expected. Areas vulnerable to corruption are land administration, tax and revenue, the justice system, telecommunications, land procurement, licensing areas and the finance sector. (http://www.ipsnews.net/2013/06/examining-the-depths-of-ethiopias-corruption/)

Lessons Learned

So far we have seen the complexity of leadership with three different forms of government in Ethiopia: (1) the aristocracy, (2) the socialist system, and (3) federalism. Western countries, including the United States, are not immune to the complexities found in government leaderships because human beings are always human beings, regardless of their geographic locations. Whatever ideology a leader follows, what matters most is how that leader relates to the founder and initiator of all leadership—God. Only those leaders who cherish and follow the moral principles set by God's system of government and standard of justice can leave a legacy for a better future because it is the root from which all right things in human life flow. Those principles can be found in the words of the wisest man on earth, King Solomon:

> The fear of the Lord is the beginning of wisdom, and the knowledge of the Holy One is understanding.
> —Proverbs 9:10

> Do not be wise in your own eyes; fear the Lord and depart from evil.
> —Proverbs 3:7

Sadly, King Solomon's wisdom did not save his kingdom from being divided when he himself broke God's commandments. From his experience and history, we learn the misery and damage caused by leaders who are wise in their own eyes and who fail to uphold God's standard of morality. Just close your eyes for a few minutes and think about such leaders in modern history: Adolf Hitler of Germany (1889–1945), Joseph Stalin of Russia (1878–1953), Benito Mussolini of Italy (1883–1945), Francisco Franco of Spain (1892–1975), and Idi Amin of Uganda (1925–2003).

The past is gone, but what have we learned from it towards shaping the future? This book is the result of my learning from what I went through. After it was all over, I asked myself why truth and justice prevailed in the tribulations I faced with the harshest government, the Derg, while the experience was not the same with the relatively democratic government, the

FDRE. The answer is that the more we move away from the principles that empower us with wisdom and victory, the more we regress.

As I mentioned earlier, I was so consumed with handling everything by myself that I did not take the time to seek the wise counsel of divine authority. I should have at least remembered the self-evaluation technique that I learned during my training of trainers at the ILO International Center for Advanced Technical and Vocational Training in Turin/Italy. During the training, they had us (trainees) give presentations and videotaped us while we were giving the presentations. Then they had us watch that video and evaluate ourselves in front of the group. At the end, they had the group evaluate our self-evaluation. That was a very interesting experience to keep me alert, but I didn't remember to use that either.

In the end, I realized that my spiritual life had deteriorated to the point that I dropped what I was called to do and settled for a wrong career. Because I did not make time to listen to God the way I had in the past, I lost focus and continued doing whatever I thought was right. Not remembering the tribulations and extreme hardship I had faced in my work with WSRA in Ethiopia prior to moving to the United States in 1994, I returned to Ethiopia in 2007 with an adoption agency, Better Future Adoption Services (BFAS), and put myself through hell.

The bad thing was that I lingered in my poor decision, boasting that I was not a quitter, still thinking that the devil was attacking me for serving God. But the voice that instructed me in the 1980s to take one step forward was also warning me that I would not be left alone to remain playing small. As Nelson Mandela said, "There is no passion to be found playing small—in settling for a life that is less than the one you are capable of living." God, who knows our weaknesses, had yet to close the wrong door, BFAS, to stop me from settling for a life that is less than the one I was predestined for.

Unfortunately, I never recognized that as a final warning to alert me to my own blind spot. Instead, I became increasingly bitter, thinking that God had not shown me justice and had let me down. By the grace of God, I finally realized that the number of problems I faced and the resulting trauma I went through with BFAS were the jolts I needed to take up the assignment the Lord had given me long ago—writing books and serving Him through His institutions and with His people. The troubles that I went through refined me, shaped me, and brought me to where God wanted me to be and to do what He called me to do. I discovered the truth of these statements:

Take away the dross from the silver, and there comes out a vessel for the smith.

—Proverbs 2:4

We can complain because rose bushes have thorns, or rejoice because thorn bushes have roses.

—President Abraham Lincoln

After it was all said and done, I picked up the call that I had received twenty-four years earlier to write books and began my first one: *The Secret to Finishing Well: Quest for Authentic Leadership.*

My next service is a bigger one: building the capacity of faith-based organizations that are committed to serving the whole person by meeting both physical and spiritual needs. When I was in Ethiopia in April 2013, the Ethiopian Evangelical Church Mekane Yesus (EECMY), Western Synod, Nedjo Parish signed a partnership agreement with me to sustain their programs and services in Nedjo. Because of a lack of funding, they could no longer run their facilities, which included a school (First through eighth grade). former missionaries' residences, a guest house, girls' and boys' hostels, and a clinic. I did not even need to raise funds to start my new assignment: building the capacity of faith-based organizations. I am using revenue from the property I owned in Addis Ababa and trusting God for the rest. The God who asks us to "give them something to eat" (Matt. 14:16) is also a God of multiplication, and He blesses to abundance what we bring to Him for service to others (Matt. 14:18–21). I am not my own, and all that I own is not mine, but His, for all good gifts are from above. He is in control; my life is in His hands, and I am not to worry about tomorrow.

The lessons I learned apply to government leaders as well. We all know that there is no perfect leader and no perfect government in the world. Problems are inevitable, and we all will face them in life in one way or another. The best thing to do is to learn from the past and draw the best out of it in order to make the future better.

The problems I pointed out in my discussion of Ethiopian government leadership exist and linger in the rest of the world as well. Even the United States, a nation with strong anticorruption safeguards such as the new Dodd-Frank corporate whistle-blower protections and a nonprofit organization named Transparency International that serves as an effective anticorruption watchdog, is not free from corruption. Discrimination and racism also exist in the United States, a country that is home to all races of the world. But the difference lies in the principles followed by the leaders in promoting the rule of law and justice. Let me share with you my personal experience of how principles with a moral root differ from the ones with a traditional root.

My youngest son, who came to the United States at age seven, started driving when he was sixteen years old. On several occasions, the police stopped him. The resulting charges for which I accompanied my son to juvenile court helped me to see the reality of the blame game surrounding racism and discrimination.

One night my son gave a ride to a friend. While driving, he saw another friend in a BMW speeding past and started competing with him, not knowing that a police officer was pursuing the other car for speeding. When my son was exiting the freeway, the officer followed him instead and arrested him on felony charges of fleeing a police officer and speeding. In my son's court hearing, the officer who charged him was truthful during cross-examination. The head of the juvenile detention center also gave witness that he found my son a well-mannered and well-disciplined young man and recommended his immediate release. I could have blamed the entire situation on racism instead of going to court with an attorney who represented my son, but I did not. In sharing this story, I am trying to stress the fact that the justice system does its job, and we parents have the responsibility to do our jobs in raising our children right and in allowing the system to work in regards to mistakes and wrongdoing.

The moral principles by which the Founding Fathers framed our Constitution remain strong to guide our leadership and to help correct its mistakes. As President Ronald Reagan once stated: "There are no easy answers, but there are simple answers. We must have the courage to do what is morally right." Let me briefly cite one example.

Although the United States Constitution banned the importation of new African slaves in 1808, slavery and racial segregation persisted for many years, giving birth to prominent civil-rights activists such as Rosa Parks and Dr. Martin Luther King Jr. To correct the mistake of slavery required the fighting of the American Civil War (1861–1865), in which more than six hundred thousand soldiers died and most of the infrastructure of the slave-holding South was destroyed. Finally, the Thirteenth Amendment of the United States Constitution was ratified on December 6, 1865, abolishing slavery in this country. [66] Furthermore, years later the US Congress named the African American activist Rosa Parks "the first lady of civil rights" and "the mother of the freedom movement" for her action against racial segregation. She received several accolades, including the Presidential Medal of Freedom, the highest honor given by the US executive branch; the Congressional Gold Medal, the highest award given by the US legislative branch; the Spingarn Medal, the NAACP's highest award; and the prestigious Martin Luther King Jr. Award.

From earlier statements I have made, you might think I make leadership too religious, and you might disagree with my stance. But the truth of the matter is, leadership *is* religious, whether we like it or not, as can be seen from the evidence I presented in chapter 1. Authorities who rule over or lead their subjects are appointed and controlled by God. Even Pilate was given the authority to fulfill the Jewish people's wishes and have Jesus crucified. Here are several Bible passages dealing with authority and earthly power:

> Jesus answered, "You would have no power over me if it were not given to you from above. Therefore the one who handed me over to you is guilty of a greater sin."
>
> —John 19:11

> Let every soul be subject to the governing authorities. For there is no authority except from God, and the authorities that exist are appointed by God.
>
> —Romans 13:1

> Therefore submit yourselves to every ordinance of man for the Lord's sake, whether to the king as supreme, or to governors, as to those who are sent by him for the punishment of evildoers and for the praise of those who do good.
>
> —1 Peter 2:13–14

You might also ask, "What about those authorities who cling to power through rigged elections or fraud?" My answer is that the just God allows it because He wants them to pay the price and also because their subjects need further refinement. As I pointed out in chapter 8, Colonel Mengistu was appointed as God's rod of anger. The London peace talks between the Derg and the TPLF guerillas that I mentioned in chapter 12 were not successful because the Derg's criminal officials were not exempt from God's anger. During my study tour in Central America in the summer of 1993, I witnessed how well peace talks between the Central American governments and the guerillas worked there. It was not that way for Colonel Mengistu's regime because those officials had to face justice. I can say with assurance that no one could have punished the evil deeds of the monarchy and the ungodly like that man, God's rod of anger, did. Likewise, no person could have punished the Derg's evildoers more so than the FDRE did. Nonetheless, the cycle must end.

Conclusion

So what did the Ethiopian government learn from its past mistakes towards building a better Ethiopia? To err is human, because no one on earth is perfect; but to remain aloof to mistakes is inhuman, to my understanding. My other question is, where does the United States stand in regards to the moral principles on which this country was established and through which it has achieved such success as the world's superpower?

From what we have covered so far, we can see that the fate of a given nation depends solely on the principles upon which that nation was built and the motives of those who govern it. God created in abundance everything that human beings need to enjoy life. After creating humanity, He gave us instructions and laws by which we can make our world a happy place to live:

> He has showed you, O man, what is good. And what does the LORD require of you? To act justly and to love mercy and to walk humbly with your God.
>
> — Micah 6:8

But much of the world's leadership (including priests) have misused their freedom and manipulated God's plan to suit their selfish desires, exposing the innocent to much misery. This is clearly seen in Hosea 4:1–2, 7–9:

> Hear the word of the Lord, you Israelites, because the Lord has a charge to bring against you who live in the land: "There is no faithfulness, no love, no acknowledgement of God in the land. There is only cursing, lying and murder, stealing and adultery. . . . The more the priests increased, the more they sinned against me; they exchanged their glory for something disgraceful. They feed on the sins of my people and relish their wickedness. Like people, like priests. I will punish both of them for their ways and repay them for their deeds."

Taking into account the evidence used in this book, I believe American leadership needs to reexamine its responsibility as a model of democracy (government of the people, by the people, for the people) towards shaping the world's leadership according to God's initial plan. There is no greater evidence to prove the validity of America's model of democracy than the cultural diversity of the people who continually immigrate to the United States from all over the world. It is an undeniable fact that those who leave their home countries and immigrate to the United States are attracted by its leadership principles that promote good governance, the rule of law, human rights, liberty, equality, and justice for all.

America's democratic system combines the rule of law with moral values and thus builds confidence in its government. As statesman, congressman, and Senator Robert C. Winthrop said in 1852:

> All societies must be governed in some way or other. The less they may have stringent state government, the more they must have individual self-government. The less they rely on public law or physical force, the more they must rely on private moral restraint. Men, in a word, must necessarily be controlled either by a power within them, or by a power without them; either by the Word of God, or by the strong arm of man.

I believe that the United States of America has a call and responsibility as a world leader to promote unbiased democracy in countries that suffer repressive regimes. I say "unbiased democracy" to caution against mistakes that could occur in promoting democracy. Mutual understanding and compromise should be taken into consideration, depending on the complexity of the situation, and promoting our national interest should never be at the expense of those who are hurting. The Bible is quite clear about that:

> He who justifies the wicked, and he who condemns the just, both of them alike are an abomination to the Lord.
> —Proverbs 17:15–16

God hears the cry of the oppressed and judges accordingly when those entrusted to protect them fail to do so:

For He will deliver the needy when he cries, the poor also, and [him] who has no helper.

—Psalm 72:12

He will bring justice to the poor of the people; He will save the children of the needy, and will break in pieces the oppressor.

—Psalm 72:4

Please do not misunderstand me, thinking that I am blindly praising America as a model of democracy. My purpose is neither to praise America nor to condemn the rest of the world; rather, I am merely sharing my evidence-based experiences as input towards shaping global leadership. I leave the judgment to you. My extensive experience with governments following different ideologies and their resulting foreign relations, as well as my visits to Central America, Europe, China, and a few parts of Africa, have offered me the privilege to collect substantial evidence towards my assessment. From the experiences that I have shared with you, I think you can see how important it is to discern what to do in any kind of intervention rather than doing nothing because of skepticism.

The Chinese government knew what it was doing when it welcomed the cheap-labor deal of the West, while Western companies were unaware of the effect of using their individual liberty to outsource so many services. China grabbed the outsourcing as an opportunity to advance its nation and promote its economic growth. Today China is the main investor in and promoter of Africa in general and the major accelerator of Ethiopia's economic growth in particular. It plays a leading role in Ethiopia in the sectors of the state-run infrastructure, investment, and trade and is the main source of its economic growth.

I am aware that the United States still maintains the long ties that it established with Ethiopia in 1952, but those should be at least equal to that of the latecomer China. As I mentioned in chapter 3, the United States, through its Point Four program in the 1950s, established the Alemaya Agricultural College (currently university); the Jimma Technical High School, the first of its kind Agricultural Extension Services; and the Debre Zeit Research Center, thereby establishing a strong foundation on which to sustain the country's progress. But why didn't American agricultural companies take advantage of the US government's longstanding contributions and invest in Ethiopian agriculture? Who else would do it better? I assure you that Ethiopians have great love for Americans and welcome them because of the bond established through the long-time ties. In my opinion, since investment in sectors like telecommunications, banking, and logistics are not open to foreign investors, the agricultural sector would be the best option for American investment.

One thing that I think is important and would like to comment on is the need for America to work on its public relations in Ethiopia. When the nation was mourning the loss of its great prime minister Meles Zenawi, something happened that reminded me of the importance of gaining visibility for good work. A woman who was being supported through USAID (the president's emergency plan for AIDS relief) was bitterly crying, "I lost my father!" though she was a beneficiary of American aid. USAID also funded life-changing programs in agriculture, nutrition, food aid, basic education, and health-care initiatives, for which the ruling party was applauded. Little was mentioned about the contributions of USAID, its presence hardly acknowledged except for the sign in front of its premises. (To see what USAID does in Ethiopia, visit their website at: http://ethiopia.usaid.gov/). In addition, on my trips to Ethiopia, I have not heard or seen anything publicizing America's long-time contributions to agriculture in Ethiopia. I believe, however, that the source of blessing needs to be properly acknowledged, because even God demands praise for what He does.

Despite my confidence in United States leadership based on the principles by which this nation achieved success, I am concerned about the threats that I see today. Those who use democracy as a masquerade to exercise their freedom wrongly are more vocal in blinding the vast majority from recognizing the danger. The idea of tolerance has gradually become one sided and is slowly displacing morals instead of maintaining the balance between the two.

When moral values decline, however, evil deeds rise because the reasoning of good and evil comes from the fear of the Lord. As President Theodore Roosevelt remarked, "To educate a man in mind but not in morals is to educate a menace to society." If that is true, then why do so many people today regard moral education as outdated? Take the issue of gun control, for example. In my opinion, gun control will never work unless there are moral values that control the hands that pull the trigger. In the absence of a gun, the hands that pull the trigger can just as easily use a different object unless moral restraint is present in the first place.

Using our freedom wrongly results in doing harm to ourselves and leading our government in the wrong direction:

> You say, "I am allowed to do anything"—but not everything is good for you. You say, "I am allowed to do anything"—but not everything is beneficial.
> —1 Corinthians 10:23

I find it hard to understand how behavior that is clearly against nature can be accepted by so many as natural. For example, it is natural to use the various parts of our bodies for their intended purposes. Imagine what would happen if you tried to use your arms for walking or your nose for drinking. Yet that is exactly what some are doing in accepting homosexuality as a "natural" alternative to heterosexuality. I am not speaking against anyone's God-given freedom to do whatever he or she chooses, but rather, I am trying to alert you to the consequences of ignoring the root cause of a problem.

If you examine the *do* and *don't* words in the Bible, you will discover that the *don't* word is always a warning against something that harms, destroys, or kills, while the *do* word is a command for good things. In Romans 1, the Bible speaks of the dangers that threaten all of us, heterosexuals and homosexuals alike. Let's start first by looking at the great danger in being given up and over by God to uncleanness, vile passions, and a debased mind:

> Although they knew God, they did not glorify Him as God, nor were thankful, but became futile in their thoughts, and their foolish hearts were darkened. Professing to be wise, they became fools. Therefore God also gave them up to *uncleanness,* in the lusts of their hearts, to dishonor their bodies among themselves. . . . For this reason God gave them up to *vile passions*. For even their women exchanged the natural use for what is against nature. Likewise also the men, leaving the natural use of the woman, burned in their lust for one another, men with men committing what is shameful, and receiving in themselves the penalty of their error which was due. And even as they did not like to retain God in their knowledge, God gave them over to a *debased mind,* to do those things which are not fitting.
> —Romans 1:21–22, 24–28, emphasis added

The chapter then goes on to list the sins that all of us face and the dangers that go with them:

241

... being filled with all unrighteousness, sexual immorality, wickedness, covetousness, maliciousness; full of envy, murder, strife, deceit, evil-mindedness; they are whisperers, backbiters, haters of God, violent, proud, boasters, inventors of evil things, disobedient to parents, undiscerning, untrustworthy, unloving, unforgiving, unmerciful; who, knowing the righteous judgment of God, that those who practice such things are deserving of death, not only do the same but also approve of those who practice them.

—Romans 1:29–31

Many argue that homosexuals are just "that way," but according to the verses above, we are all "that way" as a result of whatever God gives us up and over to because of our wickedness. On our own, it is difficult to come out from any besetting sin, but if we are willing to turn to God and honor Him, He is ready to forgive us and turn us the right way. This is the best solution because merely treating the symptoms brings only temporary relief and happiness and does not remove the internal discomfort and eternal danger.

Let's also take a look at homosexuality in the context of nature and outside of religion. The United States Declaration of Independence is centered on the idea of natural rights and individual liberty. In our day, however, the misuse of freedom is making individual liberty superior to natural rights. I ask you, is it justifiable to elevate individual liberty above natural rights on the grounds of preserving human rights? Are we not violating a child's natural urge for a father and a mother when we impose on that helpless child same-sex parenthood? When we endorse same-sex marriage, are we not preventing procreation and consequently reducing America's population? Don't we have a responsibility to prevent the resultant health consequences that claim many lives and incur high medical cost?

The Center for Disease Control (CDC) finds that gay, bisexual, and other men who have sex with men (MSM) represent approximately 2 percent of the US population, yet gay and bisexual men are more severely affected by HIV than any other group in the United States. In 2009, MSM accounted for 61 percent of all new HIV infections. In 2010, MSM accounted for 63 percent of all new HIV infections, and MSM with a history of injection drug use (MSM-IDU) accounted for an additional 3 percent of new infections. That same year, MSM ages thirteen to twenty-four accounted for 72 percent of new HIV infections among all persons in that age group and 30 percent of new infections among all MSM. At the end of 2010, an estimated 489,121 (56 percent) persons living with an HIV diagnosis in the United States were MSM or MSM-IDU[67]

I also ask, are we not violating the unborn child's right to life when we promote abortion? As a person from a developing country, where the options that exist in America do not exist, I find abortion inacceptable except for life-threatening reasons. Just imagine what the parent in particular and the world in general is missing when a woman gets rid of an unborn child.

I have read articles asserting that the Founding Fathers of America were not Christians and using that as an excuse for downplaying the importance of Christian values today. But how can anyone deny the role that religion played in the American Revolution, when the colonists themselves felt that the revolution was a righteous cause justified in the sight of God? Those colonists were men and women of deep conviction who fled religious persecution in Europe in the seventeenth century to practice their own form of religion in the new world they eventually formed. [68] The tyrants whom they fled used religion in the wrong way to retain absolute power; however, the Founding Fathers took maximum care in formulating the United States Constitution to ensure religious freedom and the separation of church and state, saying, "Congress shall make no law respecting an establishment of religion, or prohibiting the free exercise thereof."

My focus, though, is not on an individual's view of God or religion, because it is every person's God-given right to choose. Not everyone believed in Jesus when He was on this earth, for that matter. Even His own people rejected Him, and one of His twelve disciples, Judas, betrayed him for the equivalent of thirty dollars. What I am trying to do is draw attention to the standard set by the founder of leadership, the almighty God who controls the universe and everything in it.

Based on the facts, I believe the Founding Fathers tried to be neutral leaders of people with different backgrounds in giving their personal views on issues involving religion. Here are some examples of the moral values underlying the principles by which they established this great nation:

- "Of all the dispositions and habits which lead to political prosperity, religion and morality are indispensable supports." (President George Washington)
- "Whatever may be conceded to the influence of refined education on minds of peculiar structure, reason and experience both forbid us to expect that national morality can prevail in exclusion of religious principle." (President George Washington)
- "To the distinguished character of a patriot, it should be our highest glory to add the most distinguished character of a Christian." (President George Washington)
- President George Washington proclaimed a day of public thanksgiving and prayer on February 19, 1795.
- "My concern is not whether God is on our side; my greatest concern is to be on God's side, for God is always right." (President Abraham Lincoln)
- On November 1, 1800, when President John Adams arrived in the new capital city to take up residence in

the White House, he wrote to his wife from its damp, unfinished rooms, "Before I end my letter, I pray heaven to bestow the best of blessings on this house and all that shall hereafter inhabit it. May none but honest and wise men ever rule under this roof."

- Congress proclaimed national days of thanksgiving and humiliation, fasting, and prayer at least twice a year throughout the Civil War. On March 30, 1863, President Abraham Lincoln signed a congressional resolution calling for a day of fasting and prayer.

- The annual National Day of Prayer was fixed as the first Thursday of May through a bill signed into law by President Ronald Reagan on May 5, 1998. Here is his comment: "On our National Day of Prayer, then, we join together as people of many faiths to petition God to show us His mercy and His love, to heal our weariness and uphold our hope, that we might live ever mindful of His justice and thankful of his blessings."

- President Thomas Jefferson's emphasis on natural rights and individual liberty in the Declaration of Independence relates the content of the document to the biblical provisions for all human beings. The document begins with a statement: "All men are created equal, that they are endowed by their Creator with certain unalienable rights, that among these are life, liberty, and the pursuit of happiness." Inscriptions on the walls of the Jefferson Memorial in the nation's capital affirm this:

> God who gave us life gave us liberty. Can the liberties of a nation be secure when we have removed a conviction that these liberties are the gift of God? Indeed I tremble for my country when I reflect that God is just, that his justice cannot sleep forever. Commerce between master and slave is despotism. Nothing is more certainly

written in the book of fate than that these people are to be free. Establish a law for educating the common people. This it is the business of the state and on a general plan.

- In the closing statement of his State of the Union speech on January 6, 1941, President Franklin D. Roosevelt described four essential human freedoms that the United States hoped to extend to all individuals: (1) freedom of speech and expression, (2) freedom of every person to worship God in his own way, (3) freedom from want, and (4) freedom from fear.

With all that as background, why do we want to drift from the principles that underlie the very truths that brought forth such success and wealth for America, making it the most powerful country on earth? Do we have any reason to doubt our nation's motto "In God we trust," which appears on all US currencies, and to turn away from putting our trust in God? Although some may be offended by this motto, God has not failed America so far for acknowledging its trust in Him. I remember when I was in Sweden in early 1991 that a Swedish anthropologist was angered when I said to him the US dollar would remain the world's strongest currency because of the "In God we trust" inscription that appears on it. He screamed back, "No, it is not! It is in gold we trust. Americans love money!"—as if he didn't like money for himself. I calmly replied, "It is the result of what it says, whether you accept or not," but he kept on screaming, "It is in gold we trust!"

Has America fared better since we began the shift away from God? Let us remember Psalm 33:11: "Blessed is the nation whose God is the Lord." Let us also remember President Abraham Lincoln's call "to recognize the sublime truth, announced in the Holy Scriptures and proven by all history, that those nations only are blessed whose God is the

Lord." President Lincoln heeded the awakening call of the American Civil War crisis and acknowledged God as the only power, saying, "I have been driven many times upon my knees by the overwhelming conviction that I had nowhere else to go."

Some of the incidents involving Hurricane Sandy, which hit the northeastern coast on Monday, October 29, 2012, remind me of how our reliance on technology sometimes takes the place of our reliance on God. The Saturday before the storm struck, I heard about the devastating forecast from a prayer group that I joined on teleconference. The prayer group asked all of us to pray about the approaching hurricane. I wish a national call to prayer had been announced with the forecast, but of course that did not happen. After the storm, I heard one of the survivors giving thanks to technology, with no mention of God, for sparing her life. Although the storm caused great damage and much loss, it was an answer to prayer that it was only a category 1 storm and the worst did not happen.

So then, can America remain a powerful nation and maintain its leadership as a promoter of democracy? I would like to quote Mr. Charles Carroll, signer of the Declaration of Independence:

> Without morals a republic cannot subsist any length of time; they therefore who are decrying the Christian religion, whose morality is so sublime and pure . . . are undermining the solid foundation of morals, the best security for the duration of free governments.

It is my belief that America was called by God and blessed with a good start to exemplify God's initial leadership style. God promised blessings to all those who choose to serve His purpose, but included the word *if*, which determines the outcome. As an example, notice the *if* word that accompanied

God's promise to King Solomon of Israel, the wisest leader
in history:

> But if you or your sons at all turn from following Me,
> and do not keep My commandments and My statutes
> which I have set before you, but go and serve other
> gods and worship them, then I will cut off Israel from
> the land which I have given them; and this house
> which I have consecrated for My name I will cast out
> of My sight. Israel will be a proverb and a byword
> among all peoples. And as for this house, which is
> exalted, everyone who passes by it will be astonished
> and will hiss, and say, "Why has the Lord done thus
> to this land and to this house?"
>
> —1 Kings 9:6–8

What God said came to pass when King Solomon failed
to heed the *if* warning. Israel was cut off from their land
but eventually returned to it in accordance with God's
promise of mercy:

> Then say to them, "Thus says the Lord God: 'Surely I
> will take the children of Israel from among the nations,
> wherever they have gone, and will gather them from
> every side and bring them into their own land.'"
>
> —Ezekiel 37:21

Self-sufficiency gives rise to pride, and one major threat
to success is rejecting God's power and turning to pride.
Deuteronomy 8:1–18 lists the abundant blessings God had
for Israel, but God also warned them against pride, lest they
say in their hearts, "My power and the might of my hand have
gained me this wealth" (v. 17). Self-sufficiency has caused
many of us to say that our power and the might of our hands
have gained us success and wealth. Oftentimes we forget that

our lives are in the hands of our creator; we have no guarantee of tomorrow, nor do we have control over circumstances and nature. In His goodness, God sends messages to alert us about our wrong ways, but we often pay no attention.

In days past, our nation listened carefully to God's awakening calls. In turn, this helped us to pay attention to and deal with our blind spot. The way President Lincoln responded to God's awakening calls is a good example:

> When I left home to take this chair of state, I requested my countrymen to pray for me. I was not then a Christian. When my son died, the severest trial of my life, I was not a Christian. But, when I went to Gettysburg and looked upon the graves of our dead heroes who had fallen in defense of their country, I then and there consecrated myself to Christ. Yes, I do love Jesus. [69]

Here is an excerpt from President Lincoln's proclamation appointing a National Day of Prayer during the Civil War:

> And whereas it is the duty of nations, as well as of men, to own their dependence upon the overruling power of God, to confess their sins and transgressions, in humble sorrow, yet with assured hope that genuine repentance will lead to mercy and pardon; and to recognize the sublime truth, announced in the Holy Scriptures and proven by all history, that those nations only are blessed whose God is the Lord.
>
> We have been the recipients of the choicest bounties of heaven. We have been preserved, these many years, in peace and prosperity. We have grown in numbers, wealth and power, as no other nation has ever grown. But we have forgotten God. We have forgotten the gracious hand which preserved us in

peace, and multiplied and enriched and strengthened us; and we have vainly imagined, in the deceitfulness of our hearts, that all these blessings were produced by some superior wisdom and virtue of our own. Intoxicated with unbroken success, we have become too self-sufficient to feel the necessity of redeeming and preserving grace, too proud to pray to the God that made us!

It behooves us then, to humble ourselves before the offended Power, to confess our national sins, and to pray for clemency and forgiveness.

Those chosen by God need to be led by Him and acknowledge Him as the leader and provider of all good things:

And you shall remember the LORD your God, for it is He who gives you power to get wealth, that He may establish His covenant which He swore to your fathers, as it is this day. Then it shall be, if you by any means forget the LORD your God, and follow other gods, and serve them and worship them, I testify against you this day that you shall surely perish.
—Deuteronomy 8:18–20

Money is the god of our time, and the love of money is turning many people away from God. The Bible warns us that a servant cannot serve two masters (Luke 16:3) and that the love of money is the root of all evil: "For the love of money is a root of all kinds of evil, for which some have strayed from the faith in their greediness, and pierced themselves through with many sorrows" (1 Tim. 6:10). Please note that it is the *love* of money, not money itself.

America needs to heed the *if* word of God's promise of mercy upon which President Lincoln based his prayer on behalf of the American people:

If My people who are called by My name will humble themselves, and pray and seek My face, and turn from their wicked ways, then I will hear from heaven, and will forgive their sin and heal their land.
—2 Chronicles 7:14

There are many Americans today who still esteem the principles of the Founding Fathers and lift up this nation in prayer and humility before God. That raises my hope and fills me with optimism about America's future. In Genesis 18, Abraham asked God: "Suppose there were fifty righteous within the city; would You also destroy the place and not spare it for the fifty righteous that were in it? (v. 24). To that God replied, "If I find in Sodom fifty righteous within the city, then I will spare all the place for their sakes" (v. 26). Abraham continued petitioning all the way down to ten men, and God replied, "I will not destroy it for the sake of ten" (v. 32).

As I mentioned above, there are many who pray for this nation, and the focus of their prayers is not for material gain that vanishes like vapor. It is rather to get the nation back on track with the tested principles on which our forefathers established this nation and by which we will be sustained as a world leader. Herein lies the secret to finishing well.

The Pew Research Center's Forum on Religion and Public Life finds that Christianity has declined in Western countries in the last century, while it has risen in the rest of the world. The number of Christians in Europe decreased from 66.3 percent in 1910 to 25.9 percent in 2010, while that of Sub-Saharan Africa rose from 1.4 percent (9 percent of the world's Christian population) in 1910 to 23.6 percent (63 percent of the world's Christian population) in 2010. That of the Asia-Pacific area rose from 4.5 percent (3 percent of the world's Christian population) to 13.1 percent (7 percent of the world's Christian population). The research also reports that Christianity is becoming a global religion.

251

Unfortunately, Christianity is regarded as outdated in most parts of Europe, and God is left out of their affairs. This, I think, contributed to the European financial crisis. It is my wish and prayer that Europe will take the crisis as a wake-up call to return to the very God who prospered them in the years when they acknowledged and trusted Him.

Today the Netherlands is the most secularized country in the world, liberalizing abortion, homosexuality, euthanasia, and prostitution. When I traveled to the Netherlands in 1993, I asked a woman whom I knew to take me to church on Sunday. I was in Den Haag, and she took me to a Calvinist church. On that visit, I realized that Christianity was dying there. There were many empty churches just a few blocks apart from each other. I asked my friend what was going to happen to those empty churches, and she said many would be demolished. Sadly, many other church buildings are being converted to nightclubs and secular businesses. Though Calvinism was once the state religion in the Netherlands and dominated all other denominations, it and all other Christian groups are diminishing.

When I traveled to Sweden in February 1991, just a few months before the fall of the Ethiopian Communist regime, I visited a missionary who had been my music teacher in my early life. She took me to her church and asked me to speak to the congregation. Here is what I said to them: "You brought the good news to my country and gave us Jesus. We tested His goodness, and it strengthened us to endure persecution by the Communist dictators. The church grew tremendously underground. But your people are losing the invaluable treasure they gave to us. I urge you to reclaim your treasure, and this is what I owe you."

Although Christianity is the largest religion in Germany, more than 30 percent of its population are not affiliated with any church or other religious body, and the number of nonreligious people in the Federal Republic has grown since the reunification of Germany, largely because the former East German states have a large nonreligious majority [43]

Like the Swedish missionaries, German missionaries did a tremendous evangelization and development work among the Oromo people in Wollega, western Ethiopia. I witnessed their commitment when I visited the German missionaries who hosted me at their headquarters in Hemansburg in 1993. It is my prayer and wish for that light to shine over Germany again.

The above-mentioned findings of the Pew Research Center's Forum on Religion and Public Life remind me of two things: First, those who were the first in accepting and cherishing the Christian faith are becoming the last: "So the last will be first, and the first last. For many are called, but few chosen" (Matt. 20:16.) Second, the end is approaching: "This gospel of the kingdom shall be preached in the whole world as a testimony to all the nations and then the end will come" (Matt. 24:14).

Finally, I call all human beings on this planet to spiritual awakening and revival so that together we can fulfill our responsibility in turning the world into a better place (Joel 2:12–13). I call all Ethiopians to self-examination and to national repentance for the countless sins that have offended our God, for that is the only way the centuries-old cycle of misery can come to an end. Look at President Lincoln's prayer again: "It behooves us then, to humble ourselves before the offended Power, to confess our national sins, and to pray for clemency and forgiveness." If such a powerful nation could humble itself before God, why can't Ethiopia do it?

It is a good sign that Ethiopia has honored the late Prime Minister Meles Zenawi for the first time in eighty years. But repentance on behalf of all the thousands who were killed and for the living who suffered is needed for the wrong committed against the last emperor of Ethiopia. This was in violation of God's command to honor authorities. In addition, the emperor who was once named "the father of Africa" deserves a place in the hearts of all Ethiopians for the good things he did for his nation. To my fellow Ethiopians, I say you know that, for sure. I say this as a beneficiary of his good deeds (especially his commitment to education that produced great people like the late Prime Minister Meles Zenawi). As President Nelson Mandela stated, "Education is the most powerful weapon which you can use to change the world." The emperor's sin is between him and God, and we are not in a position to judge him; but his good deeds are between him and us. Ethiopians should know that Emperor Haile Selassie I was a monarch-sovereign and did not have to do all that he did to maintain his sovereignty. He did it for the good of his people.

At last, I urge my fellow Americans not to take their freedom for granted and misguide the US leadership towards turning our blessings into curses. The democratic system of the United States resembles God's system of government by giving all citizens full freedom to make their own choices and to reap the consequence of their decisions. It is not worth it to allow wrong motives to subject us to the consequences of wrong decisions and make this great nation fall short of reaching its destiny. Now, in our quest for authentic leadership, let us hold dear the secret to finishing well—the full embrace of God's moral standards and leadership example as found in His holy Word.

Glossary Notes

Ihave placed descriptions either in brackets following the sentences or as "footnote," to make it easy for readers.

In spelling and presenting Amharic terms, I have tried my best to use Amharic sounds the way I thought would conform to English spelling.

As Ethiopians are named after their fathers where the father's name becomes last name, I have used first names with father's name or only first name (the Ethiopian way) for the Ethiopian names of those I mentioned in this book.

I also avoided the Amharic prefix such as, "Ato" for Mr. and Woizero (for married woman and Woizerit for unmarried woman or single) and used Mr. and Mrs/Miss respectively. (Please note that women married in the past remains Woizeo even after being widowed or divorced and single). In all these, I have tried my hardest to avoid confusion of non-Ethiopian readers.

Calendar difference: The Ethiopian New Year is Meskerem 1 in Ethiopian Calendar and September 11 in Gregorian calendar. The Ethiopian year is 7 to 8 years behind the Gregorian year (7 years from September to December and 8 years from January to August). Ethiopia has 12 months with 30 days each and Pagume which is considered the 13th month with 5 to 6 days. There is also 7 to 10 days gap between the Ethiopian and Gregorian months of the year. Mistakes could occur in converting the Ethiopian calendar to the Gregorian calendar (especially with leap year occurrence)

Appendix List

Note: The Ethiopian way of presenting dates is: Day/Month/ Year and the dates in the English translation of the documents in the appendix lists were put that way. Gap between the Ethiopia and Gregorian calendars could result in calculation errors in converting the Ethiopian calendar to the Gregorian as well as cause confusion.

I apologize for the quality of the translation office's English in case you find their translation awkward..

1. ICC's employment termination letter
2. ICC's recommendation letter
3. Visitors' comment
4. Letter to Prime Minister Tamrat Layne petitioning the establishment of the Ethiopian Ministry of Women's Affairs (MOWA)
5. Women's Self-Reliance Association (WSRA)'s complaint filed with Region 14 Administration
6. WSRA's complaint filed with the Mayor
7. WSRA's final complaint letter to the prosecuting office dated January 27, 1994
8. Letter from the United Nations Economic and Social Council granting WSRA special consultative status
9. DHS report number 20092103 on allegations against BFAS (public information)

10. US embassy's scrutiny notice
11. letter to Charities and Societies Agency (CSA) from MOWCYA's attorney
12. lawsuit filed against MOWCYA's officers, MOWCYA and Abebe Tigabu
13B. Letter with which Abeb Tigabu set-up a family as needy
13. Email from Kathryn Joyce
14. Email communications with Jessie Hawkins
15. CSA's initial letter which BFAS's license was suspended
16B. CSA board's letter upholding the revocation of BFSA's license.

Appendix 1

ኢንተርናሽናል የልማትና የበጎ አድራጎት አስተባባሪ ኮሚቴ
የአዲስ አበባ ከተማ ፕሮግራም
INTERNATIONAL COORDINATING COMMITTEE
For Welfare and Development Programmes in Addis Ababa (ICC)*

☎ 11-55-52
✉ 24-42

ቁጥር ICC/3/87
Ref. No.

አዲስ አበባ ኢትዮጵያ ።
Addis Ababa, Ethiopia.

ቀን January 8, 1987
Date

W/ro Agitu Wodajo
ICC - SKIP Project Officer
Addis Ababa

Dear W/ro Agitu,

   I regret to inform you that after a series of meetings held with
Mr. Peter Meienberger - programme Director, Aid on the Spot, and Mr.
J.J. Bolanz - Programme Coordinator to Ethiopia, during their over
all visit & project appraisal mission here in Addis Ababa, it has been
decided not to renew your employment contract as ICC-SKIP project
officer effective December 31, 1986

   The reasons for the termination of your contract being
that:-

   1. You have proved unable to maintain proper working relations
      with the kebele authorities, with ICC - office bearers & also
      with the SKIP representative.

   2. Disappointingly little or no effective work done as a project
      officer, instead most of which is only in words which have
      not been found substantiated.

   Therefore, you are advised to handover all project property to
W/t Lemlem Berhe, Head Day Care Instructor.

                                        .../

* ICC MEMBER ORGANIZATIONS
Municipality of Addis Ababa ✳ UNICEF ✳ United Nations FAO/WFP ✳ National Children's Commission ✳ Addis Ababa
REWA ✳ Addis Ababa Schools Office ✳ Christian Relief and Development Association ✳ Red Cross Society ✳ Norwegian
Save the Children Federation (Redd Barna - Ethiopia) ✳ REWA Addis Ababa ✳ AETU (Regional Office for Addis Ababa)

259

Appendix 1, page 2

☎ 11-55-52

✉ 24-42

አዲስ አበባ ኢትዮጵያ ፡፡
Addis Ababa, Ethiopia.

ምር _____
Ref. No.

ቀን _____
Date

— 2 —

Finally, on behalf of the ICC and SKIP project, I thank you very much for the service you rendered & wish you success in your future career.

Yours Sincerely

Getahun Belay
Co-ordinator

cc.

Comrade Abebe Engidasew
Executive Committee Member
& Chairman of Social
Affairs Committee

Mr. Jean Jaques Bolanz
SKIP Programme Coordinator
to Ethiopia
Rue F. Guillmann 12,1701, FRIBOURG,
Swithrland

Kebele 23 of Higher 21 UDA

W/t Lemlem Berhe
Head, Day Care Instructor
Addis Ababa

* ICC MEMBER ORGANIZATIONS

Municipality of Addis Ababa ⁑ UNICEF ⁑ United Nations FAO/WFP ⁕ National Children's Commission ⁑ Addis Ababa REWA ⁑ Addis Ababa Schools Office ⁕ Christian Relief and Development Association ⁕ Red Cross Society ⁕ Norwegian

Appendix 2

☎ 11 55 52
✉ 2442
አዲስ አበባ ኢትዮጵያ ።
Addis Ababa, Ethiopia.

☎ኮድ ICC/71/88
Ref. No.

ቀን May 18, 1988
Date

To Whom it May Concern

This is to certify that Sister Agitu Wodajo was employed as a Project Officer in the ICC/SKIP sponsored programme at Higher 21 Kebele 23.

Her employment took effect on December 2, 1985 until the day of the termination of her employment contract i.e. May 31, 1988. During her term of office, Sister Agitu, has proved herself to be an excelle administrator & officer of the project. Besides, her positive attitu and understanding of the Community is an evidence to her geniune Committment and devotion to her work.

Apart from her normal duty as a project Officer, Sister Agitu ha precided over quite significant activities such as making an over all assessment of a Foaster Family program, studying the socio-economic conditions of the project area and also conducting a feasibility stud of different income generating activities geared to benifit the poor mothers in the Community.

Sister Agitu has invariably shown efforts to promote Various development programmes in collaboration with different governmental ar non-governmental organizations. In all her approaches, she has demonstrated a very Cooperative and skillful ability.

We are confident that Sister Agitu would prove successful in any capacity that she may be assigned for.

We wish her all the best in her future career.

Very Sincerely,

Getahun Belay
Co-ordinator

አዲስ አበባ ።
ADDIS ABABA

Municipality of Addis Ababa • UNICEF • United Nations FAO (WFP) • National Children's Commission • Addis Ababa REWA • Addis Ababa Schools Office • Christian Relief and Development Association • Red Cross Society • Norwegian Save the Children Federation (Redd Barna - Ethiopia) • REYA Addis Ababa • ETU (Regional Office for Addis Ababa) Ministry of Labour and Social Affairs (Addis Ababa Region)

Appendix 3

Note; Some of the dates of visit were cut off and are not fully visable. The following are copy of the legible comments:

Date	Name of visitor	Position of Visitor	Organization	Comments
07/07/1990	Nafis Sadik	UNFPA Executive Director	UNFPA	This is a wonderful initiative of self help by women to improve the life of their families. It deserves all our support
13 Feb 1993	Burt Tucker	UNIFEM Consultant, NECO South	C/O 60 E. 42 St. Suite 1146, New York, N.Y.10165	This project is well worth supporting. It has sound committed leadership and is operating on very solid principles of management and lucent design.
March 4, 1993	Isaac D. Russell	U.S. Information Service, Entoto Road Addis Ababa Cultural Affairs Office		I wish you great success at your fairly new projects. You should all be congratulated for your excellent work, and thank you for such a hospitable welcome
March 4, 1993	Alemtsehai Asfaw	U.S. Information Service, Entoto Road Addis Ababa	Cultural Affairs Assistant	This project is valuable for Ethiopian women. I wish you success in your endeavors.

	Pamela DeLargy	UNFPA Mission	Univ. of North Carolina, U.S.A	This project is extremely well designed and managed and the ladies here are producing good quality, reasonably priced and needed items. Good luck to all of the people involved in the Bole WSRA! You are doing impressive work.
14/9/1993	Stephen Schwartz	US Embassy	Self help Coordinator	Excellent project
	Catherin Shown	Ethiopia Aid Director	Ethiopia Aid 114 Peasecod St. Windsor SL4 IDN	We support the aim of We support this project. To give long term change to women and their families. When we have more funds we will try to help....

Appendix 4

September 13/1991

His Excellency Ato Tamerat Layne
Prime Minister
Addis Ababa

Subject: Concerning the status of Ethiopian women in the government's power structure

A holistic project titled Women's Self-Reliance Association is being established in Bole Woreda Kebele 20 through the support of donors. The objective of the project is to create job opportunity for women who were displaced, mainly from Wollo due to natural and man-made disaster and settled in temporary shelters, with no daily or monthly income to support their families.

When Dr. Nafis Sadik, Executive Director of the United Nations Fund for Population Activities and Under-Secretary General of the United Nations, visited the project on July 7/1990, she found the project's plan to integrate health care, family planning and social affair into its activities commendable. As a result, I was offered the opportunity to visit similar program in Niamey, the capital city of Niger which enabled me to acquire useful experience that could contribute towards plans that address our country's concrete situation and thereby inspired me to present my petition to your Excellency as follows:

In the past centuries, the deep-rooted traditional law and cultural heritage imposed women's status to be dependent on their husbands' free will. Just on top of this, the Derg WPE regime, through its equality masquerade, used women in promoting its political agenda in the last 17 years. According to the 1989 UNICEF study, there was not even a single woman

Appendix 4, page 2

among the 20 government ministers, although the PDRE government was propagating that it gave women equal rights in the political and economic life. There were only 15 women in the 343 member fictitious legislative committee in 1988 - 1989. The number of women employed by governmental and private organizations was only 17.9 percent. Accordingly, Ethiopian women were enslaved under the bondage of the Derg WPE rule on the one hand and the backward economic situation on the other They had to spend over 14 hours per day in arborous, un-paying hard physical labor providing care and support to their families and have been responsible for the country's backwardness. When we view the situation from the standpoint of the victory we now won, however, we can realize that EPRDF achieved the victory it won because it had women participate in its arm struggle as comrades at equal level with men. Furthermore, the attention EPRDF gave to digging Ethiopia out of economic quagmire through democratic economic initiatives reveals that it will give greater importance to women' future participation in advancing the country's progress.

When Niger got liberated from the colonial rule and was able to determine her own fate, she established a Ministry of Women's Affairs and Social Promotion which was led by a woman minister. The aim was to mobilize women toward equal participation with men in the country's reconstruction and development. We have been able to learn from the briefing given to us by the honorable minister the contribution that it made to their country.

I am confident that the honorable Prime Minister's office believes that Ethiopian women, from their natural decency, diligence, hard work and sense of patriotism, would make an immense contribution towards the country's progress. Hence, I hereby submit, with great respect, my opinion

265

Appendix 4, page 3

that establishing a women's affairs office at a ministerial level by adopting Niger's example to the national contest of and according to our country's concrete situation and ability would be of great benefit to our country. Attached please find my study-visit report and documentation of the Women's Self-Reliance Association evidencing the need for establishing the women's affair office at the level mentioned above.

With kind regards

Signed

W/o Agitu Wodajo

Appendix 5

TRANSLATION OFFICE
BUREAU DE TRADUCTION
UFFICIO TRADUZIONI

Yeshimebet Tesfaye & Family P.L. Share Co.
Addis Ababa, Ethiopia
Stadium Building No.7
Tel. (011) 515-7104, (011) 552-6312
P.O.Box 6127

የትርጉም ጽሕፈት ቤት
مكتب الترجمة
ÜBERSETZUNGSBÜRO

የሺመቤት ተስፋዬና ቤተሰቡ ኃ.የተ.የግ/ኀብረት ማ.
አዲስ አበባ - ኢትዮጵያ
እስታዲየም ሕንፃ ቁጥር 7
ስልክ (011) 515-7104, (011) 552-6312
ፖ.ሣ.ቁ. 6127

Emblem
WOMEN'S SELF RELIANCE ASSOCIATION

Date: 22/10/1993
Ref. No: WSRA/60/86

To Region 14 Administration Office
Addis Ababa

It is to be recalled that petitioner, Women's Self Reliance Association, has previously lodged petition to Region 14, Woreda 17 Office concerned bodies requesting for remedies to wrongdoings caused by Woreda 17 Kebele 20 Office against the Association in a petition Ref. No WSRA/56/86, dated 12/10/1993, which was notified to concerned bodies by copy thereof.

Basically despite the fact that we are operating activities of the organization against payment of monthly rental amount of birr 350 (three hundred fifty birr) to Woreda 17 Kebele 20 Office there can be no ground for them to interfere which in the process of our activities.

Where in essence our organization operates on the basis of assistance received from foreign donors, the existing dispute that arose with this Kebele caused freezing of external donors' funding assistance that was planned to be channeled to the Association for use in setting up and office building construction of premises of the Association, pending settlement of this dispute ; which also posed serious threat to groups beneficiary women under the organization.

Under such circumstances, we faced stoppage of sewing machines due to fault that led to bring a repair technician from outside for carry out repair and maintenance work on site; but where the technician was taking the rest of the machines to complete repair work in his own workshop, he was prevented from taking out the machines by security at exit gate, saying that they instructed to enforce prohibition for any one from take out any property of the organization out of the premises other than in to the premises, which prohibition caused serious impediment on performance of our activity.

Moreover, where workers of the organization normally used to make use of the gate at the backyard of the Kebele Office premises on entry and exit, an order has been imposed against us prohibiting our workers from using back yard gate other than front gate, followed by another stern order in which our workers are subjected to endure mandatory physical check on entry and exit.

የሺ. በሱፈቃድ
Yeshi Besufekad

267

Appendix 5, page 2

here we were anxiously waiting for rapid course of action in remedy to our petition bmitted previously, we have been condemned to endure worsened wrongdoings imposed ainst us from time to time thus far.

ius. considering the gravity of situation imposed on our organization, , which is growing orsened from time to time without any remedial course of action despite our petition thus r, we hereby kindly request prompt and appropriate course of action in remedy to this new tition alone with the previous petition filed by the Association. so that we can carry out our tivities in a smooth manner without unnecessary interference. In this respect, please find closed 3 page copy of the petition previously submitted to Woreda 17.

Regards
Signed
Agitu Wodajo
Manager

Seal

WOMEN'S SELF RELIANCE ASSOCIATION

C:

Yeshi Besufekad

Appendix 6

የትርጉም ጽሕፈት ቤት
مكتب الترجمة
ÜBERSETZUNGSBÜRO

የሺ,መቤት ተስፋዬና ቤተሰቡ ኃ.የተ.የሽርክና ማ.
አዲስ አበባ - ኢትዮጵያ
እስታዲየም ሕንፃ ቁጥር 7
ስልክ (011) 515-7104, (011) 552-6312
ፖ.ሣ.ቁ. 6127

TRANSLATION OFFICE
BUREAU DE TRADUCTION
UFFICIO TRADUZIONI

Yeshimebet Tesfaye & Family P.L. Share Co.
Addis Ababa, Ethiopia
Stadium Building No.7
Tel. (011) 515-7104, (011) 552-6312
Ref.- No. P.O. Box 6127
Date: 21/04/1994

To H.E. Ato Teffera Walwa
Region 14 Administration President
Addis Ababa

The undersigned petitioner, Women's Self Reliance Association, in accordance with the resolution passed by the Board of the Association in its 19th session held on the 30th day of March 1994, hereby kindly requests for granting order in remedy to wrong doings and unnecessary interference being imposed against our organization by Woreda 17 Kebele 20 Office, which jeopardized performance of our planned activities in violation of the law.

Our Association was established with an objective to provide integrated economic and psycho-social support to improve livelihoods of destitute women with no permanent source of income to attain sustainable self reliance by engaging in income generating activities. To realize this lofty objective, the Association is duly licensed and registered with Ministry of Internal Affairs, and Relief and Rehabilitation Commission and has also concluded 10 - year operational agreement with Ministry of Labor and Social Affairs Accordingly, the Association commenced its operations at rented office space rented in part, acquired from part of Kebele 20 Office against payment of a sum of birr 350 (three hundred fifty birr) rental fees. Performance of planned activities undertaken by the organization so far in this small rented office space resulted in training of a group of 22 beneficiary women in leather products manufacturing and a group of 12 beneficiary women in sewing. Where it is clearly known that the Association has no working relation with Kebele 20 Office other than rental contract what so ever, it turned out it has been engaged in perpetrating unlawful act of interference in our activities thus far; which included, but limited to the following:

1) Surveyors deployed by Region 14 Administration for the purpose of handing over allocation of plot of land approved for us upon erection of boundary demarcation stones on site, have been scarred away by armed guards of the Kebele by force in violation of the law which made us unable to obtain funding assistance we could have acquired from external donors for use in construction of building and operation of our activities. Moreover, we found ourselves in a difficult situation even to cover our monthly office rental fees that we lodged application to the Kebele Office in a letter dated 5/10/1995, but it turned out we received no reply other than lip service they continued to demand payment of monthly rental thus far.

2) Our flour mill which was running for above two years has come to stoppage due to their impounding order on their discretion in violation of the law and it still remains that way thus far.

3) When owners of sewing machines came over to take away the machines we borrowed from another charitable organization in Nazreth, they were prohibited from taking the machine out of the premises by Kebele armed security by force.

የሺ በሱፈቃድ
Yeshi Besufekad

4) They would always refuse to give reply to any request of the Association; which is evident in the stoppage of our flour mill as a result of impounding order issued by the Kebele with effect from May 1993.

5) Despite our relentless efforts to settle the dispute in amicable manner. in a public meeting called by the Kebele to deliberate on matters associated to land lease, they manipulated to use the floor to spread unfounded rumors aimed at damaging tarnish our reputation in public, but also caused evaluation of our organization by an Inquiry committee formed by members of their own choice without consent ; as a result of which we established clear position that the legitimate body appropriate for such purpose should be Ministry of labor and Social Affairs, which was notified to Woreda 17, and also notified to other concerned offices by copy thereof.

6) In the event where two member women from our association were carrying our product out of the premises to participate in international trade fair held in October 1993, representing our organization, they were prevented to do so by Kebele armed security by force and forced to return back to Kebele Office saying that any property of the organization cannot be taken out of the premises, we managed to release our products by lodging petition to Bole Woreda Police, though.

7) In the event when our evaluation on organization was conducted by a committee drawn from four government organizations formed by Ministry of Labor and Social Affairs, Kebele 20 Office tried to force member women of our Association to file lawsuit against the Association , and threatened to arrest those who refused to do so in the guise of failure to cooperate with the Kebele. and perpetrated unlawful act to destabilize the Association and harmony of its members, using part of our members to appear as witness against us.

8) In general Kebele 20 Office. particularly the chairman Ato Kassahun G/Michael and Ato Melese Hagos are perpetrating unlawful act of conspiracy aimed at destabilizing the association and its members in purpose to cause dissolution of the Association so as to expose beneficiary women members to difficult situation out of abuse of power and dictatorship. Thus we hereby kindly request to be granted appropriate course of action and relief in respect of the following:

(1) To release our flour mill this has been impounded by their order in violation of the law;

(2) To prevent Kebele 20 Office from any act of interference in the activities of the Association as it is operating on the basis of funding support from external donors in accordance with the law.

Regards
Signed
Agitu Wedaio
Manager

Seal
WOMEN'S SELF RELIANCE ASSOCIATION

Yeshi Besufekad
General Manager

Appendix

Appendix 7

የትርጉም ጽሕፈት ቤት
مكتب الترجمة
ÜBERSETZUNGSBÜRO

የሺመቤት ተስፋዬና ቤተሰቦ ኃ.የተ.የኅ.ርክ ማ.
አዲስ አበባ - ኢትዮጵያ
እስታዲየም ሕንጻ ቁጥር 7
ስልክ (011) 515-7104, (011) 552-6312
ፖ.ሣ.ቁ. 6127
Emblem
WOMEN'S SELF RELIANCE ASSOCIATION

TRANSLATION OFFICE
BUREAU DE TRADUCTION
UFFICIO TRADUZIONI

Yeshimebet Tesfaye & Family P.L. Share Co.
Addis Ababa, Ethiopia
Stadium Building No.7
Tel. (011) 515-7104, (011) 552-6312
P.O.Box 6127

Ref: No: WSRA/78/86
Date: 27/01/1994

To Region 14 Administration
Prosecutor's Office
Addis Ababa

The dispute that is existing between our Organization and Woreda 17 Kebele 20 Office is well known to Prosecutor's Office. It is to be recalled that by the time when Kebele Chairman, Ato Kassahun Gebremichael and Ato Melese Hagos who was said to be Chair of the Inquiry Committee of the Kebele, appeared in your office on 21/12/1994 upon the order of Prosecutor's Office I was also present by representing our organization.

Upon hearing statements of the parties Prosecutor's Office issued two directives by the day. These were:

1) For the parties to immediately dissolve the Inquiry Committee that was said to be established in the Kebele to settle the dispute in amicable manner.

2) For the parties to wait for the outcome of decision to be issued by the Legal Inquiry Committee that was established by Ministry of Labor and Social Affairs for this purpose.

Nevertheless, while we were waiting for practical implementation of the directives issued by Prosecutor's Office of the above mentioned two persons caused the wrongdoings against us which conspiracy has been growing worse from time to time thus far.

They are indirectly trying to pressure and agitate our members to file lawsuit against us. member women who refused to do so are being stigmatized against by other fellow members. and forced to sign undertaking to cooperate with the Inquiry Committee established in the Kebele threatening that those who refuse would be arrested. In general our members are under extreme threat caused by the two persons mentioned, particularly by Ato Melese Hagos.

They have divided our members against the Association, making part of them their witnesses. They are engaged in destabilizing propaganda against the Association, particularly against me, Head of the Organization, spreading unfounded rumors saying that I have committed embezzlement of property of the Association and concealed a lot of assets of the Association, and committed misappropriation of thousands of dollars in foreign aid.

271

Appendix 7, page 2

Moreover, I was summoned to appear for inquiry in Kebele Office at 9:00 am on 26/01/1994 in a letter dated 25/01/1994 which was sent by Kebele to me at home at 6:00 pm.

In general where these persons, Ato Kassahun Gebremichael and Ato Meles Hagos, were expected to bring about settlement of the dispute in amicable way by implementing the directives issued by Prosecutor's Office, they are actually disregarding the directives and are engaged in unlawful act of destabilizing the Association and harmony of our employees with an aim to cause dissolution of the Association and expose our members to social problems indirectly while also threatening the lives of our members in violation of the law. Thus, we hereby kindly request the Prosecutor's Office to take appropriate course of immediate legal action against these two persons, Ato Kassahun Gebremichael and Ato Meles Hagos. In this respect please find enclosed three page photocopy of documentary evidence in proof of the matter.

Regards
Signed
Agitu Wodajo
Manager

Seal
WOMEN'S SELF RELIANCE ASSOCIATION

Yeshi Besufekad

Appendix 8

9594

United Nations Nations Unies

NGO SECTION, DESA
1 UN Plaza, Room DC1-1477, New York, NY 10017
tel: (212) 963-8652 / fax: (212) 963-9248
www.un.org/esa/coordination/ngo
e-mail: desangosection@un.org

6 May 2003

Dear Sir/Madam:

We would like to inform you that the Economic and Social Council, at its resumed organizational session in April 2003, decided to grant Special consultative status to the organization "International Self-reliance Agency for Women".

The organization may now designate official representatives to the United Nations – to the United Nations Headquarters in New York and the United Nations offices in Geneva and Vienna. Designated representatives must pick up their passes in person at the designated site. Needless to say, the regular presence of your organization will allow your organization to implement effectively and fruitfully the provisions for this consultative relationship.

Please note, in particular, Parts II, IV, V and VII and the Council Resolution 1996/31, describing the procedures for carrying out your consultative relationship with the Council. Also, kindly note Part IX, paragraph 61c which requests that organizations in General and Special consultative status submit quadrennial reports on their activities for the four-year period in 2003-2006 to the Committee in 2007. You will be advised of the modalities for completing your report in due course. Meanwhile, we suggest that you maintain detailed records of your activities.

The United Nations issues a calendar of meetings and conferences, which can be obtained by your representatives at the United Nations sites. Every year, you will receive from this office the "Calendar of United Nations meetings open to participation by or of special interest to NGOs in consultative status". The latest copy of the calendar and other NGO-related information can also be found on the NGO Section's homepage at http://www.un.org/esa/coordination/ngo.

Finally, should you wish to indicate your status with the United Nations on your letterhead, please use the following wording: *"NGO in Special Consultative Status with the Economic and Social Council of the United Nations"*. The United Nations emblem may not be used, unless expressed approval has been granted by the Legal Office of the United Nations. This is neither granted for stationery use, nor for any printed materials describing your organization.

We look forward to a productive relationship with your organization and its representatives.

Sincerely yours,

Hanifa Mezoui, Chief
NGO Section / DESA

International Self-reliance Agency for Women

425 20th Avenue South, Suite #145
Minneapolis, MN 55454

Appendix 9

Minnesota Department of **Human Services**

November 2, 2009

Agitu Wodajo, Chairperson
Better Future Adoption Services
1429 Washington Ave. S., Suite 204
Minneapolis, MN 55454

License number: 1040795
Re: Investigation Report Number 20092103

Dear. Ms. Wodajo:

Enclosed is the Investigation Memorandum for the above referenced report number. If you have questions, please call me at (651) 297-7520.

Sincerely,

Meg McAlister, Family Systems Licensor
Division of Licensing

Enclosure

PO Box 64242 * Saint Paul, Minnesota * 55164-0242 * An Equal Opportunity and Veteran-Friendly Employer
http://www.dhs.state.mn.us/licensing

INVESTIGATION MEMORANDUM
Department of Human Services
Division of Licensing
Public Information

Report Number(s): 20092103

Date Issued: November 2, 2009

Name and Address of Program Investigated:

Better Future Adoption Services
1428 Washington Ave S, Suite #204
Minneapolis, MN 55454

Program License Number: 1040792

Rule under which Program is Licensed: Rule 4

Investigator(s):

Meg McAlister and Michelle Larsen
Division of Licensing
Minnesota Department of Human Services
PO Box 64242
Saint Paul, Minnesota 55164-0242
651-297-7520

Nature of Report(s):

It was reported that the agency failed to disclose information to an adoptive family about their adoptive child's health status.

Investigation Procedure:

Interview:

An interview was conducted in person on June 24, 2009, with an agency administrative staff person (SP).

Documents reviewed included:

- Documentation provided by the adoptive family (AF)
- The agency file for the AF

Applicable rule/statute part(s):

Minnesota Rules, part 9545.0835 **ADOPTION PLACEMENTS,** Subp. 1. **Record of child's background and history.** When an agency accepts a child for adoptive placement or facilitates an adoption between a birth parent and a prospective adoptive parent, the agency is responsible for establishing and maintaining a record that meets the requirements of Minnesota Statutes, sections 257.01 and 259.79.

Minnesota Statutes, section 257.01 **RECORDS REQUIRED.** Each person or authorized child-placing agency permitted by law to receive children, secure homes for children, or care for children, shall keep a record containing the name, age, former residence, legal status, health records, sex, race, and accumulated length of time in foster care, if applicable, of each child received; the name, former residence, occupation, health history, and character, of each birth parent; the date of reception, placing out, and adoption of each child, and the name, race, occupation, and residence of the person with whom

Better Future Adoption Services
Report Number 20092103
Page 2

a child is placed; the date of the removal of any child to another home and the reason for removal; the date of termination of the guardianship; the history of each child until the child reaches the age of 18 years, is legally adopted, or is discharged according to law; and further demographic and other information as is required by the commissioner of human services.

Minnesota Statutes, section 259.79 **ADOPTION RECORDS,** Subd. 1. **Content.** (a) The adoption records of the commissioner's agents and licensed child-placing agencies shall contain copies of all relevant legal documents, responsibly collected genetic, medical and social history of the child and the child's birth parents, the child's placement record, copies of all pertinent agreements, contracts, and correspondence relevant to the adoption, and copies of all reports and recommendations made to the court. . . .

Pertinent Information/Summary of Findings:

In a letter to the agency dated May 13, 2009, an attorney for the AF stated that information about the adoptive child's "HIV risk" was withheld from the AF by the agency.

An agency Referral Acceptance Letter signed by the AF on November 6, 2008, identified the adoptive child, described the child's health status as "very good," and stated that a "physical examination form, HIV and Hepatitis B test results, and photo(s)," were provided to the AF with the Referral Acceptance Letter.

Documentation provided by the agency reiterated that when the AF accepted the referral of the adoptive child on November 6, 2008, the AF was provided with the adoptive child's HIV test result. The agency documentation further stated that the HIV test result was negative.

Conclusion:

It was determined that the agency provided to the AF health records it had regarding the adoptive child. A licensing violation was not determined.

Action Taken by Department of Human Services, Licensing Division:

This investigation was completed on July 16, 2009. The purpose of this investigation memorandum is to summarize the findings regarding the above allegation for which no violation was determined.

Previously, on July 16, 2009, a Correction Order was issued for violations that were determined as a result of the investigation.

Appendix 10

Dear Better Futures,

Recently, the U.S. Embassy has implemented several changes to the adoption visa process, including conducting significant additional review of each case and field investigation. In light of our findings, and recent serious allegations and news reports involving Ethiopian adoptions, we will require additional time to process each case from Better Futures.

Effective immediately, the Embassy will require 8 weeks' processing time for each Better Futures adoption visa case. This means that families will not receive an immigrant visa appointment until 8 weeks after the complete case file is submitted to the Embassy. We will not accept incomplete case files in these cases under any circumstances. Additionally, we will not be able to grant extra appointment slots in March to Better Futures. **Cases that have already been submitted will continue to be processed as previously scheduled.** For cases already scheduled (for which the Embassy already has the case file), those parents should expect potentially lengthy delays in the processing of those cases.

Sincerely,

Adoption Unit
U.S. Embassy
Addis Ababa, Ethiopia

Appendix 11

የትርጉም ጽሕፈት ቤት
مكتب الترجمة
ÜBERSETZUNGSBÜRO

የሺመቤት ተስፋዬና ቤተሰቡ ኃ.የተ.የሽርክና ማ.
አዲስ አበባ - ኢትዮጵያ
አስታዲዮም ሕንፃ ቁጥር 7
ስልክ (011) 515-7104, (011) 552-6312
ፖ.ሣ.ቁ. 6127

TRANSLATION OFFICE
BUREAU DE TRADUCTION
UFFICIO TRADUZIONI

Yeshimebet Tesfaye & Family P.L. Share (
Addis Ababa, Ethiopia
Stadium Building No.7
Tel. (011) 515-7104, (011) 552-6312
P.O.Box 6127

11/10/2010

To: Charities and Societies Agency
Addis Ababa

Our Ministerial Office has received a report such that Better Future Adoption Services facilitated for the adoption of 12 children illegally using falsified documents and in collaboration with Betezata Children's Home Association and Engida Children's Aid Association. These children, according to the report made to us, were either placed with adoptive parents in the United States or prepared to leave for America. On the basis of the report, necessary inspections where conducted on our side and the Ministerial Office has instituted criminal charges at the concerned police organ in order that the case would be investigated and that the concerned officials would be charged for offences.

Whereas the above mentioned organizations were engaged in the criminal offense of trafficking children on adoption using falsified documents and in an illegal manner and, in addition, in damaging the reputation of our country, we request the agency to take the appropriate administrative measure in pursuance to the powers vested in it under Article 92 of Proclamation no. 621/2001 until such time as the case would be investigated and the necessary legal measure will be taken.

Kind regards,
Signed
Dereje Tegyobelu
Legal Affairs Officer

cc.
Office of the Honorable Minister
Office of the State Honorable State Minister
Children's Rights and Safety Enforcement Directorate
Ministry of Women's Affairs
Addis Ababa

Sealed:
The Federal Ministry of Women's, Children's and Youth's Affairs

Sea.Abr NSLSCW

...kad
... Manager

Appendix 12

የትርጉም ጽሕፈት ቤት
مكتب الترجمة
ÜBERSETZUNGSBÜRO

የሺመቤት ተስፋዬና ቤተሰቦ ኃ.የተ.የግ/ኀብና ማ.
አዲስ አበባ - ኢትዮጵያ
እስታዲየም ሕንፃ ቁጥር 7
ስልክ (011) 515-7104, (011) 552-6312
ፖ.ሣ.ቁ. 6127

TRANSLATION OFFICE
BUREAU DE TRADUCTION
UFFICIO TRADUZIONI

Yeshimebet Tesfaye & Family P.L. Share Co.
Addis Ababa, Ethiopia
Stadium Building No.7
Tel. (011) 515-7104, (011) 552-6312
P.O.Box 6127

Date: <u>01/12/2010</u>

To: Federal First Instance Court
Bole Assigned Civil Bench
Addis Ababa

Applicant: Better Future Adoption Services
Address: Bole Sub-City

Respondents:
1. Ministry of Women's, Children's and Youth's
2. Miss Mahder Bitew
3. Mr. Zibane Tadesse
4. Mr. Abebe Tigabu
Address: Addis Ababa

This petition of civil suit has been submitted under the expedited procedure as the respondents have imposed illegal prohibition upon the right of children to be adopted despite protection of such rights under the constitution

1. Introduction

1.1. The court is authorized to hear the proceedings of the case in pursuance to Article 14 of Proclamation no. 25/88;
1.2. The civil suit fulfills the requirements of Articles 222 and 223 of the Code of Civil Procedures;
1.3. The applicant follows the case through its manager or through an attorney;
1.4. The plaintiff may serve the court's summons to the defendants;

2. The theme of the petition of civil suit

2.1. The relations between the applicant and the respondents

279

Appendix 12, page 2

The applicant is engaged in provision of services related to children to be given for adoption and prospective adoptive parents in compliance with the international conventions, the laws of Ethiopia, the directives issued by the Ministry of Justice and that of the 1st respondent as well as the relevant laws, rules and regulations.

The duties of the 1st respondent are signing operation agreement with the applicant, giving opinions on contracts of adoption and facilitation for the obtainment of certificates of births and passport to children in relation to adoption services.

The duties of the second and the third respondents are to see to it that the 1st respondent discharges its duties and powers in an appropriate manner.

The 4th respondent was engaged in the applicant organization with the duty of undertaking the objectives and duties thereof until such that as he was discharged from his management position due to defects in performance.

2.2. The cause of the liabilities of the respondents towards the civil suit

The 1st respondent has gone beyond the limits of the powers and duties given to it and refuses to sign operation agreement and to give confirmation which allows adopted children to leave for abroad. The decision it has made in this regard is not supported by the law and, hence, such respondent is liable to this civil suit.

The second and the third respondents are liable towards the civil suit on the grounds that they have hindered the discharging of duties and powers by the first respondent on the basis of the law and evidences.

The forth respondent, without there being legal grounds and evidences, reported to the 1st respondent that the operations of the applicant are illegal. Further, he has made false allegations over electronic media and the newspapers which have caused damages to the 1st respondent. Therefore, such party is responsible towards the civil suit.

3. Details

3.1. The first respondent has caused Mr. Joseph Gilliam and Mrs. Pamela Gilliam not to obtain contract of adoption, certificate

280

Appendix 12, page 3

of birth and passport to the children whom they have adopted from Andnet Children's and Family Aid Association;

3.2.   The 1ˢᵗ respondent caused Mr. ████████ ████ and Mrs. ████ ████, adoptive family, not to be granted with visa of entry into Ethiopia when attempting to travel to the country to take their adopted child named ████ ████. In addition, the 1ˢᵗ respondent has refused granting contract of adoption, certificate of birth and passport to child █████ ████ whereby denying prohibiting his placement with his adoptive family.

4. Judgment requested

4.1.   We request the court to cause cessation of the prohibitions made by the respondents stated from 1through 3 and to discharge the duties given to them under the law. We also request the court to cause issuance of evidences and provision of support within the scope of their duties.

4.2.   We request the court to cause the 4ᵗʰ respondent to reverse the allegations he made against us.

With respects,

The civil suit is true and correct;

281

Appendix 12, page 4

የትርጉም ጽሕፈት ቤት
مكتب الترجمة
ÜBERSETZUNGSBÜRO

የሺመቤት ተስፋዬና ቤተሰቡ ኃ.የተየፃርከና ማ.
አዲስ አበባ - ኢትዮጵያ
እስታዲየም ሕንፃ ቁጥር 7
ስልክ (011) 515-7104, (011) 552-6312
ፖ.ሣ.ቁ. 6127

TRANSLATION OFFICE
BUREAU DE TRADUCTION
UFFICIO TRADUZIONI

Yeshimebet Testaye & Family P.L. Share Co.
Addis Ababa, Ethiopia
Stadium Building No.7
Tel. (011) 515-7104, (011) 552-6312
P.O Box 6127

Date: <u>01/12/2010</u>

To: Federal First Instance Court
Bole Assigned Civil Bench
<u>**Addis Ababa**</u>

Applicant: Better Future Adoption Services
Address: Bole Sub-City

Respondents:
1. Ministry of Women's, Children's and Youth's
2. Miss Mahder Bitew
3. Mr. Zibane Tadesse
4. Mr. Abebe Tigabu
   Address: Addis Ababa

Statements of Evidences of the applicant

1. The illegal prohibition made by the first respondent against provision of support for the obtainment of certificate of birth and passport, 02 pages photocopy; the original is in the hands of the Ministerial Office;

2. The statements made by Mr. Christopher Conner and Mrs. Mona Conner under the title "Ups and Downs in Ethiopia" which they faced during the times that they had come to Ethiopia to take their adopted child. The English version's copy constitutes 08 pages while the translation contains 07 pages. The originals are kept with Mr. Christopher Conner;

3. Evidence for completion of the adoption of child Fitsum Chafengim, 03 pages copy; the Original is kept at the Ministry of Women's and Children's and Youth's Affairs;

Appendix 12, page 5

4. The letter addressed to the Ministry of Women's, Children's and Youth's Affairs concerning child ███████, 02 pages copy; the original is kept with the Ministerial Office;

5. The letter addressed by the Attorney and Consultant at Law of Better Future Adoption Services to the Ministry of Women's, Children's and Youth's Affairs stating the illegality of prohibition made by the Office hindering placement of child ███████ with his adoptive parents; (02 pages copy – the original is at the Ministerial Office);

6. The letter submitted to the Office of the Minister by Better Future Adoption Services detailing the outline of the misdeeds of the Ministerial Office, 03 pages copy; the original is kept with the Ministerial Office;

7. The letter addressed by the Attorney and Consultant at Law of Better Future Adoption Services to the Ministry of Women's, Children's and Youth's Affairs, dated 25/10/2010, 01 page; the original is kept at the Office of the Ministerial Office;

8. The defamatory articles written by the forth respondent on Sendek and Gogda Newspapers, 01 page copy; the original is kept with the editor.

End of evidences;

Kind regards,

Appendix 12 B

TRANSLATION ENTITY
Yoseph Petros
19219 Larch Way
Lynnwood, WA 98037
Phone #: 425 245-5844

Date: 18/10/2002 E.C .

To Better Future Adoption Service
Addis Ababa

Subject: Adoptee Child Faven's Family Financial Support

We, the family of child Faven residing in the Oromia National Region, due to serious difficulty we are in, sincerely request for Birr 5000 to be allowed and given to us as assistance from Better Future Agency organization through which our child received adoption service.

Applicant,

W/o Fozia Mohammed,   Signature

Ato Ermias Hailu,   Signature

To Ato Assefa
Considering the life difficulty the applicants have shared dispensing the requested money will support them and I suggest to be submitted for payment

Signature
Abebe Tigabu

To Finance

Execute as suggested by the Deputy Director Abebe Tigabu

Signature
Dated: 18/10/2002 E.C.

Note from BFAS Executive Director – added (not translated)
The application shown above and the instruction to pay the family were all fraudulently prepared, written, and signed in Abebe Tigabu (the Deputy Director)'s own handwriting while he was actively engaged in embezzling and malicious libel intent to destroy the agency. We have never paid adoptees' families before or after this incident. We don't even allow adoptive parents to give any gift to birth parents. He has done unimaginable damage and gotten away with it so far. Never have we heard of a case where a needy family determines and requests for assistance in an exact amount (birr 5,000.- in this case). Mr. Tigabu's unprofessional and unethical practices have produced this. This is only one tiny example of what he had been involved in as a disguised lawyer and Deputy Director of the agency.

Appendix 13

From: Kathryn Joyce <███████████████> (Email address shaded)
Date: Mon., Dec. 12, 2011 at 11:12 a.m.
Subject: Press inquiry—Newsweek International
To: info@betterfutureadoption.org

Hello, I'm a journalist working on a story for *Newsweek International* about adoption in Ethiopia. I'm hoping to speak to someone at BFAS about the accusations made against the agency by the Ethiopian government and the revocation of its license. Is there someone I can call today or tomorrow for a brief phone interview? The story is expected to close later this week, so please let me know as soon as possible.

Thanks very much.

Best regards,

Kathryn Joyce
███████████ (Telephone number shaded)

Appendix 14

Note: Contact information for Jessie Hawkins and director of the youth homeless shelter as well as the adoptive child's name (Subject of the email) are shaded.

From: " _____ " < _____ >
To: Agitu <agitu@betterfutureadoption.org>
Sent: Sat, May 8, 2010 1:56:59 AM
Subject:

Hi Agitu,

How have you been? Busy I imagine! ▮▮▮▮▮ is doing very well and loves it here. She is picking up more and more English and starting to tell us stories about her life in Ethiopia. She seems to remember some details that we didn't have through the adoption but being so young, I'd like to see if I can verify any of them with you. Do you have any additional information about her past? We really know nothing and I'd love to have any pieces of information we can for her since she spent so many of her youngest years in Ethiopia.

She remembers having a mother in Ethiopia, but no father. She remembers her mother being sick and taking her to the care center. Do you have any details about this? We'd love to have details of that for her; it would mean so much for us and as she grows, that kind of information is priceless.

Thanks again for all you did for our family. We think of you and pray for you often.

▮▮▮▮▮▮▮, ▮▮▮▮▮▮▮▮▮
Vintage Remedies Inc.
▮▮▮▮▮▮▮▮▮▮▮▮▮▮ office: ▮▮▮▮

On May 8, 2010, at 3:00 PM, agitu@betterfutureadoption.org wrote:

Hi,

It is so good to hear from you. I treasure your prayers and thoughtfulness. As we have faced this kind of drama last month and have gained the needed experience, I will do a though investigation on ▮▮▮▮ case and will do my best to get the information for you. I am aware how import it is for your family and ▮▮▮▮.

Thank you

Appendix 14, page 2

-------- Original Message --------

Subject: Re: ███████████
From: "███████████, MH" <███████████>
Date: Mon, May 10, 2010 10:06 am

To: agitu@betterfutureadoption.org

Thank you so much!

███████, ███████████
Vintage Remedies Inc.
███████████████████████ office:

On May 11, 2010, at 8:11 AM, agitu@betterfutureadoption.org wrote:

Hello,

I started working on this right away. No one from our agency here knows Hayats mom. Today, I heard that a woman who is an employee of an NGO that works with young women who are exposed to street life knows her. I will continue with my search and will keep you posted of the progress.

Thank you

From: ███████████, MH [mailto:███████████]
Sent: Tuesday, May 25, 2010 9:46 AM
To: agitu@betterfutureadoption.org
Subject: Re: ███████████

Hi Agitu,
Just checking in to see if you were able to find anything else about ███████'s birthmother. We would really do anything to get that information for her.
Thanks for all your hard work!

███████, ███████████
Vintage Remedies Inc.
███████████████████████ office:

From: Agitu Wodajo [mailto:agitu@betterfutureadoption.org]
Sent: Tuesday, May 25, 2010 3:49 PM
To: ███████████, MH'
Subject: RE: ███████████

287

Appendix 14, page 3

Hello,

I just got back from Ethiopia. I did try my hardest to locate ████ birth mom with no avail. It will take time to come to a conclusion, but I don't want to give up. I beg your patience while we continue our search.

Thank you

On Jul 6, 2010, at 11:06 AM, Agitu Wodajo wrote:

Hello,

Our staff in Addis tried so hard to locate ████ birth mom and finally gave up. If ██ knows the name of her birth mom, I think it would be helpful. I personally prefer that you email us her full name and we try one more time before we give up. Please let me know if you agree to that.

Thank you

From: ████, MH [mailto: ████████]
Sent: Friday, July 09, 2010 7:25 AM
To: Agitu Wodajo
Subject: Re: ██

Thank you so much! She tries hard, but can't remember her mother's name. She has described their "house" where she slept, what they did together and so many other things, but she can't remember her name! She sometimes tells us Beti is her mom, and she recognizes the names of the nannies in the pictures we have from when we were there, but she still can't remember her birthmother's name. I'm trying to help her. Did any of the nannies get her name when she dropped ████ off?

Even without her name, any information about her would be great to have. For example, was she sick? or well? Did ████ have birthsiblings (she seems to think so)? Was she homeless? Did she give a reason for needing to bring ████ into the care center... anything would be so beneficial for her! Thanks again.

If I can help her to remember any more information, I will let you know. Thanks so much for working so hard to help us!

████, ████████
Vintage Remedies Inc.
████████
office: ████████

Appendix 14, page 4

On Jul 10, 2010, at 12:59 PM, Agitu Wodajo wrote:

Dear █████,

First of all, I would like to thank you very much for the love and concern you have for █████. Because of you, we worked so hard to locate █████ birth mom and achieved success.

I have a good news. I got so excited when I got the contact number for the director of the youth homeless shelter yesterday and kept on calling until it was 11:00 PM in Addis Ababa. I had to call him first thing today. He picked up the phone when I called and we talked for almost an hour. His name is █████. He too was exited that I called him. He was my successor for a Swiss project that I led from 1986 – 1989 and knows me very well. He told me that █████ birth mom is 17 years old and that she lived in his shelter with her mom. He went on to tell me that she is among the children on his organization's website: █████. I viewed his website right after I hang up with him, but couldn't identify █████ I am sure you will visit this website immediately. Please let me know if you identify her.

Mr. █████ has accepted my request to have our staff in Addis Ababa video tape █████ birth mother's story. We have a professional video producer who does live DVDs for our families. As the live DVDs done in Ethiopia were not that good, we bring the video recording here and have the live DVD produced here. If you want this live DVD, the fee is $375. Please let me know if you want us to go ahead with the live DVD.

Mr. █████ has asked me for █████ pictures. If you email me her pictures with her adoptive family included, I will forward it to him. Just in case you also want to help one of his projects (█████ former home), we are tax exempt and all donations are tax deductable.

Thank you

From: █████, MH [█████]
Sent: Thursday, July 15, 2010 7:20 PM
To: Agitu Wodajo
Subject: Re: █████

Thank you so much! We are so excited! I'm sorry it took me so long to get back to you; we had been on a little vacation.

I couldn't find a picture of █████on the website, but she did recognize the pictures on the site and remembers being there. I would love to have the video made and learn anything about her birthmother that we can. How do we get that started?

Jessie Hawkins, Executive Director
Vintage Remedies Inc.
█████ office:

Appendix 15

Logo
Ref Number 011C&SA – 2562/S – 1232
The Federal Democratic Republic of Ethiopia
Date: December 9, 2010 E.C.
Charities and Societies Agency

TO: Better Future Adoption Services
         Addis Ababa

RE: Regards Notice of Revocation of the Organization's Permit

Better Future Adoption Services is an international Non-Governmental Organization (NGO) re-registered under the Charities and Societies Agency (CSA) proclamation number 621/2001 section 111(2) with a certificate number 1232 to engage in adoption work. Based on a study of adoption agencies and orphanage in Addis Ababa by CSA and MOWCYA after the organization's re-registration as well as the verification of tips that the Ministry of Women and Youth/Children received about the organization, the organization was in illegal manner involved in trafficking and adoption practices of children. Among the illegal practices that the organization was involved in are:

1/   After bringing about 7 children from around Shashamenne through illegal transfer to the adoption agency, faked as if the children were abandoned at various parts of Addis Ababa city administration with false documents prepared for them in order to use for its illegal purpose.

Appendix 15. page 2

2/ Using false documentations of children who have families and faking that they were abandoned in alignment with orphanages that were engaged in illegal operation and obtain decisions and send the children for adoption and other problems were confirmed through investigation with evidences

Hence, the Charities and Societies Agency, based on proclamation 621/2001 paragraph 67 sub section (3) and (4), and the notification by Ministry of Women Children and Youth Affairs on their decision to cancel the organization permit based on the investigation that was carried out and according to proclamation Article 92 sub section 2(b), has found that the organization used its re-registration permit to involve in illegal purpose which harms the children's right and benefits and hereby decided the permit canceled. Accordingly the organization's leadership be notified to do the necessary safeguard of the organization's assets and property.

With greetings,
Signature
Ali Siraj Mohammed
Director General

CC: Ministry of Foreign Affairs
        Ministry of Federal Affairs
        Ministry of Women and Youth/Children
        Ministry of Justice
        Addis Ababa Administration Bureau of Women & Children
        Board of Charities and Societies Agency
        Agency's Registration & Oversight Process, CSA

Appendix 15 B

<table>
<tr>
<td>

የትርጉም ጽሕፈት ቤት
مكتب الترجمة
ÜBERSETZUNGSBÜRO

የሺመቤት ተስፋዬና ቤተሰቡ ኃ.የተ.የሽርክና ማ.
አዲስ አበባ - ኢትዮጵያ
አስታዲዮም ሕንጻ ቁጥር 7
ስልክ (011) 515-7104, (011) 552-6312
ፖ.ሣ.ቁ. 6127

</td>
<td>

TRANSLATION OFFICE
BUREAU DE TRADUCTION
UFFICIO TRADUZIONI

Yeshimebet Tesfaye & Family P.L. Share Co.
Addis Ababa, Ethiopia
Stadium Building No.7
Tel. (011) 515-7104, (011) 552-6312
P.O.Box 6127

</td>
</tr>
</table>

<u>Decision rendered on the compliant filed by better future adoption service</u>

It is stated that the cause for the conciliation of the license of Better Future Adoption Organization is the study conducted through the ministry of Women Children and Youth Affairs children's right and safety enforcement directorate. The study team has collected documentary evidences that show Better Future has been involved in a number of illegal activities with Engida orphanage and Betezata Children's Home Association and besides that it has assigned a team that will investigate the case in detail and based on the assessment it has made, as per articles 67/3 and 4 of the proclamation No. 621/2001 it has outlined the offences committed by the adoption agency and presented to the charities and societies agency to take the necessary measure as stated in their letter. Based on this after care fully investigation the evidences furnished to it, the agency has found better future adoption agency has committed the following offences working out of the license issued to it.

1. While Child Feven Jimma is from Nazareth and both her parents namely Mr. Ermias Hailu and Mrs. Fozya Mohammed are alive; the adoption agency has presented a document which stated the child was found abandoned in Jimma Area and that she has no any parent to care for and raise her up and it has given the child to the adopting family. Moreover, as the mother of the child asked them the whereabouts of her child, they have paid birr 5000.00 (Five Hundred) to keep the secret the officials of the adoption agency and make the case to remain undiscovered. They have also explained that the check of such payment is attached as evidence with the presented document.

አቶ. የሺ በሱፈቃድ
Yeshi Besufekad
ዋና ሥራ አስኪያጅ
General Manager

Appendix 15 B, page 2

2. On the other hand the organization has presented untrue documents about around 5 children stating as if the children were found abandoned in different S/cities of Addis Ababa and presented to court for approval of adoption. However, as the court has told them that it doesn't accept and entertain adoption filed, the organization has transferred the children from Addis Ababa to West Arsi zone Assosa Woreda to illegal orphanage center which is known by the name Kiyanazrawi Orphanage Center and as it was trying to start the adoption process preparing forged documents, they have heard that the women's and children's affairs office of the woreda is informed about the case, they tried to transport the children through Shashemene. The Shashemene Police has caught them and performed the necessary investigation and finally they have let the officials of Kiyanazrawi Orphanage Center and the woreda officer who issued the document to be punished. They have also stated that the necessary warrant of the court was received ordering to catch the officers of better future adoption agency, around 10 families have filed their grievance against better future stating that they don't know the whereabouts of their children to the police office and the case is under investigation as stated by the team that organized to investigate the case. The above stated situations by themselves clearly show that how far the organization has gone in illegal activities and that it is not working towards the enforcement of the right, safety and interest of the children which should have priority in its licensed activity.

3. They have also declared that the organization is financing Engda Orphanage center and Betezata children's home association who have licensed orphanage centers to illegally process the adoption case of children and use such organizations for its illegal activity as it is confirmed from the evidence received from the Ministry Office.

The director general has stated that it is appropriate action of the Ministry of Women Children and Youth Affairs to request the charities and societies

Vashi Besufekad

Appendix 15 B, page 3

agency to take the necessary legal measure as per article 67/3 and 4 of the Proclamation No. 621/2001 listing the offences committed by the organization as per the investigation carried out.

In relation with this the organization has argued in its complaint that the Ministry of Women, Children and Youth Affairs has stated in its report for the agency to take the necessary measure but not to cancel the license of better future adoption organization, it has received the evidence/document from Mr. Abebe Tigabu who is termination the organization that they have taken the necessary disciplinary measure against the persons who committed offences. However, such arguments can not make the organization to be relieved from the liability of the offence committed and they have declared that the agency doesn't use any document or information received from Mr. Abebe Tigabu who is said terminated from the organization; rather its decision was based on the evidence and report received from the Ministry of Women Children and Youth Affairs.

Besides the fact that the illegal activity committed by the organization is substantiated with sufficient evidence; knowing that it is not possible to make decision of cancelation in the absence of the registration certificate issued from the ministry office, it is appropriate action to list the details of the offences and illegal activities that committed by the organization and present same to the charities and societies agency for the necessary decision and legal measure and to make decision to cancel the license issued to better future organization as it has used it for illegal activity as per article 92/2/B/ of the proclamation No. 621/2001; as they have declared and explained to the members of the board.

After making the necessary deliberation and detailed discussion on the case at hand; board members have reached on agreement to make the following decision without needing to undertake further the investigation understanding that the offence is substantiated with evidence and clear cheating activity is carried out as per the evidence.

Yeshi Besufekad

Appendix 15 B, page 4

Decision

After examining the complaint, evidence of the organization and the decision and related documents of the agency; as the case is not acceptable and the offence and illegal activity committed by the organization leads and consequences further legal measure as substantiated with evidence, subject to the power of the charities and societies agency to use any kind of source of information for such kind of investigation; the board doesn't found the complaint presented by the organization against the information obtaining from the Ministry of Women and Children Affairs which is the basis for the measure taken against the organization. Finally as the case should not end up with the license cancelation measure of the agency, the board has fully reaffirmed the decision of the agency saying that the offence and illegal activity should be brought to the court of justice through the prosecutor as part of the measures and actions of the charities and societies agency.

Seal
Charities and Society Agency
Record and Documentation

Yeshi Besufekad
General Manager

References

1. Gary Wills, *Certain Trumpet: The call of Leaders*, 1994 by Literary research, Inc. p.12
2. Gary Wills, p. 106.
3. Michael Hopkin, "Ethiopia Is Top Choice for Cradle of Homo Sapiens," *Nature*, February 16, 2005, doi:10.1038/news050214-10.
4. Harold G. Markus *A History of Ethiopia*, Updated edition, by Regents of the University of California, p. 17.
5. *"Causes of Poverty in Developing Nations"*, http://www.neoperspectives.com/causesofpoverty.htm
6. Harold G. Marcus, p. 19
7. Harold G. Marcus, p. 77
8. Harold G. Markus, p. 81
9. Harold G. Markus, p. 122-123, Emperor Haile Selassie I (Part I), http://www.angelfire.com/ny/ethiocrown/Haile.html
10. Harold G. Marcus, p. 118
11. Emmanuel Abraham, *Reminiscences of my life*, 1995 Addis Ababa, Ethiopia
12. Harold G. Marcus, p. 128–129
13. Haile Selassie, *My Life and Ethiopia's Progress: The Autobiography of Emperor Haile Selassie I*, translated by U. L. Lendorff, Chicago

14. Keller, *Revolutionary Ethiopia*, Bloomington, Indiana University Press, 1991, p. 69
15. Harold G. Marcus, p. 165–166
16. http://www.angelfire.com/ny/ethiocrown/Constitution.html, http://dsttietod2012.blogspot.com/
17. Harold G. Marcus, p. 131
18. Harold G. Markus, p. 111
19. Gebru Tareke, 1996. *Ethiopia: Power and Protest: Peasant Revolution in the Twentieth Century.* Lawrenceville: The Red Sea Press, p. 15
20. Harold G. Markus, p. 22–23
21. Rev. Gamachu Danuu, 2012, *HOW DID WE GET THE GOSPEL OF CHRIST?*, p. 37
22. Ras Gobena (1821 – 1889), http://www.ethiopians.com/tse8.html
23. http://www.dacb.org/stories/ethiopia/onesimus_nesib.html, Gammachu Danuu, 2012; Arén, Gustav, 1978, *Evangelical Pioneers in Ethiopia*, Stockholm: EFF_Vorlage
24. Emmanuel Abraham, p. 35; Harold G. Marcus, pp. 144–145
25. Harold G. Marcus, p. 152
26. *My Life and Ethiopia's Progress,* vol. 2, 1999, p. 165
27. Harold G. Marcus, p. 160
28. Peter P. Hinks, John R. McKivigan, R. Owen Williams, *Encyclopedia of Antislavery and Abolition*, 2007, p. 248
29. David Hamilton Shinn and Thomas P. Ofcansky, *Historical Dictionary of Ethiopia*, 2004, p. 201
30. http://2001-2009.state.gov/documents/organization/67407.pdf; http://www.presidency.ucsb.edu/ws/index.php?pid=2118#ixzz1wxTGZrlX .
31. Harold G. Marcus, p. 135–136
32. Harold G. Marcus,, p. 167
33. Harold. G. Marcus, p. 168
34. Emanuel Abraham, 1995, p. 191

35. Emmanuel Abraham, p. 64–66
36. Harold G. Marcus, p. 131, 136
37. www.jewishvirtuallibrary.org/jsource/Politics/africa. htm, Erlich, p. 59; Raman Bhardwaj, *The Dilemma of the Horn of Africa*, India: Sterling Publishers, Ltd., 1979, p. 159; Gitelson, in Curtis and Gitelson, pp. 192–196
38. Louis Rapoport, *The Lost Jews*, New York: Stein and Day, 1980, p. 192
39. Bar-Zohar, *Ben-Gurion*, pp. 263–264
40. Walter Eytan, *The First Ten Years,* London: Weidenfeld and Nicolson, 1958, p. 178; Bar-Zohar, p. 261; Rapoport, 1980, p. 192; Churba, pp. 140–141; Erlich, p. 57.
41. Rapoport, 1980, p. 192; Haggai Erlich, *The Struggle Over Eritrea,* California, Hoover Institution Press, 1983, p. 57
42. http://www.jewishvirtuallibrary.org/jsource/Politics/ africa.html, Chanan Aynor, interview with former Israeli ambassador to Ethiopia, April 1987.
43. Raman Bhardwaj, *The Dilemma of the Horn of Africa,* India: Sterling Publishers, Ltd., 1979, p. 159; Gitelson, in Curtis and Gitelson, pp. 192–196
44. Harold G. Marcus 2000, pp. 161–162
45. William B. Quandt, *Peace Process: American Diplomacy and the Arab-Israeli Conflict Since 1967*, p. 104
46. Published *Airpower Journal*, spring 1989
47. Daniel Yergin, *The Prize: The Epic Quest for Oil, Money, and Power*, New York: Simon and Schuster, 2008, p. 589
48. Daniel Yergin, *The Prize: The Epic Quest for Oil, Money, and Power*, New York: Simon and Schuster, 2008, p. 587

49. Daniel Yergin, *The Prize: The Epic Quest for Oil, Money, and Power*, New York: Simon and Schuster, 2008, p. 587), (Walter J. Boyne, "Nickel Grass," *Air Force Magazine*, December 1998
50. http://history.state.gov/milestones/1969–1976/OPEC
51. Daniel Dickson, *The Last Ethiopian Emperor*, BBC, May 2005, Harold G, Marcus, p. 181
52. http://www.angelfire.com/ny/ethiocrown/HaileIII.html
53. Erlich, pp. 58–59.
54. http://www.mongabay.com/history/ethiopia/ethio-pia-the_establishment_of_the_derg.html
55. Marina and David Ottaway, *Ethiopia: Empire in Revolution*, New York: Africana, 1978, p. 52
56. Dr. Paulos Milkiya, "Mengistu Haile Mariam: The Profile of a Dictator," reprinted from the February 1994 *Ethiopian Review*, accessed July 30, 2009
57. *Tortured for Christ*, Richard Wurmbrand, 30th anniversary ed., p. 36
58. http://allafrica.com/stories/201102081019.html, Ethiopia: Board Upholds Revocation of NGOs, Licences, Accounts Freeze, By Mahlet Mesfin, 7 February 2011
59. www.addisfortune.com/ Addis Fortune, Published Feb. 06, 2011, (Board Upholds Revocation of NGOs, Licences, Accounts Freeze
60. http://www.hrw.org/en/news/2001/10/16/ethiopia-government-attacks-women-lawyers
61. http://arefe.wordpress.com/2009/08/01/ewla-director-in-hiding/
62. John M. Cohen, Peter H. Koehn, *Rural and Urban Land Reform in Ethiopia)*, Markakis, 1974, pp. 168–169). MARKAKIS, John (1974) *Ethiopia: Anatomy of a Traditional Polity*. London: Oxford University Press.
63. http://ilri.org/InfoServ/Webpub/fulldocs/wp39/3Evo-lutiona.htm

64. *A Country Study: Ethiopia*, Thomas P. Ofcansky and LaVerle Berry, eds., Library of Congress Federal Research Division, 1991).

65. www.ey.com/Publication/vwLUAssets/2012.../2012%20TI%20CPI.pdf

66. XIII—"Slavery Abolished," the Avalon Project, Passed by Congress January 31, 1865. Ratified December 6, 1865.).

67. http://www.cdc.gov/hiv/topics/msm/index.htm, HIV Among Gay, Bisexual, and Other Men Who Have Sex With Men

68. http://www.loc.gov/exhibits/religion/, **Religion** and the Founding of the American Republic, Library of Congress

69. *Freeport Weekly Journal*, "The Victory of Truth, a Discourse Preached on the Day of National Thanksgiving, November 24, 1864, in the First Presbyterian Church of Freeport, Illinois, by Isaac E. Carey, December 7, 1864, p. 1

70. http://www.thedailybeast.com/witw/articles/2013/04/24/kathryn-joyce-s-the-child-catchers-inside-the-shadowy-world-of-adoption-trafficking.html

CPSIA information can be obtained at www.ICGtesting.com
Printed in the USA
BVOW04s1402091114

374199BV00002B/3/P